Ekphrasis, Memory and Narrative after Proust

Ekphrasis, Memory and Narrative after Proust

Prose Pictures and Fictional Recollection

Leonid Bilmes

BLOOMSBURY ACADEMIC
LONDON • NEW YORK • OXFORD • NEW DELHI • SYDNEY

BLOOMSBURY ACADEMIC
Bloomsbury Publishing Plc
50 Bedford Square, London, WC1B 3DP, UK
1385 Broadway, New York, NY 10018, USA
29 Earlsfort Terrace, Dublin 2, Ireland

BLOOMSBURY, BLOOMSBURY ACADEMIC and the Diana logo are
trademarks of Bloomsbury Publishing Plc

First published in Great Britain 2023
Paperback edition published 2024

Copyright © Leonid Bilmes, 2023, 2024

Leonid Bilmes has asserted his right under the Copyright, Designs and
Patents Act, 1988, to be identified as Author of this work.

For legal purposes the Acknowledgements on pp. ix–x constitute an
extension of this copyright page.

Cover design by Rebecca Heselton
Cover image © Natali_Mis/Shutterstock

All rights reserved. No part of this publication may be reproduced or transmitted
in any form or by any means, electronic or mechanical, including photocopying,
recording, or any information storage or retrieval system, without prior
permission in writing from the publishers.

Bloomsbury Publishing Plc does not have any control over, or responsibility for,
any third-party websites referred to or in this book. All internet addresses given
in this book were correct at the time of going to press. The author and publisher
regret any inconvenience caused if addresses have changed or sites have
ceased to exist, but can accept no responsibility for any such changes.

A catalogue record for this book is available from the British Library.

Library of Congress Cataloging-in-Publication Data

Names: Bilmes, Leonid, author.
Title: Ekphrasis, memory and narrative after Proust : prose pictures and fictional
recollection / Leonid Bilmes. Description: London ; New York : Bloomsbury Academic, 2023. |
Includes bibliographical references and index. | Summary: "This book explores the relationship between
ekphrasis and memory in the novel after Marcel Proust. Drawing on A` la recherche du temps perdu as a model,
Leonid Bilmes considers how Vladimir Nabokov, W.G. Sebald, Lydia Davis, Ali Smith and Ben Lerner have employed
and reshaped Proust's way of depicting the recollected past. In each of these writers' works, memory
images are variously transformed into alluring intermedial objects that inform the narrator's story, just
as they shape the reader's own memory of the text. Ekphrasis in the novel after Proust, Bilmes argues,
is more than mere descriptive ornament or plot device: it is a pivotal textual site where image
and text, past and present, memory and forgetting, self and other continuously contest one another.
Ekphrasis, Memory and Narrative after Proust surveys a wide field of critical inquiry, encompassing classic
accounts of ekphrasis and memory in Horace, Henri Bergson and Paul Ricoeur, as well as more recent
interventions by theorists including W.J.T. Mitchell, Jean-Luc Nancy and Liliane Louvel. The book's open dialogue
between literature and theory presents a cogent argument in favour of the bond between ekphrasis
and memory in the novel, one as yet underexplored"– Provided by publisher.
Identifiers: LCCN 2022031210 | ISBN 9781350336834 (hardback) | ISBN 9781350336872 (paperback) |
ISBN 9781350336841 (ebook) | ISBN 9781350336858 (epub) | ISBN 9781350336865
Subjects: LCSH: Proust, Marcel, 1871-1922–Literary style. | Proust, Marcel,
1871-1922–Influence. | Ekphrasis. | Memory in literature. | LCGFT: Literary criticism.
Classification: LCC PQ2631.R63 Z54425 2023 | DDC 843/.912–dc23/eng/20220915
LC record available at https://lccn.loc.gov/2022031210

ISBN: HB: 978-1-3503-3683-4
PB: 978-1-3503-3687-2
ePDF: 978-1-3503-3684-1
eBook: 978-1-3503-3685-8

Typeset by Integra Software Services Pvt. Ltd.

To find out more about our authors and books visit www.bloomsbury.com
and sign up for our newsletters.

For my family

Contents

List of illustrations	viii
Acknowledgements	ix
Introduction: On seeing prose pictures	1
1 Proust's way: Ekphrasis, memory, narrative	27
2 After Proust: By way of ironized nostalgia	67
3 Description and narration in Vladimir Nabokov's *Ada or Ardor*	87
4 Narration's looming of the archive in W. G. Sebald's *Austerlitz*	117
5 Retrospect, prospect and the fiction of the face in Ben Lerner's *10:04*	149
6 Commemoration via intermedial lamination in Ali Smith's *How to Be Both*	161
7 Writing forgetting in Lydia Davis's *The End of the Story*	187
Conclusion	213
Works cited	221
Index	235

Illustrations

1. *The Skate*, 1727, by Jean-Baptiste-Siméon Chardin (1699–1779), oil on canvas, 114.5 × 146 cm. Courtesy DeAgostini Getty Images — 2
2. Adapted from Bergson's original diagram — 68
3. Poster for *Divan Japonais*, by Henri de Toulouse-Lautrec (1864–1901). Courtesy DeAgostini Getty Images — 101
4. Face on Mars (Photo by © CORBIS). Courtesy Corbis Getty Images — 157
5. Triumph of Minerva, Sign of Aries and Borso d'Este, who administers justice and goes hunting, scenes from *Month of March*, c. 1470, by Francesco del Cossa (c. 1435–1477), fresco, east wall of Hall of the Months, Palazzo Schifanoia (Palace of Joy), Ferrara, Emilia-Romagna. Detail. Italy, fifteenth century. Courtesy DeAgostini Getty Images — 172
6. Idyllic love, detail from Triumph of Venus, scene from *Month of April*, c. 1470, by Francesco del Cossa (c. 1435–1477), fresco, east wall, Hall of the Months, Palazzo Schifanoia (Palace of Joy), Ferrara, Emilia-Romagna. Italy, fifteenth century. Courtesy DeAgostini Getty Images — 183

Acknowledgements

This book began life as a PhD thesis on memory in the novel after Proust at Queen Mary University of London, and I want to first thank my supervisors, Mark Currie and Molly Macdonald. The book's theoretical foundation owes a big debt to Mark's prescient guidance and his freeing advice to follow the scent of inquiry wherever it might lead. Mark's writing is a model of clarity and cogency, qualities that I have tried to emulate in my own scholarly work, such as it is. Thank you to Molly for reading early chapter drafts with a most scrupulous eye. I also wish to thank my examiners, Peter Boxall and Paul Hamilton. The present book would not be what it is without their combined feedback, and I am especially grateful to Peter for his advice and encouragement, which have gone a long way to helping me see this project through to the end.

At Bloomsbury, thank you to the editorial team, Ben Doyle and Laura Cope. I am especially grateful to Ben for his enthusiasm about the book and for his continued support throughout the publishing process. Thank you to Laura for her help during the final stages of manuscript preparation. I also thank my two anonymous reviewers for their valuable comments and suggestions.

Several friends and colleagues, both at Queen Mary's School of English and Drama and elsewhere, deserve thanks. To Vincenzo Torromacco, thank you for the stimulating conversations and for reading parts of the manuscript and offering invaluable feedback; it is no exaggeration to say that the writing has said what it needed to say more elegantly and rigorously with your help. To John O'Meara Dunn, Daichi Ishikawa, Ellen C. Jones, Tatjana Kijaniza, Sam Quill, Julie Tanner, James Reay Williams and Denise Wong, thank you for making the PhD experience far more rewarding than it would have been in your absence. To Huw Marsh, thank you for reading the proposal and for generously giving advice whenever I have asked for it. To Kate Wilkinson, thank you for reading drafts of earlier publications that have helped shape this book's argument. To Erica Wickerson and Mary Ann Caws, thank you for your most generous and warm responses to conference papers presented at St John's College, Cambridge, and the Graduate Center at CUNY.

I would also like to thank friends living in different cities and on different continents: Matthew Greenway, Craig and Tracey Harris, Elizaveta Kuznetsova,

Ignatius Zaaijman and Warrick Zipp. Over the years, you have all been patient enough to listen to my (often unasked for) perorations about the subjects and ideas that have now found their way onto this book's pages.

I owe an inexpressible debt of gratitude to my ever supportive parents, Tatiana and Clive Jandrell, and my big-hearted grandparents, Roza and Valentin Arinine. If not for their unfailing support this book could not have been written, and I dedicate it to them.

Finally, I am daily grateful to Diana Davidian. Thank you, Diana, for helping me to live outside the book.

Introduction: On seeing prose pictures

In his essay on Jean-Baptiste-Siméon Chardin, Marcel Proust presents us with the following tableau:

> Now come into the kitchen, where the entrance is strictly guarded by a feudality of crocks of all sizes, faithful, hardworking servants, a handsome industrious race. Knives, brisk plain-dealers, lie on the table in a menacing idleness that intends no harm. But a strange monster hangs above your head, a skate, still fresh as the sea it rippled in; and the sight of it mixes the foreign charm of the sea, the calms, the tempests it matched and outrode, with the cravings of gluttony, as though a recollection of the Museum of Natural History traversed the delicious smell of food in a restaurant. It has been gutted, and you can admire the beauty of its delicate immense structural design, painted with red blood, azure nerves, and white sinews like the nave of a polychrome cathedral. … Then there are oysters again, and a cat, counterpointing this fishy creation with the covert vitality of its subtler contours and with its glittering eyes fixed on the skate, picks its velvet-footed way in unhurried haste among the opened shells.
>
> ('Chardin' 327–328)

On display here are all the distinctive features of the kind of immersive, elaborate description that is so compelling in Proust's writing. The opening phrase invites us to share the world of the narrator as we participate in this act of seeing. The metaphors – the knives, 'brisk plain-dealers' which lie upon the table in 'menacing idleness that intends no harm', and the skate's sinews shaped like 'the nave of a polychrome cathedral' – make these objects come alive in our imagination. We can see the crockery, knives, skate, oysters and prowling cat, even if we have not seen the Chardin still life that Proust's prose is picturing (see Figure 1).

Proust's verbal portrait also lends this scene a sense of movement that the painting can only represent in its arrest – the cat 'picks its velvet-footed way'

Figure 1 *The Skate*, 1727, by Jean-Baptiste-Siméon Chardin (1699–1779), oil on canvas, 114.5 × 146 cm. Courtesy DeAgostini Getty Images.

over the oyster shells – and here we start to discern the very form of Proustian narration. Proust continues:

> An eye practiced in trafficking with the other senses, and in reconstituting by means of a few strokes of colour not merely a whole past, but a whole future, can already feel the freshness of the oysters that will dabble the cat's paws, and hear … the thunder of their fall, as the precarious heap of frail splintered shells gives way under the cat's weight.
>
> (328)

Reading Proust's *In Search of Lost Time*, we are likewise left suspended between Marcel's past, as he ekphrastically resurrects the scenes of forgotten memory retrieved by chance recall, while we also anticipate, through the narrator's proleptic remarks, the future that will shortly unfold before the 'I' that he once was.

This book traces the form of Proust's novel as a modulation between descriptive delay and narrational progress, as Marcel's ekphrastic evocations of his memories overflow into the story about his life. Erich Auerbach has observed that the so-called secondary senses that allow Marcel to recover his past function in the novel as invocations of vision: as he puts it, 'the world of his childhood [then] emerges into light, becomes *depictable*, as more genuine and more real than any experienced present – and he begins to narrate' (my emphasis 54). Indeed, description in Proust is really depiction, precisely as it so often evokes the world of visual art, with Marcel repeatedly comparing his memories to paintings and photographs as he wrestles with the limits of his (author's) own medium of expression. But, despite description's close ties with visual art, ekphrasis in Proust is not reducible to invocations of artists and artworks. Ekphrasis plays a much larger role in the novel than the reproduction of either actual or imaginary pictures: it is structurally vital to the novel's architecture. The vast 'cathedral' that is *In Search of Lost Time* could not presence itself as lucidly as it does in the mind of the reader, were it not for Marcel's ekphrastic conjurations of his past.

Ekphrasis, Memory and Narrative after Proust explores a distinct genre of the novel about recapturing the past, exemplified by Proust's *Search*. Ekphrastic description in Proust, this book argues, is not merely an aesthetic preference: it is indicative of a writerly strategy for bequeathing memory's intangible visions to indelible words. The word 'pictures' in the subtitle is intended to be read in two ways, encompassing the book's central analytical concerns. Read as a noun, prose 'pictures' are metaphorically elaborate descriptions, rich in pictorial overtones, which feature in Proustian narratives at the *textual site* of ekphrasis. Read as a verb, ekphrastic prose is writing that *pictures* the narrator's inner sights, bringing about a vicarious experience of recollection through a text-effected seeing. The generic form of the *Search* may thus be conceived as a kind of discourse mould within which mnemonic prose – prose that is both itself memorable and that evokes memory – has been shaped, and this book reads Vladimir Nabokov's *Ada*, W. G. Sebald's *Austerlitz*, Ben Lerner's *10:04*, Ali Smith's *How to Be Both* and Lydia Davis's *The End of the Story* as singular iterations of Proust's novel. Like the *Search*, these novels celebrate the sights words can conjure even as their narrators acknowledge the limitations of writing, whenever it is confronted with the immediacy of actual pictures. This self-reflexivity enables these novelistic representations of recollection to express, by means of their form, what various theorists and philosophers have said about memory's reliance on images actual and virtual, and who have also conceived narrative as media-assisted figuration of the absent self, scene and sight.

In the introduction to the 2012 edition of *Novel*, 'The Contemporary Novel: Imagining the Twenty-First Century', Timothy Bewes suggested that contemporary writers increasingly express an 'ontological' interest in the novel, an interest in 'the very world that opens itself up for presentation' (160). One way that this preoccupation manifests, Bewes argues, is 'the ekphrastic mode, in which a work undertakes an extended analysis of another artistic work' (160). Cara L. Lewis, building on Rita Felski's 'postcritical' approach to the study of literary texts,[1] similarly contends that the novel is currently 'in the midst of a visual turn' (130), citing, among others, W. G. Sebald, Karl Ove Knausgård, Teju Cole, Aleksandar Hemon, Zadie Smith, Ali Smith and Ben Lerner as practitioners of 'contemporary ekphrasis', whose writing challenges criticism's assumptions about artistic interpretation, and compels readers to consider both 'what art is' and literature's ways of answering this question (131). Lewis reads *How to Be Both* as a novel that 'insist[s] on its capacity to *be both* a temporal object and a spatial object like a painting that we may see' (137), requiring the critic to adopt an intermedial approach. This is precisely the kind of approach that I will be adopting in this book, but I would also like to extend Bewes and Lewis's claims: the contemporary ekphrastic novel – certainly the kinds of past-haunted novels written by the writers whom Lewis mentions – thinks not only about visual art but also about the visual's close ties with memory's representation. In the novels that this book will be examining, there is an intimate relationship between memory and ekphrasis, a relationship best captured by Proust's *Search*, and one which is presently being rediscovered in what Lewis calls 'the artistic turn of the contemporary novel' (133).

A study of ekphrasis in Proust and after is clearly timely, and interest in Proust's writing and its relation to visual media has only grown over the past two decades.[2] A recent essay about Proust and visuality opens with the question: 'Is there anything more to say about Proust and the image?' (Haddad 115). Considering the mass of scholarship on the subject, the anxiety behind this question is certainly understandable; however, as said essay's original reading

---

[1] See Felski, *The Limits of Critique* 162–185. Felski draws on Bruno Latour's actor-network theory to move away from a hermeneutics of suspicion towards a more open approach to a literary text, one that sees it as a kind of non-human 'actor' that can generate interpretation inasmuch as soliciting it (168).

[2] For an overview of recent scholarship on Proust and the visual arts, see Adam Watt, *Cambridge Introduction to Proust* 110–112, and Watt, 'Late-Twentieth- and Twenty-First-Century Responses' 211–213. Mieke Bal's *The Mottled Screen: Reading Proust Visually* remains an important contribution in this area; Bal thinks about the ways in which Proust's text foregrounds semantic exchange, examining how painting, photography and various optical instruments act as 'figurations' of writing in the novel – a way of representing the external world with their mediation (3). While her book goes a long way in unpacking visual media-and-text relations in Proust's writing, Bal does not explicitly address *memory*'s own reliance upon (even its calling out for) intermedial ekphrasis. See also Richard Bales 183–199, where Bales discusses not only the significance of painting (Elstir) and literature (Bergotte) for Proust's aesthetic but also music (Vinteuil).

of the image in Proust shows, the answer remains a resounding 'Yes'. Not only is there much left 'to say about Proust and the image' but, more specifically, about Proust and the *memory* image.

Discussions of ekphrasis in Proust almost invariably restrict this term to either the explicit or implicit invocation of visual art. While this is an important aspect of Proustian description, it limits ekphrasis' original scope. Ekphrasis is more than an allusion to, or a description of, visual art: it designates any description that makes its object immediate, vivid and as if present. Ekphrasis in Proust is also, vitally, where subject (the narrator) and object (the past) are fleetingly, mimetically reconciled. It is a textual site/sight where the presence that is writing's elusive dream appears to be attained – only to vanish as soon as it appears, as description is overtaken by narration, immersed in story-time's flow. At these textual sites of mnemonic ekphrasis, picture and text are in a symbiotic relation, where the representation of a memory *as if* it were a picture acquires a semantic density, making it appear more present than a past diegetically sketched.

In recent years, there has happily been renewed interest in ekphrasis and the questions it has never ceased to pose about verbal and visual relations. Renate Brosch, Ruth Webb, Janice Hewlett Koelb and Liliane Louvel have all made significant contributions here,[3] and Louvel is especially helpful in her discussion of the significance of description for the study of image, text and their dialectical exchange:

> The descriptive may be a means of renewing criticism and exploring theory from another angle, that of intermedial criticism, a term that is preferable to that of 'intersemiotics', which is heavily loaded with theories of the sign and the reduction of the image to a code. The literary text is … conceived in terms of a plateau, or a rhizome, a configuration and an apparatus that is open to an interplay between the elements that superimpose, intersect, and interpenetrate each other, on a smooth, flat level.
>
> (*Pictorial Third* 157)

Louvel's metaphor of the literary text as a 'plateau' upon which intermedial elements play is particularly fitting for ekphrastic prose narratives, where a tangible image beyond the text's borders ever intrudes, interrupting the text's sovereignty. We might say: wherever description proliferates in its quest for

---

[3] See in particular Brosch's overview of ekphrasis' resurgence in contemporary literature, 'Ekphrasis in the Digital Age'.

verbal visioning, there beckons the image. In this sense, ekphrasis poses broader theoretical questions about mimesis and the limits of linguistic representation. Far from having been exhausted since the zenith of poststructuralist critiques of language, the issue of seeing things with words remains as pressing as ever, and Proustian narratives, by their very form, speak to these concerns. Mark Currie, for instance, here draws attention to this topic in contemporary critical debate:

> Recently, there has been renewed interest in the interaction of words and images, not only as multimedia juxtapositions, but in the ekphrastic power of the written word to construct pictures. The subject is often broached in terms of a kind of power struggle between words and images, or through the broad idea that words are somehow on the retreat in an age which is dominated by images.
>
> (*Postmodern Theory* 129)

This power struggle, as we shall observe throughout the course of this book, is precisely what motivates writers of memory to continue to find novel ways (and to find the novel's way) to depict both actual and mnemonic images with the written word – without neglecting to interrogate the limitations of verbal imaging.

While ekphrasis has made a comeback in literary studies, and while description in Proust has been examined over the years,[4] what has not been explicitly addressed is the relationship between *ekphrasis and memory*. This book thus hopes to contribute to a clearer understanding of the relationship between image and text that characterizes not only ekphrasis but the 'picture' of memory that Proustian writing presents to us. To do so, it shows the ways in which ekphrases of memory both reflect and elaborate the conception of ekphrasis as theorized in classical rhetorical manuals. As we will see, the rhetoricians' emphasis on the fact that ekphrastic speech is composed with a view to being not only 'visual' but also memorable for the audience correlates with the function of memory's description in Proust. Proust's ekphrases of the past are nothing if not memorable, and their unforgettable quality is conveyed to the reader by means of figurative imagery – predominantly, visual analogies. Where Proust's ekphrastic practice elaborates the classical conception is in the retrospective overlaying of perspective that occurs whenever the older Marcel

---

[4] Edward J. Hughes's book *Marcel Proust: A Study in the Quality of Awareness* provides a painstaking analysis of how many of Proust's descriptive scenes were revised during the composition of the *Search* and what these revisions tell us about changes in the novel's conception. Hughes argues that description in Proust allows readers to vicariously experience the maturation of Marcel's artistic consciousness; see 98–132. See also Genette's reading of Proustian description in *Narrative Discourse* 99–106.

re-presents – that is, *rewrites* – scenes previously depicted and subsequently recognized by our mind's eye. This kind of layering of perspective occurs, for the most part, late in the novel, ensuring that the reader of Proust is presented with both the young Marcel's brightly coloured recollections and their reinvocation in more pensive, mortality-tinged hues.

On picturing memory

One thinker whose work remains essential to a consideration of prose pictures is W. J. T. Mitchell. Mitchell's *Picture Theory* (1994) has come to be recognized as having heralded a 'pictorial turn' in the humanities (Curtis 95). Mitchell's call for a 'pictorial turn' arose out of a sense that, in the wake of the linguistic turn in philosophy at the beginning of the twentieth century, pictorial images were in danger of becoming reduced to their verbal signification (*Picture Theory* 16). In an early essay, 'The Civilization of the Image', Roland Barthes had also called for the need to make better sense of a culture increasingly rife with extra-textual images:

> The very acute sense we have now of a 'rise' of images leads us to forget that, in this civilisation of the image, the image is never, as it were, wordless. ... This prompts the thought that the study of this modern world of images – which hasn't really been undertaken yet – is in danger of being distorted in advance if we do not work directly on an original object that is neither just image or language but image coupled with language in a form we might term logo-iconic communication.
>
> (*Signs and Images* 60)

Barthes's call for the study of 'logo-iconic communication' acknowledges the intermedial complexity of images, but the tenor of this call clearly favours language over image ('the image is never, as it were, wordless'). Since his first monograph on the bond between printed image and poetry in William Blake – *Blake's Composite Art* (1978) – Mitchell has instead sought to defend pictures' perennially troubled independence from the text. The 'pictorial turn', as Mitchell conceives it, is an endeavour to grasp pictures' extralinguistic significations, however difficult these might be to express. The most important critical tool that *Picture Theory* provides for an examination of 'pictures' in prose, though, is Mitchell's neologism, 'imagetext'. Mitchell suggests that when we are confronted by artforms that blend the visual and the verbal (for instance, Blake's logo-iconic poetry volumes), then not only are we caught up in a tangle of allusions between two media, but neither medium is *reducible* to the other. Text and image produce meaning jointly, and for Mitchell each party maintains its jurisdiction. When we read a literary text that either invokes or alludes to a painting, photograph or other visual medium, we are likewise faced with the problem of this kind of semantic lamination:[5] the image that we see *arises* out of the literary description, but the literary description has had to *withdraw* this image from elsewhere, translating it into words. Indeed, even when the image being conjured by the text happens to be fictional, mnemonic, or both these things at the same time, we still read its verbal depiction *as if* an extant image (a picture) magnetized and informed it.

In both theory and literature, the word 'image' is often used to mean 'picture', as the above discussion attests. 'Image' covers the entire spectrum of visual phenomena, including ones externally perceived, internally conceived or textually produced. In *What Do Pictures Want*, on the other hand, Mitchell makes a pertinent distinction between 'image' and 'picture' which will be helpful in clarifying the kind of seeing realized by prose pictures: 'You can hang a picture, but you cannot hang an image. ... The image is the "intellectual property" that escapes the materiality of the picture when it is copied. The picture is the image plus the support; it is the appearance of the immaterial image in a material production' (85). Proustian memory writing, I have suggested, is about a narrator's resurrection of memory's sights as if they were pictures. However, like memory's sights, the scenes that words conjure cannot be hung up in a gallery. Prose pictures, in effect, are immaterial yet indelible verbally produced images – this is why Proustian narratives so often gravitate towards the bright zones of visual media, at times invoking real pictures in an effort to render memory's images all the more *present* on the page.

Mitchell suggests that whenever we speak of memory – whether our own, in phenomenological terms, or another's, as encountered in art and literature – we might do better to speak of it neither as 'image' nor as 'text', but to adopt the figure of imagetext (*Picture Theory* 192).[6]

> It may seem odd to speak of memory as a medium, but the term seems appropriate in a number of senses. Since antiquity, memory has been figured

---

[5] I am grateful to Vincenzo Torromacco for suggesting the word 'lamination' in this context.
[6] Aside from Mitchell's *Picture Theory*, there is a marked absence of studies dealing with ekphrasis in relation to memory and narration. Linguistics-based approaches are generally unhelpful here, as they tend to encourage the *divide* between word and image, rather than examining their

not just as a disembodied, invisible power, but as a specific technology, a mechanism, a material and semiotic process subject to artifice and alteration. More specifically, memory takes the form in classical rhetoric of a dialectic between the same modalities (space and time), the same sensory channels (the visual and the aural), and the same codes (image and word) that underlie the narrative/descriptive boundary.

(Mitchell, ibid., 192)

If we recall Proust's depiction of Chardin's painting, we can appreciate the extent to which our comprehension arose out of an exchange between painted image and text, seeing and hearing. But memory's *own* form also involves a 'dialectic' between mnemonic image and text that, in turn, reflects on the distinction, within narrative discourse, between description and narration (Mitchell 191). While the distinction between the descriptive and narrational functions is of course applicable to all narrative discourse, in Proustian narratives the descriptive function is given far greater emphasis than in earlier efforts of writing memory.

The reason that this is significant to this book's attempt to understand ekphrastic memory writing can be discerned in an observation made by Henri Bergson in *Matter and Memory*, a book that made a lasting impact on Proust.[7] Bergson here distinguishes between two kinds of memories, what he calls visual or contemplative memory, and 'motor' or habit memory:

> [T]hese two extreme states, the one of an entirely contemplative memory which apprehends only the singular in its *vision*, the other of a purely motor memory which stamps the note of generality on its *action*, are really apart and are fully visible only in exceptional cases. In normal life they are interpenetrating, so that each has to abandon some part of its original purity.
>
> (155)

If we apply Bergson's distinction between 'visual' and 'motor' memory to a reading of narrative, then we find a correspondence of two kinds of recollection available for the reading experience. When we read sections of narrative

---

entanglement. Exemplary of this trend is John Bateman's *Text and Image*, where Bateman signposts his methodology as jettisoning the very question of memory as imagetext: 'Memories of the image, descriptions of questions that we can offer after the fact ... scenes conjured up mentally by skillful uses of language ... are explicitly excluded. ... The crucial restriction drawn is then: *intended* co-presence of concrete text-material with concrete image-material' (25).

[7] Proust insisted that his conception of memory differs from Bergson's: 'my work is based on the distinction between involuntary and voluntary memory, a distinction which not only does not appear in M. Bergson's philosophy, but is even contradicted by it' (qtd. in Lennon 55). As we will see in Chapter 2, though, Bergson also points to contingently induced recollection. As Joshua Landy has argued, 'though Proust himself vehemently denies it, Bergson shares with him a belief that some of the memories return unbidden' (7).

text relating action and incident, we are exercising the equivalent of 'motor' memory – we know that this is how narratives operate, and these minor diegetic incidents tend not to make much of an impression on our memory of the text. On the other hand, when we encounter lengthy visual description – ekphrasis – we exercise the equivalent of contemplative or visual memory, for we continue seeing these images while the description lasts, and certainly afterwards. Diegetic time *seems* to become suspended while we are momentarily absorbed in a kind of prose-induced seeing.

When Marcel, having tasted the proverbial madeleine dunked in tea, first sees his forgotten past brighten, this is how he describes the experience:

> I place in position before my mind's eye the still recent taste of that first mouthful, and I feel something start within me, something that leaves its resting place and attempts to rise. … Undoubtedly what is thus palpitating in the depths of my being must be *the image, the visual memory* ['ce doit être *l'image, le souvenir visuel*'], which, being linked to that taste, is trying to follow it into my conscious mind.
>
> (my emphasis, *Swann's Way* 53; *À la recherche* 46)

Prior to tasting the madeleine, all that Marcel can recall of Combray is his mother's goodnight kiss and her reading to him from Georges Sand's novel *François le Champi*. Note the visual analogies that Marcel uses to describe his struggle to remember those distant childhood days:

> [F]or a long time afterwards, when I lay awake at night and revived old memories of Combray, I saw no more of it than this sort of luminous panel, sharply defined against a vague and shadowy background, like the panels which the glow of a Bengal light or a searchlight beam will cut out and illuminate in a building the other parts of which remain plunged in darkness.
>
> (*Swann's Way* 49)

After tasting the little tea-soaked cake, he waits patiently for 'the elusive whirling medley of stirred-up colours' (53) to fuse and coalesce. Then,

> as soon as I had recognized the taste of the piece of madeleine soaked in her decoction of lime-blossom which my aunt used to give me … immediately the old grey house upon the street, where her room was, rose up like a stage set to attach itself to the little pavilion opening on to the garden which had been built out behind it for my parents (the isolated segment which until that moment had been all that I could see); and with the house the town, from morning to night and in all weathers, the square where I used to be sent before lunch, the streets along which I used to run errands, the country roads we took when it

was fine. And as in the game wherein the Japanese amuse themselves by filling a porcelain bowl with water and steeping in it little pieces of paper which until then are without character or form, but, the moment they become wet, stretch and twist and take on colour and distinctive shape, become flowers or houses or people, solid and recognisable, so in that moment all the flowers in our garden and in M. Swann's park, and the water-lilies on the Vivonne and the good folk of the village and their little dwellings and the parish church and the whole of Combray and its surroundings, *taking their shape and solidity*, sprang into being, town and gardens alike, from my cup of tea.

(my emphasis 54–55)

This famous passage encapsulates the 'Combray' section of *Swann's Way*, where Marcel describes just these places and people, often in remarkably visual terms. The image of folded paper flowers blooming in water can be read as a metaphor of the effects of ekphrastic description in the novel. For, when we come across Proustian description with its artful metaphors, it is indeed as if 'the whole of Combray and its surroundings' unfold on the page and spring into being before our mind's eye.

Ekphrasis and memory

It would of course be untrue to say that *all* that we find in Proust's novel is descriptive prose. The richness of Proust's writing is its generic polychromy, coloured as it is by elements of the essay, satire, philosophical dialogue, autobiography.[8] Nonetheless, formally the Proustian novel might be conceived as a series of vivid descriptions sewn into an intricate tapestry of plot that unfolds in time. As Georges Poulet has argued in the classic *L'Espace proustien* (*Proustian Space*): 'The Proustian novel is often this: a series of images that, from the depths where they have been buried, rise to the light of day … they present themselves isolated, distinct, and nonetheless simultaneously to the gaze' (94).[9] The 'series' of images in Proust is conveyed to the reader precisely by means of

---

[8] On this topic see William C. Carter 25–41. See also Suzanne Nalbantian 69–99, where Nalbantian suggestively reads the *Search* as a kind of creative 'misrepresentation' of Proust's life.

[9] Poulet is the first Proust scholar, to my knowledge, to suggest that Proust 'conceived the temporality of his universe under the form of a series of pictures' (106). Poulet's book certainly emphasizes visuality in Proust, but it does not specify its mode of realization – and its stylistic distinctness – as mnemonic ekphrasis. Poulet also downplays the temporal aspect of Proust's novel in favour of the spatial, whereas my own reading of the *Search* proposes that the two are mutually dependent. See Chapter 2.

descriptive ekphrasis, producing textual sites of heightened visuality in the novel. Concerning the effect of descriptive delay in narrative fiction, Mitchell notes: 'Description threatens the function of the system [of narrative] by stopping to look too closely and too long at its parts – those "places" with their "images" in the storehouse of memory' (*Picture Theory* 194). Ekphrastic description in Proust would thus seem to sabotage the speedy functioning of the narrative 'system', and yet, as I have suggested, it also best serves the needs of memory by presenting to the mind's eye the prose pictures issuing out of its 'storehouse' of images.

The conception of memory as a 'storehouse' of images has a long history. When it comes to autobiographical writing, we first encounter it in Augustine's *Confessions*. In Book X, Augustine presents his inspired reflections on recollection, where memory's visual figuration gets eloquently voiced:

> I come to the fields and vast palaces of memory, where are the treasuries of innumerable images of all kinds of objects brought in by sense-perception. … When I am in this storehouse, I ask that it produce what I want to recall, and immediately certain things come out; some things require a longer search, and have to be drawn out as it were from more recondite receptacles … until what I want is freed of mist and emerges from its hiding places.
>
> (185)

Writing more than a millennium after Augustine, Jean-Jacques Rousseau opens his own *Confessions* with a preamble that adopts the language of the visual artist: 'This is the only portrait of a man, painted exactly according to nature and in all its truth, that exists and will probably ever exist' (3). Nevertheless, despite Augustine's figuration of memory as a 'storehouse' of images, and Rousseau's figuration of his autobiography as a truthful 'portrait', what distinguishes the writings of Augustine, Rousseau, and confessional literature more broadly from Proust is a notable *absence* of ekphrastic description.

Let us compare two scenes. The first scene comes from Rousseau's *Confessions*. In Book I, Rousseau thus describes a childhood memory of his beloved aunt:

> Her good humour, her gentleness, her agreeable features, all these have so imprinted themselves on my memory, that I can still see in my mind's eye her manner, her glance, her whole air; I *could* describe how she was dressed, how she wore her hair, even to the two black curls which, after the fashion of the day, framed her temples.
>
> (my emphasis 10)

It is striking that Rousseau here uses a modal verb, 'could', so that he is, in effect, not describing his aunt at all well. All that we see of her through our ears, so to speak, are the 'two black curls' framing her temples. Vladimir Nabokov's approach is quite different. In *Speak, Memory* – in some respects a very Proustian autobiography[10] – this is how he depicts a childhood memory of his mother:

> With great clarity, I can see her sitting at a table and serenely considering the laid-out cards of a game of solitaire: she leans on her left elbow and presses to her cheek the free thumb of her left hand, in which, close to her mouth, she holds a cigarette, while her right hand stretches towards the next card. The double gleam on her fourth finger is two marriage rings – her own and my father's, which, being too large for her, is fastened to hers by a bit of black thread.
>
> (29)

We immediately apprehend the greater vividness of Nabokov's description and its more painterly character; we can certainly *picture* this framed textual scene with far greater ease than in Rousseau's example (with perhaps a few exceptions, vivid description is seldom encountered in Rousseau's autobiography).

Ekphrasis is textual framing: in Nabokov's description of his mother, our inner gaze is directed towards her image captured by his evocative prose. Lest my account of ekphrasis (conceived as vivid *prose* description) seem eccentric, it is worth re-examining ekphrasis' definitions. Ekphrasis is nowadays commonly understood to mean a poetic representation of a visual work of art, and oft-cited examples of ekphrastic poetry range over the canon of Western literature, beginning with the depiction of Achilles's shield in Book XVIII of Homer's *Iliad*;[11] John Keats's 'Ode on a Grecian Urn';[12] W. H. Auden's 'In the Musée des Beaux Arts'; or May Swenson's lean poetic portrait, 'The Tall Figures of Giacometti'. This conception of ekphrasis is commonly traced back to Horace, who, in *The Art of Poetry*, first used the Latin phrase beloved by art criticism: *ut pictura, poesis*. As Horace explains it: 'A poem is like a painting: the closer you stand to this one the more it will impress you, whereas you have to stand a good distance from that one; this one demands a rather dark corner, but that one needs to be seen in full light, and will stand up to the keen-eyed scrutiny of the critic' (108). The problem

---

[10] Despite a shared penchant for visual description, Nabokov's autobiography departs from Proust's *Search* in that Nabokov celebrates *voluntary* recollection; see John Burt Foster 119–21.
[11] See Martin Squire for a discussion of Homer's importance to an understanding of visual-verbal exchange. 'By forging in words its description of Hephaestus forging the shield', Squire argues, 'the poet of the *Iliad* also forged an intellectual paradigm for figuring visual and verbal relations – one that permeated … the Western cultural imaginary at large' (157–158). I revisit the ekphrasis of Achilles's shield in Chapter 1.
[12] See Leo Spitzer, 'The "Ode on a Grecian Urn"' 72. Spitzer's essay is important not least because it arguably instituted modern criticism's understanding of ekphrasis as a poetic genre concerned *exclusively* with visual art.

with confining ekphrasis to poetry, however, is that Horace at no point specified that *prose* could not also be 'like a painting'. In fact, ekphrasis, as Murray Krieger observes in *Ekphrasis: The Illusion of the Natural Sign*, originally 'referred, most broadly, to a verbal description of something, almost anything, in life or art' (7). Rather than confining ekphrasis to representations of visual art, Krieger argues that ekphrasis may be more comprehensively defined as 'a set verbal device that encouraged an extravagance of detail and vividness in representation, so that – as it was sometimes put – our ears could serve as our eyes, since "ekphrasis" must through hearing operate to bring about seeing' (7). And it is precisely this kind of 'extravagance of detail and vividness in representation' that we find in Proust's descriptions of memory's retrieved sights.

When did ekphrasis, then, get confined to poetic representations of art? Before the late nineteenth century, according to Ruth Webb, '[o]ne searches in vain for any unambiguous use of the term to mean "description of a work of art"' (*Ekphrasis, Imagination* 5–6). Webb suggests that it was Leo Spitzer's 1955 essay on Keats's 'Ode on a Grecian Urn' that helped spread the notion that ekphrasis denotes *poetic* evocations of painting and sculpture (33–35). Janice Koelb, in turn, argues that Spitzer likely drew on John Dewar Denniston's entry in the 1949 *Oxford Classical Dictionary*.[13] 'The modern English restrictive application of the term to works of art', Koelb sums up, 'has no classical precedent; it is entirely a twentieth century innovation, authorized initially by Denniston and taken up by Spitzer' (2).

To understand how ekphrasis was originally conceived in antiquity, and why this might be important for a study of contemporary prose pictures, we need to turn to Webb's *Ekphrasis, Imagination and Persuasion in Ancient Rhetorical Theory and Practice*. Like Krieger's earlier study, this book seeks to restore to ekphrasis the capaciousness it once possessed. Webb consults the *progymnasmata* (ancient rhetoric manuals) where we find the earliest known theorizations of ekphrasis. What the manuals all agree on, Webb argues, is that ekphrasis aims to make 'the listener "see" the subject matter in their mind's eye' (2). A good orator, for example, needed to know his audience intimately to select the most fitting and *recognizable* visual referents. The theoretical picture upon which this understanding of ekphrasis was based is as follows: 'By activating the *images already stored* in the listener's mind, the speaker creates a feeling *like*

---

[13] To add one more turn to the screw of definitional complication: Denniston derived *his* restricted definition of ekphrasis via a mistranslation from the German, having consulted Friedrich Lüger's definition in *Reallexikon des klassischen Altertums* (1914), itself the model for the first edition of the *Oxford Classical Dictionary* (Webb, *Ekphrasis, Imagination* 7).

that of direct perception, a simulacrum of perception itself. It is the *act of seeing* that is imitated, not the object itself' (Webb 127–128). Common subjects which appear in the rhetoric manuals include descriptions of people; places (cities, harbours); events (battles, earthquakes, calamities); the seasons; festival days, and so on (Webb 61). For the burgeoning orator, what was important was not the subject but their way of presenting it in precisely chosen words to their audience. If a speaker is addressing a court, for instance, he must use his words in such a way as to make, in Webb's words, 'the audience into virtual witnesses' (90). The speakers able to achieve this illusion best were those who not only spoke eloquently, but who also knew intimately their audience's stock of common cultural references: the 'raw material' of everyday life. If the speaker succeeded, then his speech produced the effect of *enargeia* (not to be confused with a related quality *energeia* or forcefulness), which may be defined as a sense of presence as well as the desired emotions associated with these verbally depicted objects or events.[14] *Enargeia*, in sum, is the *vividness* produced by an ekphrastic description, conjuring before the reader's attention that which is no longer there. As Quintilian put it, 'images of absent things are presented to the mind in such a way that we seem to see them with our eyes and to be in their presence' (qtd. in Webb 95).

Making present that which is absent is precisely what is required of a writer of memory seeking to capture its images in words. Unlike an orator who faces his audience and can gauge the effectiveness of his speech by reading faces, an author writes memory's images in the dark. Nonetheless, the rhetoricians' understanding of language's ability to mimic visual perception – indeed, their emphasis on the fact that it is the 'act of seeing' that is evoked within the hearer – is precisely the dream of ekphrastic writing. For, when reading Proust and those who wrote after his manner, we always witness the past appearing as if through the narrator-protagonist's eyes.

In the wake of post-structuralism, this conception of ekphrastic visioning may certainly appear naive. However, if we fail to address our *sense* of seeing prose pictures, then we risk giving up the visions of our own reading experience in exchange for a theoretical model demanding this sacrifice. As Currie frames this question,

> there seem to be two different orders of vision involved in realistic narrative: we see the written word on the page and we see the fictional world of represented

---

[14] In Richard Lanham's definition, *energeia* and *enargeia* denote, respectively, a speech's 'vigour and verve' and its powers of ocular demonstration (40).

events, characters and places which constitute the content of the narrative. Any narratology which denies this spits in the face of common sense. But it was from this counter-intuitive claim that structuralist narratology derived its radical force: that the ability of narrative to refer to something other than itself was an illusion.

(*Postmodern Narrative* 43)

Currie is referring here to classic texts of structuralist narratology, such as Barthes's essay 'Introduction to the Structural Analysis of Narrative', where Barthes provocatively concluded that 'the function of narrative is not to "represent", it is to constitute a spectacle still very enigmatic for us but in any case not of a mimetic order' (*Image, Music* 123–124). In his aptly titled book, *Literature, Theory and Common Sense*, Antoine Compagnon, Barthes's erstwhile colleague at the Collège de France, critiques these kinds of radical claims that ground structuralist thought, when he argues that structural linguistics

> gave a privileged place to narration as an element of literature, and consequently to the development of French narratology as an analysis of the structural properties of literary discourse. This was an analysis of the syntax of literary narrative structures to the detriment of anything in texts that concerns semantics, mimesis, the representation of the real, and especially description. In the duality of narration and description, conventionally thought to constitute literature, every effort was directed to a single god, narration, and to its syntax (not to its semantics).
>
> (72)[15]

An approach focused solely on diegesis and narration, in sum, fails to shed light on what is so distinctive about *ekphrastic* narratives, and the following chapters attempt to redress this disequilibrium by giving greater weight to the significance of description. As I have suggested, it is description that is privileged in Proustian evocations of memory, and, as a result, what distinguishes these narratives from non-ekphrastic texts is that reading them alters the nature of our encounter with a literary text. Reading these narratives, that is, we perceive duration differently than in less-descriptive writing; as Gérard Genette observes apropos of the long descriptive scenes in Proust, their reading 'often seems to take longer, much longer, than the diegetic time that such scenes are supposed

---

[15] Koelb makes an even broader indictment: 'two-and-a-half millennia of Western literary criticism have produced very few inquiries into literary description, notwithstanding the fact that poets and novelists obsess about getting it right' (5).

to be covering' (*Narrative Discourse* 95). And this is indeed one of the functions of ekphrasis as practised in antiquity: by riveting our attention upon a person, object or moment, ekphrasis, in Krieger's phrase, 'interrupt[s] the temporality of discourse' and indulges 'in spatial exploration' (7).

Framing memories

Mary Ann Caws, in *Reading Frames in Modern Fiction*, shares my own point of departure for reading (and writing about) prose pictures, opening her book as follows:

> This book had its origin in the hypothesis that many readers recall the same scenes from even the longest novels, that frequently the same passages have stood out from the whole in successive readings, and are *represented in the memory as condensations of action and vision*. They could be compared to a static arrest, within the normal flow of the text, for the presentation of a scene whose borders are so marked as to enhance and enclose its denser, or more 'dramatic,' more pictorial, or more musical, or sometimes more 'poetic' consistency. The actions and gestures seem to participate in a space larger than ordinary narrative space, and yet a heavily bordered one; their importance seems heightened.
>
> (my emphasis 3)

What Caws refers to as 'a space larger than ordinary narrative space, and yet a heavily bordered one' is ubiquitous in Proust's writing.[16] For instance, the following passage depicts – after much reflection on memory's unpredictable unfolding – young Marcel's recollection of Albertine in Balbec:

> When walking with others she would often stop, forcing her friends, who seemed greatly to respect her, to stop also. Thus it is, coming to a halt, her eyes sparkling beneath her polo-cap, that I still see her again today, silhouetted against the screen which the sea spreads out behind her, and separated from me by a transparent sky-blue space, the interval of time that has elapsed since then – the first impression, faint and tenuous in my memory, desired, pursued, then

---

[16] Caws's conception of 'framing' is broader than my own, for Caws is interested in any instance where another genre (for example, an inserted theatrical episode, or a poetic or even musical citation) can be said to interrupt the flow of narration. In her reading of Proust, moreover, Caws focuses primarily on the theatrical and musical framing effects in the novel, whereas I focus exclusively on moments of ekphrastic description and the significance of these moments to both the novel's plot and the reader's apprehension of the narrator's verbal evocation of what he 'sees' inwardly.

forgotten, then recaptured, of a face which I have many times since projected upon the cloud of the past in order to be able to say to myself, of a girl who was actually in my room: 'It is she!'

(*Within a Budding Grove* 473)

By Proust's own standards, this is certainly not the longest of descriptions, but it demonstrates the essential features of this mode of writing. As if highlighting what visual description is made to do – create a moment of narrational *delay*, giving the mind time for visualization – Proust's description shows us Albertine silhouetted against the blue 'screen' of the sea, and this memory has imprinted itself, Marcel says, on his mind. Indeed, this is the kind of scene that acts in the novel as a 'condensation of action and vision', exemplifying Albertine's significance for Marcel at that time – a significance subsequently imparted to the reader's *own* memory of the novel.

In *What We See When We Read*, Peter Mendelsund draws on his experience as designer of book cover art to reflect on this question of recalling prose pictures. Mendelsund tries to grasp how the individual scenes of a narrative blend into one another to form an apparently seamless whole; characters in a narrative, he writes, seem to 'perform in panels – scenes – which, though not encapsulated by visual frames, are delineated verbally. These scenes/panels are strung together by the reader, who renders the passages into a plausible whole' (287). Mendelsund is here describing the way a parataxis of individual events is always already becoming the hypotactic arrangement of a plotted whole, and this process might be seen as the structural blueprint for narrative sense-making in general. The narrative comes to us plotted, in other words, so we *expect* hypotactic completion even as we are confronted with the parataxis of actions and events.

In talking about reading as a process of parataxis being articulated via hypotaxis, Mendelsund invokes a whole tradition of reader-response criticism, the premises of which are clearly stated by one of its founders, Roman Ingarden:

> In moving along with the new phases of the work which are revealing themselves to us, we 'see' the previous parts of the work under constantly new phenomena of temporal perspective, usually in a selection which is at least partly determined by the content of the part of the work we are just reading. These changes in our way of 'seeing' what we have read reveal not only the dynamics of the work itself … but also the type of its unified structure, which is based in the peculiarities of its composition. We perceive … these features of composition during the course of the reading.
>
> (142)

Ingarden adds that we can never 'perceive' the entirety of the narrative 'in a single aesthetic apprehension', precisely because of the literary work's temporal nature; hence, only 'in the succession of all the parts of the work during reading do we obtain the whole system of its temporal aspects' (143). The narrative whole cannot be experienced in a single moment, as one experiences (a portion of) a painting – the narrative can only be experienced as temporal flow and gradual unravelling. For Ingarden, it is only when the reading process is over and the book is finished that we are able, as it were, to 'gaze' upon what we have read in more stable, because recollected, form. It is only after reading, during retrospection – what Ingarden calls the narrative's 'concretization' in our memory – that we are able 'to survey the whole process in its phases; the process then takes on the form of something which has already happened, which has become static, which is fixed for all time' (112–113). Significantly, Ingarden then describes this kind of retrospection of the read with the help of a visual analogy: 'The whole remembered situation is always surrounded by a horizon of obscurity and vagueness, out of which it moves, as it were, for just a moment *into the cone of light cast by memory*, soon to sink again into the twilight of what is only incidentally remembered' (my emphasis 122).

This book considers the situations depicted by ekphrasis to be more memorable in precisely this way: they appear to our recollection as (if) illuminated scenes, framed against the umbrous background of diegetic text. Metaphorically elaborate ekphrastic passages, such as the description of Albertine silhouetted against the blue 'screen' of the sea, are thus mnemonic in two senses. First, they represent the metaphor-produced picturing of Marcel's memory, conveying recalled scenes in arresting analogies. Second, these prose pictures are themselves memorable: over the course of the novel, they will serve as *reminders* of all the associated impressions, themes and events that surround them, and which such ekphrases encapsulate. Prose pictures, in this sense, are crucial building blocks within a novel that encompasses its narrator's artistic maturation, precisely because, as I will demonstrate in the next chapter, they are so often recalled by the narrator himself, to serve as reminders-cum-indices of the self he once was and for whom such scenes were so dear. Thus, the prose pictures of Marcel's past become visual 'condensations' of it in our own memory, capturing, both in the choice of image and in the choice of language, not only the self Marcel was when he first saw these indelible sights but also the self he has become when he remembers them.

Prose pictures in theory

Continental philosophy's repudiation of the 'eye' and its elevation of word above picture only confirm ekphrasis' importance to both literary and philosophical reflections on verbal representation. A more helpful way of thinking about this inveterate opposition of *eye* versus *ear* is to consider their *imbrication* during one's encounters with prose pictures. The chapters ahead aim to show that such encounters are radically intermedial and synaesthetic, suggesting that the borders between text and picture, 'inside' and 'outside' have always been porous, impossible to delineate with precision. It is this uncertain threshold, and the way the Proustian novel guides its reader across it, that this book attempts to illuminate.

There is a singular instance of this kind of intermedial complication in twentieth-century continental philosophy. The opening chapter of Michel Foucault's *The Order of Things* is memorably devoted to Diego Velázquez's *Las Meninas*. Foucault's ekphrasis is among the longest evocations of a painting in philosophical writing. The mind's eye is guided over Velázquez's canvas in prose so evocative, over many pages, that it seems as if we were seeing it without having to look at the painting itself:

> The painter is standing a little back from his canvas. He is glancing at his model; perhaps he is considering whether to add some finishing touch, though it is also possible that the first stroke has not yet been made. The arm holding the brush is bent to the left, towards the palette; it is motionless, for an instant, between canvas and paints. The skilled hand is suspended in mid-air, arrested in rapt attention on the painter's gaze; and the gaze, in return, waits upon the arrested gesture. Between the fine point of the brush and the steely gaze, the scene is about to yield up its volume …
>
> His dark torso and bright face are half-way between the visible and the invisible: emerging from that canvas beyond our view, he moves into our gaze; but when, in a moment, he makes a step to the right, removing himself from our gaze, he will be standing exactly in front of the canvas he is painting.
>
> (Foucault 3–4)

Foucault gives us this verbal portrait of the artist as he appears on his own canvas and, more importantly, as Foucault's *eye* studies him. Reading this description, we join Foucault's looking, as he unfolds his deconstruction of the tenets of classical representation, and he can only do so by conjuring the painting itself with precise, evocative phrases ('arrested in rapt attention'; 'the steely gaze';

'dark torso and bright face'). And, as we saw in Proust, a description of a static representation cannot help but convey the *time* that the narrative impulse gives it: 'in a moment', the artist will step to the right behind the canvas, hiding himself from our gaze.

I invoke this instance of ekphrastic portraiture in Foucault in order to point to ekphrasis' often unacknowledged presence in philosophical texts concerned with deconstructing representational practices.[17] But the verbal presence of an absent painting, in a text by a philosopher who was among the most incisive critics of ocularcentrism, also points to a bigger picture. In *The Triangle of Representation*, Christopher Prendergast suggests that the very idea of framing the real in any given medium is

> one of the master concepts of modernity underpinning the emergence of what Heidegger called the Age of the World Picture, based on the epistemological subject/object split of the scientific outlook: the knowing subject who observes ... the world-out-there in order to make it over into an object of representation. 'Observation' here is a strongly loaded term, indicating not only empirical observation but also the primacy accorded to a relation of looking, and this priority given to the visual and vision ... as the very ground of apprehending and understanding the world is quite fundamental.
>
> (2)

I want to suggest that ekphrastic depiction, as it appears in a particular novelistic genre, *stages* this process of picturing: it is that mode of writing which demarcates, presenting before its reader the 'enframed' object of description. Prendergast's

---

[17] To the same extent that the modern representational aesthetic has been shaped by the idea of the framed picture, twentieth-century philosophical accounts of modernity have been critical of this privileging of vision. As Martin Jay puts it, 'The development of Western philosophy cannot be understood ... without attending to its habitual dependence on visual metaphors of one sort or another. From the shadows on the wall in Plato's cave to Augustine's praise of the divine light to Descartes's ideas available to a "steadfast mental gaze" and the Enlightenment's faith in the data of our senses, the ocularcentric underpinnings of our philosophical tradition have been undeniably pervasive' (187). Two texts by Jacques Derrida merit citation in this context. In 'White Mythology', Derrida deconstructs philosophy's reliance on visual figures, arguing that philosophical writing, since Aristotle, habitually sees metaphor as 'putting something before our eyes, making a picture' (39). In a related essay, 'The Parergon', Derrida examines the Kantian aesthetic judgement and how it understands an object of art, an object that is by definition demarcated by a frame. He argues that Kant's critique of aesthetics has its own interior *parergon*, a 'frame' within the work created by Kant's importation of 'an analytic of logical judgments to an analytic of aesthetic judgements' (26). This conceptual frame acts as a kind of prosthesis for the lack or missing centre in Kant's *Critique of Judgement* (and, by implication, any philosophical exposition), what Derrida calls 'an infirmity within the thesis which requires compensation by a prosthesis. ... Framing always sustains and contains that which, by itself, collapses forthwith' (37). Ekphrasis, from this perspective, is the 'framing' that sustains the vast architecture of the *Search*, and it is also the 'prosthesis' without which memory's depiction could not be affectingly enacted.

book, in unpacking the implicit power structures and epistemological questions posed by this practice of framing,[18] invokes in its title Barthes's idea, precisely, of a 'triangle of representation' that structures every act of enframing the real for observation and imitation. In 'Diderot, Brecht, Eisenstein', an essay on mimesis in literature, theatre and film, Barthes argues that representation occurs 'so long as a subject (author, reader, spectator or voyeur) casts his gaze towards a horizon on which he cuts out the base of a triangle, his eye (or his mind) forming the apex' (*Image, Music* 69). Barthes adds that this 'tableau (pictorial, theatrical, literary) is a pure cut-out segment with clearly defined edges … everything that it admits within its field is promoted into essence, into light, into view' (70). If modernity, as Heidegger, Prendergast and Barthes all insist, is distinguished by its fixation upon a framed 'portrait' of the real, then ekphrasis encapsulates this modernist representational aesthetic. An ekphrastic representation of the past is all about 'a relation of looking', in Prendergast's phrase, where vision is often given priority – but not without voicing a subtextual anxiety about language's limits. This is another way of saying that Proust and those who write after not only express this modernist aesthetic but also voice a suspicion of their own mode of staging it in the self-reflexive form of their novels.

The Proustian narrative is about memory in a specific sense, I have suggested, and this aboutness is what the following chapters seek to elucidate by bringing each novel into dialogue with philosophical accounts of recollection and writing. Louvel's remark on how theory and literature echo one another pertains to my own approach to this question: 'Theory … seems to figure in the work or to be figured by it, both because it is at the origin of the vision and of its conception and because it reflects it' (*Poetics of the Iconotext* 18). The Proustian novel and its understanding of memory are seen distinctly when looked at through theory's lens, but this is also the kind of understanding, captured by this genre's singular form, that allows theory to see more clearly its own conceptions. An ekphrasis of the memory image, as practised by Proust, Nabokov, Sebald, Lerner, Smith and Davis, contains its own self-critical subtext, in that their novels acknowledge the figurative plenitude of verbal expression, while still earning after the felt immediacy of memory's visions. In each of these writers, we discern the features of a distinct type of memory narration, one distinguished not only by ekphrasis

---

[18] See Heidegger: 'The fundamental event of the modern age is the conquest of the world as picture. The word "picture" now means structured image that is the creature of man's producing which represents and sets before. In such producing, man contends for the position in which he can be that particular being who gives the measure and draws up the guidelines for everything that is' (134). For an incisive analysis of Heidegger's repudiation of Western ocularcentrism, see Jay 269–275.

but also by a kind of theorizing of recollection itself. This is not to suggest that each novel presents a 'philosophy' of memory, in any grand sense of this term.[19] Instead, these fictional narratives formally enact, and thus allow their reader to vicariously experience, their narrators' memory *through* vivid depiction and thereby bear witness to both description's limits before and its metaphor-produced evocation of ocular sight.

Chapter 1 defines mnemonic ekphrasis in Proust as a metaphorically elaborate visual description of a recalled moment from the narrator's past. I here draw on Webb's study of varied kinds of ekphrasis practised during antiquity and bring her reflections into dialogue with those of Genette, one of Proust's most penetrating readers. The chapter then examines Proust's conception of involuntary memory and the crucial role of the senses in bringing it about, suggesting that the narrator's analogies often enable him to impart to the reader both visual *and* nonvisual impressions. The chapter next turns to Flaubert's descriptive method, presenting it as a kind of prototype for Proustian ekphrases with their intermedial allusions and the momentous delays that such descriptions produce. I claim that mnemonic ekphrases reproduce within the reader of the *Search* the *sense* of revelation gifted to Marcel by involuntary memory. This is achieved via metaphor because Proustian metaphor – like Viktor Shklovsky's idea of *ostranenie* with which it finds resonance – revivifies perception by awakening it from habit-induced purblindness. The chapter concludes by examining several memorable ekphrases in Proust's novel, suggesting that Marcel's *restaging* of such prose pictures over the course of his narrative enables him to understand the self he once was, precisely because the Marcel who re-invokes them has changed. The self's otherness to itself is here reflected by means of the new accents of meaning with which the newly recalled-cum-depicted prose pictures are invested.

Chapter 2 explores the theoretical concerns that an ekphrasis of memory elicits. The chapter begins by examining the structural role of visual description in the *Search*, arguing that it is the key formal aspect of the novel that leads Marcel to formulate his philosophical conclusions about the nature of time and memory. I here unpack the inherent paradox in Marcel's crowning metaphor of finding himself perched upon time's 'stilts' (objective time), and yet looking down within himself (subjective time) at the landscape of the represented past below him, suggesting that ekphrasis is the textual site/sight that thinks through

---

[19] The idea that Proust's novel expresses a 'philosophy' informs Vincent Descombes's *Proust: Philosophy of the Novel*. For Descombes, the *Search* represents an artist's journey, via the cumulative gains of metaphor, from error and misrecognition towards artistic truth, and therein lies its philosophical claim.

this paradox, enabling the narrator to reconcile these opposing views of time. The chapter concludes by suggesting that the Proustian novel blends the modes of nostalgic reverie and ironic self-distance that set it apart from the mode of confessional autobiography. Here, ekphrasis plays a vital role by fusing two opposing attitudes towards the represented past and the time-sundered self who inhabits it.

Chapter 3 proposes that we can think of ekphrastic narratives about the past as virtual 'memory theatres' with textual *topoi* (places) that store the images to be remembered (both by the narrator, from whom they originate, and by the reader, who recollects the textual 'memory theatre' upon rereading the novel). With this figure in mind, the chapter argues that Nabokov's novel *Ada* exhibits memory's gravitation towards not only extensive but also imaginatively elaborate description, even as description remains the servant of narration with its progress towards an ending. The chapter concludes by turning to the narrator's treatise on time. I argue that Van derives his idea of a deterministic future from the 'picture' of the past that the descriptive narrative has produced within him: he pictures the future as if an unillumined area of a memory theatre that he cannot yet see, but which (he fears) might already pre-exist him. Drawing on Mark Currie's explication of the future perfect tense in narrative, the chapter contends that Nabokov's novel, contrary to Van's philosophizing, thinks futurity as the readiness to describe memories of moments that – whatever they might be – will have happened and, therefore, become retrospectively grasped.

Chapter 4 turns to Sebald's *Austerlitz*, a novel that expands the generic framework informing the *Search*. The chapter examines how Sebald's text represents personal memory's confrontation with the archive, suggesting that Jacques Austerlitz's story enacts the hypotactical ordering of the archive's parataxis of unremembered events. Far from being an 'archival subject', as some readers of the novel have called him, Austerlitz is a narrating subject who *constitutes* the archive, incorporating its visual contents alongside his own verbally captured memories. Austerlitz internalizes the archival real, represented in the novel by Sebald's pensive photographs, via narration, but without being able to *recognize* the retrieved traces of his past as memories – and therein lies his tragedy.

Chapter 5 reads Lerner's fiction as a self-reflexive response to Proustian retrospection. In Lerner's second novel *10:04*, memory's description is temporally fluctuating, as the kind of palimpsestic layering of time past, present and future that occurs in Proust over many pages gets condensed into a single paragraph. The chapter also focuses on seeing faces on digital screens and in fiction, a subject that often compels Lerner's narrators, and one that reflects on the spiral of ekphrastic hope and ekphrastic fear that begins turning whenever writing turns towards visuality.[20] This is a preoccupation best captured by pareidolia: the tendency of seeing human characteristics in the external world, which is also the kind of effect that ekphrasis aims to produce on the page, although, as Lerner's writing attests, in ekphrasis one encounters a more artful kind of visualization. Chapter 5 acts as an interlude, separating the chapters on Nabokov and Sebald, which are primarily concerned with 'seeing', from the final two chapters on Smith and Davis, which are equally concerned with 'hearing'.

'Seeing' and 'hearing' are constitutive of reading fiction, and *How to Be Both* and *The End of the Story* are particularly attuned to hearing's function in bringing about ekphrastic evocation (in Smith's novel) and pointing to its blind spots (in Davis). Chapter 6 begins by addressing the inseverable link between commemoration and intermediality in Proust and Smith, where one preserves one's memory of the departed with the help of visual prostheses that often challenge memory inasmuch as they assist it. The chapter reads *How to Be Both* as typographically rendering the narrational rhythm particular to the contemplation of what is no longer there and proposes two modulations of narrative voice in the novel: namely *enargeiac* (vivid) and diegetic (plain) narration, corresponding with picturing and sequencing. As per its original conception, ekphrasis elicits a verbally produced vision, and in *How to Be Both* the reader can *hear* more distinctly the lexical and rhythmic alteration (signalled by the unusual punctuation in the novel) that telling undergoes once prose picturing takes over.

Chapter 7 turns to a writer who has perhaps the closest connection to Proust. Lydia Davis's only novel to date, *The End of the Story*, is concerned with capturing not only memory, as in the *Search*, but also forgetting. The novel, I contend, reflects on forgetting's active presence in shaping what is written, as forgetting's agency is indexed (both seen and heard) by the profusion of the conjunction 'or'. The chapter concludes by addressing Samuel Beckett's importance both

---

[20] I am here indebted to Mitchell's distinction, in *Picture Theory*, between what he calls the three moments of 'ekphrastic fascination', namely 'fear, hope and indifference' (156). Mitchell's idea of 'ekphrastic hope' is one I adopt above, but 'ekphrastic fear' I intend differently. For Mitchell, the 'fear' is not about language *failing* to conjure the visual, as I am proposing, but almost the exact opposite; it occurs 'when we sense that the difference between the verbal and visual representation might collapse and the figurative, imaginary desire of ekphrasis might be realized literally and actually' (154). This is a fear that, paradoxically, is ekphrasis' own undoing (since, if realized, ekphrasis as text disappears), but it does not characterize Proustian narratives, where this kind of 'tangible' realization of ekphrastic hopes, though earned for, is always deferred.

to Davis's novel and to mnemonic ekphrasis as descriptive mode. By placing Beckett's writing as a foil beneath Davis and Proust, I suggest, we can see more clearly that which haunts memory's visual description: namely black words lying upon a white page, whose sounds not only produce prose pictures but can also erase them.

*

Ekphrasis is motivated, in Krieger's phrase, by the dream 'of a language that can, in spite of its limits, recover the immediacy of a sightless vision built into our habit of perceptual desire since Plato' (10). This dream has always been shadowed by its double, the fear of blindness, of language's insufficiency to make absent things come back into the present. Horace believed that 'the mind is less actively stimulated by what it takes in through the ear than by what is presented to it through the trustworthy agency of the eyes' (103). Ekphrastic writing of memory promises to restore memory's visions, a line of prose at a time: making seeing happen through the far more speculative agency of a reading eye. This promise, as the next chapter will show, has been kept in Proust.

1

Proust's way: Ekphrasis, memory, narrative

Defining mnemonic ekphrasis

According to its earliest theorizations, we have seen, ekphrasis was thought of not only as a description of a work of art as is now commonly supposed, but an evocation of anything, so long as it was both vivid and visually immersive. In *Ekphrasis, Imagination and Persuasion*, Webb highlights two properties of ekphrasis that will inform this chapter's reading of visual description in Proust:

> While the visual arts may be literally absent from this definition of ekphrasis, and from most discussions by ancient rhetoricians, the *idea* of the visual underpins this mode of speech which rivals the effects of painting or sculpture, creating virtual images in the listener's mind.
>
> (8–9)

> An ekphrasis was distinguished from a *diēgēsis* not by the nature of the subject matter, but by the degree of reference to visible phenomena and the effect it had on the audience.
>
> (67)

Hence, ekphrasis always accretes around a visual scene (not necessarily artistic) and it is distinguished by the effect it has on its audience. Ekphrasis is *distinct* from narration precisely by virtue of its simulation of 'the act of seeing'.

One of the *progymnasmata* authors, Nikolaos, describes the effect produced by ekphrasis as follows: 'Vividly [*enargōs*] is added because it is in this respect particularly that ekphrasis differs from *diēgēsis* (narration). The latter sets out the events plainly, while the former tries to make the listeners into *spectators*' (my emphasis, qtd. in Webb 71). An example of an ekphrasis that channels *enargeia* (vividness) is given by Quintilian, who cites a fragment from a lost speech by Cicero, describing the after-effects of a drunken celebration: 'I seemed to see some coming, others going, some staggering with effect of the wine, some yawning from the previous day's drinking. The floor was filthy, smeared with wine, covered with wilting wreaths and fish bones' (qtd. in Webb 91). Cicero's description presents itself as a scene, immersing our attention within the ambit of his uncertain gaze. (Was the speaker himself inebriated, we wonder, and only 'seemed to see' the banquet hall?) The speaker is presenting a series of actions and, at first, the scene does not seem very vivid. However, as we read on a pictorial logic gradually takes over and diegesis (narration) becomes description. Many figures are said to be coming and going, while others are yawning, suggesting a broad, almost painterly perspective and giving the scene a stilled quality that prepares the listener/reader for the precise details to come. 'Wilting wreaths' and 'fish bones' covering a filthy floor 'smeared with wine' convey a vivid sense of the mess left over from the night's carousing. Had Cicero said something along the lines of 'The banquet hall had a dirty floor and was filled with hungover carousers', then, clearly, his account would not have been as vivid as the one he gives. In short, he would have produced a diegetic sentence sans *enargeia*: he would have employed diegetic narration without incorporating an *enargeiac* modulation.

In Cicero's example, the speaker is not merely describing the banquet hall but also recalling the state of mind he was in while seeing it, when he tells us 'I seem*ed* to see'. Mnemonic ekphrasis is thus a kind of simulation of what was *once* experienced and may *now* be 'seen' through words alone. I suggest that it is precisely this aspect of mnemonic ekphrasis that makes it such an effective tool for the representation of the past in the novel after Proust. Of course, this does not mean that ekphrasis cannot also feature descriptions of the sensations of sound, taste, hearing and touch.[1] The detail of the floor 'smeared with wine', for instance, conveys a sensation of tackiness as we can easily imagine walking over its sticky surface. But there is no denying that we are first and foremost contemplating a visual scene: Cicero's fragment stages the mimesis of retrospective sight.

According to the *progymnasmata* authors, ekphrasis can portray events and actions of various kinds, and what distinguishes it from narration is the degree to which it tries to make them inwardly 'seeable'. However, even an ekphrastic passage presenting us with images of events still stands out from the text, as if surrounded by a frame that sets it apart from the larger narrative to which

---

[1] In Proust, the senses of touch, taste, smell and hearing are crucial in that they serve to transport the past back into Marcel's present. However, as readers we do not have access to these sensations in the same way that we have access to the depicted images that follow right on their heels, and around which the vast swathes of diegetic narration unfold and spread before us over many pages.

it belongs. This is perhaps best illustrated by the well-known example of the forging of Achilles's shield in Homer. In Book XVIII of the *Iliad*, the poet relates how the god Hephaestus forged Achilles's shield, so that as readers we are both attending to the shield being made and contemplating the scenes decorating its surface. We are presented with striking descriptions of sky and sea; a wedding feast and a violent quarrel; a battle; ploughmen ploughing fields and labourers harvesting grain; boys and girls picking grapes in a vineyard; a huge bull being ravaged by lions; and so on (Homer 483–487). Each of these scenes contains its own micro-narrative, but the depicted events *belong to a different order of time* than the narrative proper. Webb, too, suggests that what we have in Homer is 'a prime example of a narrative ekphrasis that *interrupts* a larger framing narrative' (my emphasis 68). The scenes depicted on the shield are literally framed, with Ocean 'girdling/round the outmost rim of the welded indestructible shield' (487). Suggestively, in Robert Fagles's translation of this passage the ekphrasis commences in the present tense: 'first Hephaestus makes a great and massive shield', the stanza concluding with the lines, 'across its vast expanse with all his craft and cunning/the god creates a world of gorgeous immortal work' (483). Although the events depicted on the shield are narrated in the past tense, their framing and vivid presentation consign them to a different (as it were, more present) temporality than the events recounted in the epic that this ekphrasis interrupts.

The delay of descriptive ekphrasis is not the stasis of a painted canvas, and it is only experienced as such relative to the kinesis of narration. To clarify this point, I want to briefly invoke Gérard Genette's distinction between narration and description in the novel. Genette defines their functions as follows:

> [Narration] is concerned with actions or events considered as pure processes, and by that very fact it stresses the temporal, dramatic aspect of the narrative; description, on the other hand, because it *lingers* on objects and beings considered in their simultaneity, and because it considers the processes themselves as spectacles, *seems to suspend the course of time and to contribute to spreading the narrative in space.*
>
> (my emphasis, *Figures* 136)

A total suspension of narrative time is, of course, impossible. The parataxis of visual detail can only be rendered via its hypotactic arrangement in a sentence, and this arrangement already carries traces of narrational logic. Nonetheless, when we encounter the kinds of lingering descriptions of recollected moments at which Proust excels, time does *seem* to stand still: a past moment becomes (as if) present, as narration becomes (as if) arrested. When description accretes around its object, narrative speed slows, and reading slows down with it; as Genette remarks apropos of Proustian description: 'the quantity of information is solidly in inverse ratio to the speed of the narrative' (*Narrative Discourse* 166).

D. P. Fowler, in an incisive article, 'Narrate and Describe: The Problem of Ekphrasis', argues that 'with any passage where in any sense we for a moment "stand back" from the narrative we have the presence of two realities: the passage taken in isolation and its wider context' (35). As I aim to show in this chapter, ekphrases of memory in Proust do just this: they make present a past scene by decelerating time; then, as we read on, the scene's broader significance within plot's complex tapestry is made apparent and becomes still more heightened during our retrospection of the novel. Fowler also draws attention to the fact that while 'narration often continues through a description (there is rarely a complete pause) … the needs of the plot can usually be satisfied by a much more exiguous account than we are offered in ekphrasis' (27).[2] This suggests that there is a 'something', a surplus of meaning produced by ekphrasis that cannot be *reduced* to narration, 'the needs of the plot'. In Proust, this 'something', I am suggesting, is the needs of memory, needs not fully subservient to plot's dictates and which require mnemonic ekphrasis to fulfil them. While the descriptive function exercises its short-lived duration, the progression of events is deferred: ekphrasis thus captivates the mind's eye, riveting it on the past moment made present. All too soon, though, the stillness passes as the portrayed scene is submerged within narration's flow. As Genette memorably puts it, 'narration cannot exist without description, but this dependence does not prevent it from constantly playing the major role. Description is quite naturally *ancilla narrationis*, the ever-necessary, ever-submissive, never-emancipated slave of narrative' (*Figures* 134).

Description remains submissive to narration, and this is particularly apparent in the forging of Achilles's shield example. In some of the scenes, description plays a more central role; for instance, the highly descriptive scene of the grape harvest features action and movement but has minimal story elements (Homer 485–486). In other scenes, like the wedding feast where a violent quarrel has broken out in the marketplace, narration is more dominant, infusing the depicted moments with plot as we learn the backstory to the quarrel (Homer 483–484). Webb, in fact, refers to the forging of Achilles's shield as a 'narrative

---

[2] Fowler stresses that description has historically been relegated to the wings of criticism's stage, with plot kept firmly under the spotlight: 'this primacy of plot and almost moral distaste for description has been very deeply ingrained in the Western tradition' (26).

ekphrasis', where the descriptive and narrational functions compose meaning jointly, but where narration generally has the upper hand. Indeed, as Webb has shown, the modern distinction between description and narration did not always hold in antiquity.[3] Instead, a distinction was often made between *diegesis* (plain narration) and *enargeia* (vivid narration), the latter being understood as 'an intensification of the narrative, introducing a degree of detail which would involve the audience both imaginatively and emotionally' (Webb, 'Ekphrasis ancient and modern' 14). 'Narrative ekphrasis' typically evoked events 'unfolding in time, like a battle, a murder or the sack of a city' (Webb 14). To make such complex events more comprehensible, a speaker would usually provide his audience with context, by telling them, for instance, what happened before a battle took place or relating what happened after a murder was committed (Webb, *Ekphrasis, Imagination* 67). In the *Search*, on the other hand, the 'before' and 'after' of the recalled moment belong to the narrative whole, so that, while the ekphrastically evoked scene is incorporated within the narrative – forming a key part of the novel's plot – it still preserves its visual (as if there) and temporal (as if present) distinction.

Mnemonic ekphrasis, in my sense, corresponds closely to what Webb calls

> ekphraseis [*sic*] of places, times, 'the manner in which' and persons – precisely the types of ekphrasis which recall the common modern conception of description as a separate block inserted into the flow of narrative ... The supporting role which seems to be attributed to these ekphraseis *in setting the scene* corresponds to the conception of description as the faithful 'ancilla narrationis' identified by Genette as one of the characteristics of the modern conception of description.
>
> (my emphasis, *Ekphrasis, Imagination* 66)

'If some types of ekphrasis correspond to the description-as-opposed-to-narration which Genette identified as characteristic of modern conceptions of literature,' Webb continues, 'others blur the boundaries', as the shield of Achilles demonstrates (67).[4] I want to suggest that the kinds of ekphrases that we encounter in the *Search*, and in those novels that share some of its aesthetic

---

[3] See also Frank J. D'Angelo 441–442 and 445.
[4] Besides Achilles's shield, perhaps the most noteworthy example from antiquity that 'blurs the boundaries' between description and narration is the *Eikones* (*Imagines*) of Philostratus the Elder; Philostratus describes a series of paintings which he once saw in a gallery in Naples to a group of young men and a boy. He also talks about the paintings' method of composition, interprets the mythological scenes shown on them and gives an account of his first visit to the gallery (Webb, *Ekphrasis, Imagination* 187–188). Webb suggests that Philostratus's *Eikones*, because of the ways in which it both foregrounds questions of descriptive interpretation *and* narrativizes the paintings, 'is an example both of an ekphrasis in the ancient sense and in the modern sense' (189).

aims, correspond to Genette's distinction. In Proust and after, that is, we are presented with both memory images (description) as well as their significance in the plot (narration), but a significance fully realized *retrospectively*. Mnemonic ekphrasis in Proust always concerns a particular moment from the narrator's past: a *memorable* moment overwhelming in its immediacy. These recaptured moments require diegetic delay, giving description the time needed to depict them. In Proustian narratives, mnemonic ekphrasis thus 'intensifies' the story, creating a narrational pause with the kind of descriptive detail necessary to evoke the narrator's experience of a recalled moment, to be shared with the reader.

When reading descriptive narratives, to borrow Fowler's phrase, 'we move from detail to whole' (34), and this movement defines the structure of the kinds of novels that will be examined in this book. For Proust, Nabokov, Sebald, Lerner, Smith and Davis memory's sights of past moments, persons and places become verbal tableaux animated within a life recounted – the narrative whole wherein these moments find retrospective meaning.[5] Clearly, such mnemonic ekphrases, despite the delays they produce, often represent actions and gestures that transmit an implicit narrative charge. Nonetheless, the depicted scenes of memory stand out from the preterite narration that they designedly, artfully suspend. For a moment, 'It is just as if we were there ourselves' (Fowler 26).

Involuntary memory revisited

To understand Proust's way with mnemonic ekphrasis, let us first turn to *Contre Sainte-Beuve*, the text that presages many of the themes that will occupy the seven volumes of the *Search*.[6] Part critical essay and part novelized autobiography, it is where Proust first introduces his distinction between voluntary and involuntary memory. Voluntary memory is ruled by the intellect, and the intellect is unhelpful where the past is concerned. 'What the intellect restores to us under the name of the past', Proust writes, 'is not the past. In reality, as soon as each hour of one's life has died, it embodies itself in some material object, as do the souls of the dead

---

[5] Kathryn Stelmach, in a suggestively titled essay, 'From Text to Tableau', describes Virginia Woolf's novels as enacting a similar movement from ekphrastically rendered moment to narrative whole. In Woolf's fiction, Stenmach argues, we often encounter moments of temporal suspension that serve to underscore 'the endlessly cyclical nature of ekphrasis: tableaus and texts become virtually indistinguishable as they oscillate between the realms of spatial imagination and sequential narration' (306).

[6] For a succinct account of the importance of *Contre Sainte-Beuve* to the gestation of the *Search*, see Nathalie Mauriac Dyer 34–37.

in certain folk-stories, and hides there' (*Contre Sainte-Beuve* 19). The forgotten past is only restored to us when we chance upon such an object-reminder, but, as the narrator laments, 'there is so little likelihood that we shall come across it' (19). He then relates a chance meeting with just such an object, one that will appear in slightly different form in *Swann's Way*. One winter evening, he returns home and sits down to read in his cold bedroom, trying to get warm. His old cook brings him tea – which he doesn't ordinarily drink – and two slices of dry toast. Dunking the toast in the tea and tasting it, he can suddenly smell flowers – geraniums, orange blossoms – and 'a sensation of extraordinary radiance and happiness' overwhelms him (20). He remembers the summers he'd spent in this house as a child, and one summer morning, when he came down into his grandfather's bedroom and his grandfather let him taste a rusk dipped in tea. He sees vanished childhood scenes appear before his mind's eye:

> But as soon as I had tasted the rusk [toast], a whole garden, up till then vague and dim, mirrored itself, with its forgotten walks and all their urns with all their flowers, in the little cup of tea, like those Japanese flowers which do not re-open as flowers until one drops them in water. In the same way, many days in Venice, which intellect had not been able to give back, were dead for me until last year, when crossing a courtyard I came to a standstill among the glittering uneven paving-stones … in the depths of my being I felt the flutter of a past I did not recognise. … It was the same sensation underfoot that I had felt on the smooth, slightly uneven pavement of the baptistry of Saint Mark's. The shadow which had lain that day on the canal where a gondola waited for me, and all the happiness, all the wealth of those hours – this recognised sensation brought them hurrying after it, and that very day came alive for me.
>
> (20–21)

These scenes disclosed by involuntary memory reappear in the *Search*: the episodes of the madeleine cake dunked in tea and the feel of uneven-paving stones appear, respectively, in the first and last volumes of the novel.

The reason that voluntary memory cannot retrieve the past on its own is that it is caught up in a habit-deadened perception of the world. 'In the broad daylight of habitual memory,' Marcel says, 'the images of the past turn gradually pale and fade out of sight, nothing remains of them' (*Within a Budding Grove* 254). We are reminded here of Bergson's distinction between habit memory (which rules quotidian life) and contemplative memory (which presents us with images of the past). In Proust's own philosophical conception, habit operates in *both* kinds of recollection, in that, while contemplative memory shows us images of the remembered, these images have been viewed so many times that they soon 'fade out of sight' and no longer hold revelation in store. It is the so-called secondary senses that furnish us with the most poignant images of things past. 'It is not primarily the sense of sight,' Harold Weinrich argues, 'the most acute and most intelligent sense, that should be memory's course; instead Proust calls on the other, less acute senses to put themselves in the service of memory' (148). Indeed, the senses of smell, taste, hearing and touch act as temporal conduits in Proust's novel: they effect a kind of phenomenological teleportation, transporting the narrator's past *back into* his present, thus reconciling two moments separated in time. The taste (and smell) of the madeleine dunked in tea, the feel of uneven paving stones, the touch of a napkin and the sound of a spoon tinkling on a saucer – these are some of the key sensations that reveal the past for Marcel.

In 'The *Madeleine* Revisualized', Lauren Walsh suggests that such moments of recall in Proust produce 'a full emotive recapture of the past', whereby the narrator re-apprehends the past moment with all his senses and where the visual sense is 'one component' (102). While I share Walsh's view concerning the multisensory nature of involuntary memory, I want to suggest that the visual sense plays a specific and structurally pivotal role in the novel, both in the framing effect of key recollections that are so often encountered in Proust, as well as in the way the narrator's analogies allow the reader to apprehend more substantially the sensations of the other senses, by producing synaesthetic effects enacted via visual *vehicles*.[7] The present chapter thus makes two claims concerning the function and significance of prose pictures in Proust. The first is that while the sensations of smell, taste, touch and hearing perform the vital role of transporting a forgotten moment back into Marcel's consciousness, the retrieved moment itself is, typically, rendered in strikingly visual terms. It is *around* this moment – often steeped in light, colour, and presented to the reader as if within an emotionally charged frame – that the vast narration, which of course encompasses other kinds of sensations, coalesces.[8] This kind of memorable framing of key moments from the narrator's past, I suggest in the

---

[7] See Augustine's examination of the way we use the verb 'see' in everyday expressions: 'Seeing is the property of our eyes. But we also use this word in other senses, when we apply the power of vision to knowledge generally. We do not say "Hear how that flashes", or "Smell how bright that is", or "Taste how that shines" or "Touch how that gleams". Of all these things we say "see". But we say not only "See how that light shines", which only the eyes can perceive, but also "See how that sounds, see what smells, see what tastes, see how hard that is". So the general experience of the senses is the lust, as scripture says, of the eyes, because seeing is a function in which eyes hold the first place but other senses *claim the word for themselves by analogy* when they are exploring any department of knowledge' (my emphasis 211). In Proustian ekphrases, this is particularly felt when involuntary memory has done its work.

[8] Walsh has also commented on the significance of colour and light in involuntary recollection (103).

chapter's closing section, plays an important role within the philosophy of time excursus upon which the novel concludes. The chapter's second claim concerns the distinctness of ekphrastic description in the *Search*: what makes Proustian ekphrases distinct (and, crucially, distinctly memorable) are precisely the *visual metaphors* that compose them. Mnemonic ekphrasis in Proust, recapturing 'the act of seeing', is the locus where visually compelled metaphors proliferate, producing a 'seeing-as' of the past that distinguishes Proustian prose pictures from pictures in the strictly pictorial sense.

Concerning the senses' role in involuntary memory, Thomas Lennon has made a suggestive observation in his reading of the novel in 'Proust and the Phenomenology of Memory', tracing a correspondence of ideas in Proust and the seventeenth-century philosopher, Nicholas Malebranche. Lennon argues that while Malebranche does not make the connection with memory that we find in Proust, he does point to an intriguing phenomenological distinction between the visual and other kinds of sensations.[9] Drawing on Malebranche's thought, Lennon sums up the difference between the senses as follows:

> [W]hile, taste, odor, sound, pain are all localizable, none is either spatial or quantifiable. I might have a pain in my index and middle fingers and not in the others, but it makes no sense to say, except metaphorically, that one pain is twice the size of the other. There is no geometry of any sensation but the visual. Visual sensations are extensive magnitudes; all the rest, intensive. What we see is in, or can be regarded as in space; but what we taste, smell, hear, feel is, it might be argued, only in time. In the *search* after lost time, the visual is irrelevant.
>
> (my emphasis, Lennon 60)

As in Proust's own conception of voluntary memory, the visual sense is powerless to bring back the past. Sight, however, is 'irrelevant' only in the *search* after lost time; once the past moment has been retrieved, via the mediation of the senses, visual imagery and detail become vital within the moment's verbal transcription. 'Visual sensations are extensive magnitudes', Lennon argues, and, for this very reason, they require extensive description to lay out, in a manner commensurate with the vividness of the impressions retrieved, the remembered scene that, to a significant degree, is spatial. Lennon recognizes the significance of the visual in Proust's writing, arguing: 'visual imagery abounds in Proust and is more than just a vehicle of figuration. It is so systematized and scientifically sophisticated that it is not inappropriate to talk of a Proustian optics' (61). What has arisen

---

[9] Proust, as Lennon (52–53) has discovered, was familiar with Malebranche's philosophy, quoting him in a letter to Robert de Montesquiou.

unbidden from within – the 'intensive' sensation – is precisely what calls out for a sophisticated system of visual imagery, an 'optics' to use Lennon's apt word, needed to portray it. One cannot, in Proust's sense, wilfully 'see' the true past; one may only apprehend it via the indirect, intensive route of the other senses. And yet these returned sensations are so often depicted, made vivid via visual metaphors to become the extensive prose pictures that the metaphors jointly shape.

We saw in the previous chapter that when Marcel first tastes the tea-soaked madeleine, he feels something stirring deep within him, as follows: 'Undoubtedly what is thus palpitating in the depths of my being must be the image, the visual memory, which, being linked to that taste, is trying to follow it into my conscious mind.' Modern neuroscience has shed light on what has come to be known as 'the madeleine episode'. A very readable book in this area is Cretien van Campen's *The Proust Effect*. The 'Proust effect' occurs, van Campen explains, when the amygdalae (located at the basal part of the cerebrum that joins the optic tract), stimulated by particularly affective sensations, produces a strong emotional response, and the hippocampus provides a broader context for this memory (143). The provided context is, of course, multisensory, yet the recalled sensory impressions, triggered by a smell, taste, touch or sound, are always anchored within a specific setting, created by the hippocampus – a *scene*, in short, which might then be rendered in descriptive prose. Van Campen describes the process as follows:

> For Marcel, the taste of the cake triggered feelings of joy and happiness even before he explicitly remembered the time and place to which those feelings referred. The emotions are gradually given form by the actions of the hippocampus, which is located close to the amygdalae and is responsible for organizing the memory. Where the amygdalae are concerned with assessing the emotional value of an event, for example, the danger of an abyss or a loving smile, the nearby hippocampus *maintains an overview and lays down the circumstances in the memory*. This ensures that we know later *where the abyss was or what clothes the person with the loving smile was wearing at that time.*
>
> (my emphasis 143)

Recent neuropsychological studies have produced a detailed description of this process. Rereading the madeleine episode through a neurological lens, Barry C. Smith argues that it is, in fact, the taste of the madeleine-and-tea combined with their aroma that triggers Marcel's memory. Marcel, it should be said, is himself aware of the power of taste and smell to retrieve the distant past; as he puts it, 'taste and smell alone, more fragile but more enduring … bear unflinchingly, in the tiny and almost impalpable drop of their essence, the vast structure of recollection'

(*Swann's Way* 54). There are two functions performed by smell: orthonasal olfaction registers external smells, while retronasal olfaction processes smells of objects placed inside the mouth. The taste of something, in other words, is inextricably bound to its smell, as Smith explains: 'Odours processed retronasally allow us to access the quality of what we have just eaten ... though we don't recognize these experiences as involving smell and usually think of them as tastes' (40). 'Smell has a special capacity to trigger memories,' Smith argues, 'because of the direct connections olfaction has with parts of the limbic system involved in generating emotion and memory' (39).[10] 'The extraordinary power of smell,' Smith continues, 'is that it can retrieve not just a memory of what was previously smelled but *visual images* of a house, gardens, the trees at Combray. The involuntary recreation of a world of sights and sounds goes far beyond memories of past smells, and this shows that the memory of *the scene*, like the original experience itself, is multisensory, drawing on the collaborative workings of all our senses to put us in touch with our *surroundings* and ourselves' (my emphasis 40–41).

Recent neuroscientific contributions to our understanding of Proustian involuntary recall, such as the studies sketched above, point to the fact that, while the experience of the retrieved past is multisensory, visuality often figures prominently within its representation. As Mary Ann Caws puts it, 'the reader depends upon the narrator's backward reference for the alignment of one episode under another's time and place, the remembered sight or sound apprehended once more, literally, brought back by the triggering moment, through which the past can be seen, as through a transparency' (207). Auerbach, we recollect, describes Marcel's resurgence of recall following the madeleine moment in similarly visual terms: 'from recovered remembrance, the world of his childhood emerges into light, becomes depictable'. Impressively, in *The Imagery of Proust* Victor E. Graham has calculated the total numbers of auditory, visual, kinaesthetic, mental, gustatory and olfactory images to be found in the *Search*. According to Graham's findings, visual images emerge on top at 62 per cent (260–261). Graham's investigative feat has also revealed that the imagery associated with memory is predominately visual in Proust, while the effect of involuntary memory is that 'it serves to recall a flood of visual memories that have long since sunk below the level of the conscious memory of recall' (107).

---

[10] E. Leigh Gibson expands on this point, citing a functional magnetic resonance imaging study, which 'showed that odour-evoked autobiographical memories were associated with greater activation of emotional brain circuitry, *particularly for earlier memories*, than those evoked by words, whereas the latter produced more involvement of brain areas involved in higher cognition, such as executive function' (my emphasis 43).

Of course, Proust's novel is formally complex, consisting of extended satirical scenes (the soirée at the Verdurins'); lengthy dialogues about contemporary issues (the Dreyfus affair); philosophical meditations about art, music, time, love, jealousy and much else besides, where visual images do not always feature prominently. Nonetheless, I suggest that where memory is concerned visual description plays a crucial (but not exclusive) role in conveying to the reader the narrator's involuntarily recalled scenes, *together* with their attendant sensory impressions and emotions.

Besides the kinds of extensive mnemonic ekphrases that will be examined in this chapter, Proust's narrator also employs visual images to capture the workings of the senses of touch, smell and especially hearing. Towards the conclusion of the novel's opening volume, for example, when, for the second time, Swann hears 'the little phrase' from Vinteuil's sonata, his memories are described as having been kept 'invisible in the depths of his being' until that moment (*Swann's Way* 415). The phrase's revelatory effect upon his mind is then conveyed by means of visual imagery:

> Swann felt that the composer had been content … to unveil [the unseen], to make it visible … the sound altered at every moment, softening and blurring to indicate a shadow, springing back into life when it must follow the curve of some bolder projection … it [the phrase] was still there, like an iridescent bubble that floats for a while unbroken. As a rainbow whose brightness is fading seems to subside, then soars again and, before it is extinguished, shines forth with greater splendour than it has ever shown.
>
> (422; 424)

In *The Captive*, Marcel's descriptions of both Vinteuil's sonata and septet, as well as his recollection of the musical soirée at the Verdurins', are similarly replete with visual analogies.[11] To cite just one example, when Marcel hears the opening bars of Vinteuil's septet, this is how he describes the music's effect on him:

> Whereas the sonata opened upon a lily-white pastoral dawn, dividing its fragile purity only to hover in the delicate yet compact entanglement of a rustic bower

---

[11] When Marcel describes hearing for the first time the 'little phrase' from Vinteuil's sonata, he too uses a visual analogy to capture the difficulties he has in understanding it. 'For our memory,' he says, 'relatively to the complexity of the impressions which it has to face while we are listening, is infinitesimal … Of these multiple impressions our memory is not capable of furnishing us with an immediate picture. But that picture gradually takes shape in memory … even when I had heard the sonata from beginning to end, it remained almost wholly invisible to me, like a monument of which distance or a haze allows us to catch but a faint and fragmentary glimpse' (*Within a Budding Grove* 118–119). Marcel here anticipates the detailed 'picture' that will have taken shape in his memory by the time he describes both the sonata and septet so vividly in *The Captive*.

of honeysuckle against white geraniums, it was upon flat, unbroken surfaces like those of the sea on a morning that threatens storm, in the midst of an eerie silence, in an infinite void, that this new work [the septet] began, and it was into a rose-red daybreak that this unknown universe was drawn from the silence and the night to build up gradually before me. This redness, so new, so absent from the tender, pastoral, unadorned sonata, tinged all the sky, as dawn does, with a mysterious hope.

(282)

The music's ineffableness – what Marcel calls its 'transposition of profundity into terms of sound' (290) – is given expression by means of visual metaphor, imparting to the reader the sonata's tender pastoral mood in contrast to the sombre soundscape of the septet's opening, pictured as a storm-threatened seascape. The ensuing description of the septet, over nearly ten pages, repeatedly invokes painterly allusions, such as the work's triumphant concluding motif being pictured as 'an ineffable joy which seemed to come from paradise, a joy as different from the sonata as some scarlet-clad Mantegna archangel sounding a trumpet from a grave and gentle Bellini seraph strumming a theorbo' (294). Marcel then compares the art of Elstir with the music of Vinteuil: reflecting on what he has learned from them both, he writes, 'The only true voyage … would not be to visit strange lands but to possess other eyes, to see the universe through the eyes of another, of a hundred others, to see the hundred universes that each of them sees, that each of them is' (291).

Considering the plenitude of visual detail in the novel, even in descriptions of impressions made by the other senses, it seems a necessary critical endeavour to examine more closely the implications of 'a Proustian optics', not least where memory is concerned. This kind of endeavour motivates Thomas Baldwin's recent essay, 'Proust's Picture Plane'. Baldwin's argument echoes my own reading of the novel, in that he contends that the *Search* presents its reader with a kind of 'picture plane', whereby the narrator's descriptions act as 'virtual paintings under an ekphrastic description' (134). For Baldwin, the 'picture plane' is a 'phenomenological "modelling tool" for Proust, marking areas of the novel where the limits at which our perception of the world occur are brought vividly to our attention' (135). Proust's narrator often conjures remembered objects and scenes as if they were paintings, Baldwin argues, and, in so doing, establishes a fundamental difference between 'subject' (the narrator) and 'object' (the depicted world). In this way, Proust's 'text conjures glimpses or flashes of pictorial surface to show that consciousness is limited and oblique' (Baldwin 136). Like a framed picture, consciousness apprehends at the cost of what it leaves outside the sensory 'frame', and whatever it contemplates (including the past) can only be seen from the 'oblique' view of the present. The significance of Baldwin's essay, though, is not only that it alerts us to the presence of a 'picture plane' within Proust's text with its attendant epistemological implications, but that it discloses the figuration implied by it. A 'picture plane', that is, can only be conjured within a text by means of *analogies* – the tried-and-true way of metaphor.[12] As Baldwin aptly defines it: 'Picturing – a literalization of metaphor as ekphrasis or quasi-ekphrasis' (135). The following examples from the novel will illustrate that ekphrases of the past in Proust are, indeed, literalized metaphors: in this book's terms, prose pictures.

Before analysing key instances of prose pictures in the *Search*, though, I want to explore further how ekphrasis operates in narrative by turning to Gustave Flaubert, a writer who had a formative influence on Proust's descriptive style.

Reading painterly prose

In *Realist Vision*, a book which re-establishes the significance of visual description in the study of the novel,[13] Peter Brooks argues that realism in prose fiction shares intimate ties with realism in painting:

> For realism is almost by definition highly visual, concerned with registering what the world looks like ... It needs to give the thereness of the physical world, as in a

---

[12] My discussion of metaphor in Proust finds resonance in Jan Zwicky's understanding of analogical thought: 'By "metaphor" I mean the linguistic expression of the results of focused analogical thinking ... Similes and analogies, too, are metaphorical in the sense I am concerned with. The "like" in such figures is merely a nod in the direction of the metaphor's implicit "is not"' (5). 'The implied "is not" in a metaphor,' in Zwicky's striking formulation, 'points to a gap in language through which we glimpse the world. That which we glimpse is what the "is" in a metaphor points to' (10).

[13] Visual description has been part of the novel's architecture since the novel's conception. Among the earliest texts that can be loosely called novelistic is Achilles Tatius's *Leucippe and Clitophon*, written c. 300 CE, and it begins with an extraordinary ekphrasis. A traveller, having survived a storm, arrives at Sidon. On his way to make an offering to the goddess Astarte, he comes across a painting hanging inside a temple: 'I saw a picture hanging up which was a landscape and a seascape in one. The painting was of Europa: the sea depicted was the Phoenician ocean; the land, Sidon. On the land part was a meadow and a troop of girls: in the sea a bull was swimming, and on his back sat a beautiful maiden, borne by the bull toward Crete ... The painter had put the girls at one end of the meadow where the land jutted out into the sea. Their look was compounded of joy and fear: garlands were bound about their brows; their hair had been allowed to flow loose on their shoulders ... their eyes were fixed wide open upon the sea, and their lips were slightly parted, as if they were about to utter a cry of fear; their hands were stretched out in the direction of the bull' (3–9). For an analysis of this ekphrasis and its subversive connotations in Tatius's text, see Helen Morales, *Vision and Narrative* 36–60. See also Webb, *Ekphrasis, Imagination* 178–185, where Webb examines ekphrasis in Tatius and other Greek novels from antiquity, arguing that ekphrasis has always been 'central to the novel as genre' (179).

still-life painting. In fact, realism as a critical and polemical term comes into the culture, in the early 1850s, to characterize painting ... and then by extension is taken to describe a literary style. It is a term resolutely attached to the visual, to those works that seek *to inventory* the immediate perceptible world.

(my emphasis 16)

Flaubert's descriptive prose style was being formed contemporaneously with realism's painterly conception,[14] between the 1840s and 1850s, and his works reflect modernity's obsession with capturing the contingent details that compose everyday life, inventorying the visual minutiae of mundane reality. In *Madame Bovary*, for example, 'everything is perfectly rendered. As in a Brueghel painting, nothing is missing. The more you look at it, the more you find that all the details are in place' (Brooks 70). This kind of exhaustive approach to description meant that Flaubert's novels tended to upset readers' expectations of surprizing revelations and the predictably unpredictable ending – the structuring principle of the serialized novel exemplified in the work of Charles Dickens and Alexandre Dumas. As Auerbach argues, 'Flaubert ... lingers as a matter of principle over insignificant events and everyday circumstances which hardly advance the action' (547). For Auerbach, Flaubert's *depiction* of the insignificant is the advent of modernity in literature, in that his aim – as it was also to become for Proust, Woolf, Joyce and those in their wakes – 'was to put the emphasis on the random occurrence, to exploit it not in the service of a planned continuity of action but in itself. And in the process something new and elemental appeared: nothing

---

[14] In *S/Z*, Barthes has also examined the painterly aspirations of the realist novelist, who is said to carry around a kind of 'empty frame' with which to delimit 'a collection or continuum of objects' (54). 'Thus, realism ... consists not in copying the real but in copying a (depicted) copy of the real: this famous *reality*, as though suffering from a fearfulness which keeps it from being touched directly, is *set farther away*, postponed, or at least captured through the pictorial matrix in which it has been steeped before being put into words: code upon code, known as realism' (Barthes 55). Another way to think about the relation between painting and literature is provided by Ricoeur. Ricoeur argues that instead of seeing realism as a 'copying' of the extant, we can conceive it as an augmentation enriching our apprehension of the real ('Function of Fiction' 136). Ricoeur does not deny that our understanding of reality is mediated by codes, *pace* Barthes; what he is interested in is how the painterly 'models' through which we look at the world can also create the new, rather than reproduce the old. As he argues: 'To the extent that models are not models of ... i.e., still pictures of a previously given reality, but models for ..., i.e., heuristic fictions for redescribing reality, the work of the model becomes in turn a model for constituting in a meaningful way the concept of the productive reference of all fictions' (141). Reading Proustian description through Ricoeur's remarks, we can appreciate how the painterly models that Proust's writing draws on act as a kind of raw material for the novel's unforgettable instances of ekphrastic scenes, which are not only descriptions of Marcel's memories but also metaphor-effected redescriptions of his apprehension of the real. Proustian description, that is, *refreshes* the staid, conventional representation of reality. It may issue out of the 'empty frame' that every writer and artist must 'look' through, but the view it presents to the reader is far from orthodox. Perhaps this explains why the mimesis of memory in Proust is so often a surprise that, paradoxically, seems deeply familiar.

less than the wealth of reality and depth of life in every moment to which we surrender ourselves without prejudice' (552). As Flaubert himself famously described the novelist's goal in a letter: '[it is] to represent the little detail as powerfully as the other kind ... to make you feel almost *materially* the objects he reproduces' (*Selected Letters* 170).

'If we wish to find in the modern novel a model or a precursor of Proustian description,' Genette observes, 'we should think of Flaubert' (*Narrative Discourse* 101). Genette points to an important distinction between description as it appears in Flaubert and as it was practised before him. While extended description is also pervasive in Balzac's novels, Genette argues, there the omniscient narrator will often 'describe a scene that ... no one, strictly speaking, is looking at', whereas Flaubertian description, while it does not exclude this kind of omniscience, tends to focalize what is being described through the eyes of a character (*Narrative Discourse* 101).[15] In Proust, description is likewise 'always bound to the perceptual activity of the hero. Proustian descriptions are rigorously focalized ... their content never exceeds what is actually perceived by the contemplator' (Genette 204). I would only add that while what we see in Proustian description is indeed what Marcel the 'hero' sees, we also notice how this ekphrastic seeing is *brought about* by Marcel the narrator. The content of what is being depicted belongs to the perspective of the 'contemplator' – his younger self – but the *form* of its expression (the descriptive language and metaphorical imagery) derives from the older, narrating self. In this way, even at the level of individual descriptive passages, a suturing of temporalities is already happening in the novel. Marcel's language presences his future self *within the very lines* of narration about his past, and this is why, in Genette's memorable sentence, when reading Proust we experience '[e]xtreme mediation, and at the same time utmost immediacy' (168–169).[16]

---

[15] See also Jonathan Culler 79–88 and 96–98. Culler argues that while Balzacian description is thematically motivated and always invested with a clear symbolic connotation, in Flaubert descriptive details are seldom causally or even symbolically connected.

[16] In an essay titled 'Narrate or Describe', this is how Georg Lukács reads the well-known agricultural fair scene in *Madame Bovary*: 'The description of the agricultural fair ... is among the most celebrated achievements of description in modern realism. But Flaubert presents only a "setting". ... The "setting" has an independent existence as an element in the representation of the environment. The characters, however, are nothing but observers of this setting. ... They become dabs of colour in a painting which rises above a lifeless level only insofar as it is elevated to an ironic symbol of philistinism. The painting assumes an importance which does not arise out of the subjective importance of the events, to which it is scarcely related, but from the artifice of its formal stylization' (114–115). Flaubertian description, in Lukács's assessment, signifies an artist's refusal to 'participate actively' in society and his being content with ironical observation, so that description becomes 'the writer's substitute for the epic significance that has been lost' (127). Lukács thus denounces

Description, in sum, is a key formal component in both Flaubert and Proust, because of the way it slows narration, introducing the seeming randomness of the real within an ordered whole, thus permitting us to occupy moments of rescued time as we contemplate them through the eyes and words of the narrator. From this perspective, Flaubert's novella *November* can be seen as a prototype of Proustian narration. This early text – described by Jonathan Culler as 'Flaubert's most ambitious work before the first [version of] *Education sentimentale*' (22) – is a retrospective narrative that recounts the romantic dreaming and frustrated desires of the unnamed narrator. 'We can sometimes spend centuries in exhaustive recollection of a certain hour that will never return, that has passed, that has forever ceased to exist, and that we would gladly give the whole future to get back' (*November* 104), writes Flaubert's romantic in a sentence so reminiscent of Marcel that Flaubert appears here to have channelled the voice of a fictional narrator from the future. The narrator continues: 'Those memories are flaming torches arranged here and there in some great dim hall, gleaming in the murk; only by their glimmer can you see anything at all; what is near them is brightly lit, while everything else is darker, covered over with shadows and gloom' (104). The narrator sees his memories glimmering in a dark place (for Marcel, the 'depths' out of which the Combray of his childhood emerges into light), and, like a shady hall containing 'flaming torches', his story consists of 'brightly lit' prose pictures of the past.

The productive distinction between the visually descriptive and narrational functions, characteristic of Flaubert's mature style, is captured in the following scene. The narrator has here returned to the bedroom of his lover, Marie, for their second tryst:

> She was alone, as she had been that morning; she was sitting in the same place, almost in the same posture; but she had changed her dress: this one was black, and the lace trimming around the neck quivered with a life of its own on her

---

the (seemingly) disinterested descriptive novel as a product of capitalist dehumanization (127). However, in his denunciation Lukács actually points to what is perhaps most significant about description in Flaubert, and certainly in Proust. 'Description', he writes, 'contemporizes everything. Narration recounts the past. One describes what one sees, and the spatial "present" confers a temporal "present" on men and objects. But it is an illusory present, not the present of immediate action and drama' (130). Lukács rightly places the 'present' in scare quotes, but he is wrong to imply that it could ever be otherwise. He claims that description even poses a danger for narration: 'The false contemporaneity in description brings a disintegration of the composition into disconnected and autonomous details' (132). In a Proustian narrative, though, memory's description 'contemporizes' the recalled moment but without compromising the novel formally. The reason for this is that the novel after Proust consists not of 'a series of *static* pictures', but of a series of descriptively delayed moments which become animated within the flow of narration in which they form an inextricable, though distinct, part.

white breast; her flesh was glowing, and her face had that lascivious pallor that the flicker of candlelight creates; her mouth half-opened, her hair hanging in curls around her shoulder and her eyes raised to the sky …

Straight away, she leapt joyfully up, dashed over to me and clasped me firmly in her arms. For us it was one of those shuddering embraces that lovers at night must enjoy when they meet.

(120)

The difference between these paragraphs is that the first one is all about *depiction*, as we contemplate a candlelit scene. Note the proliferation of descriptive nouns and adjectives, such as 'posture', 'dress', 'lace trimming', 'flicker of candlelight', 'lascivious pallor', 'curls', 'eye', creating a paratactic sequence of visual detail held together by semicolons. The second paragraph, on the other hand, is all about *action*, marked by such energetic verbs as 'leapt', 'dashed' and 'clasped'. Description is thus supplanted, even uprooted by narration – as indeed it must be, narrative configuration being a hypotactic ordering of paratactic events. What these two paragraphs illustrate, therefore, is the very *form* of descriptive narration, where the reader is lost among the specificities and details of description until he or she is again reminded that all of this is taking place in a plotted sequence of events.[17]

Ekphrastic evocations often feature allusions to visual media, predisposing us to read them as though they took on said media's formal properties. We often read a visual description, that is, as if it was depicted in a painting, photograph or film – we visualize it according to a visual medium's grammar. For instance, consider the narrator's evocation of contemplating the sea:

Then I found myself on a plateau in a mown field; I had the sea ahead of me, it was bright blue, the sun shed over it a profusion of gleaming pearls, and furrows of fire ran through the waves; between the azure sky and the dark blue of the sea the horizon shone in flaming splendour; the vault of the heavens rose over my head and then sank behind the waves that rose to meet it as if to close the circle of an invisible infinitude.

(*November* 105)

Puis je me suis trouvé sur un plateau, dans un champ fauché. J'avais la mer devant moi; elle était toute bleue; le soleil répandait dessus une profusion de perles lumineuses, des sillons de feu s'étendaient sur les flots; entre le ciel azuré et la mer plus foncée l'horizon rayonnait, flamboyait; la voûte commençait sur

---

[17] In Jacques Rancière's reading, *Madame Bovary* is similarly said to be composed out of two sequences of events: the story events proper, which are causally linked and propel the reader from beginning to ending with 'intrigue and denouement'; and 'micro-events', which do not advance the plot and are purely descriptive (*Emancipated Spectator* 123–124).

ma tête et s'abaissait derrière les flots, qui remontaient vers elle, faisant comme le cercle d'un infini invisible.

(*Novembre* 83–84)

This verbal seascape might conjure any number of mental images, and these images will blend into one another as we read.[18] To stay with the medium of painting: we might picture this scene as an amalgam of a landscape by Caspar David Friedrich (such as one of his *Rückenfigur* series, where a solitary figure is depicted with his or her back to the viewer, contemplating a grand view of nature) and J. M. W. Turner's vistas of swirling fiery light above the sea. Such painterly images aid us in visualizing the 'furrows of fire' ('des sillons de feu') and the 'flaming splendour' of the horizon ('l'horizon rayonnait, flamboyait'); when we reach the verb 'rose' ('remontaient') referring to the waves, the waves begin to move. The still scene has already, imperceptibly, become a moving one.

In this attempt to describe in phenomenological terms the painterly images that Flaubert's prose draws to itself, I have merely given an account of these images, not how they are brought about.[19] They are obviously brought about by the sentences that describe them, but it is rather difficult to account for why it is these words, arranged precisely in this manner, that work so effectively (even in translation) in evoking this scene. A useful concept to shed light on this interplay between image and text is Jacques Rancière's 'sentence-image'. The reason that this concept is useful in interpreting narratives, Rancière explains, is that it allows us to see how a 'paratactic syntax' can be effectuated within stories (*Future of Image* 43). In combining 'sentence' and 'image' into a hyphenated noun, Rancière attempts to account for narrative's ability to represent arresting moments *without* these moments' being removed from narrative time. The Flaubert passage above is a complex sentence depicting a moment of contemplation: we are first presented with the image of the field; then our eye is directed ahead, towards the sea and then on to the horizon glowing in fiery colours; finally, we look upwards at 'the vault of the heavens' and down again to see it sink 'behind the waves'

---

[18] In *Contre Sainte-Beuve*, Proust notes that when we read literature, 'To each sentence we attach a meaning, or at any rate a mental image, which is often a mistranslation. … When I read of the shepherd in *L'Ensorcelée* I see a man like a figure by Mantegna with the colouring of Botticelli's T [*sic*] … Perhaps this is not in the least what Barbey saw; but in Barbey's description there is a consort of statements, which, given the false premise of my mistranslation, leads to an equally beautiful shepherd' (267). See also Marielle Macé 222–228. Macé suggests that the *Search* 'offers a complete phenomenology of literary experience' (223).

[19] Peter Brooks has pointed to description as the literary mode connecting realism in the novel with phenomenology (*Realist Vision* 210–211). What distinguishes phenomenology from other kinds of philosophical discourse is its defamiliarizing *redescription* of our perception of everyday objects. See, for example, Alphonso Lingis 47–70. Lingis's prose ekphrastically evokes, among other things, a table, a sun-bleached log, a chunk of lava, a painting, a grapefruit, giant sequoias and a walk along the beach.

that meet it, as sea greets sky. This complex 'sentence-image' expresses an articulation of visuality (parataxis) to narrative grammar, the 'syntax' that makes the visual narratively presentable. By capturing this articulation of stillness and motion, the idea of a 'sentence-image' allows us to grasp the image's belonging to narrative temporality; although ekphrastic prose may seek to slow time and interrupt narrational progress, it nonetheless still belongs to it, as the sentence which forms it already performs its narratively syntactical role.

Rancière adds that in the 'sentence-image', '[t]he sentence function is still that of linking. But the sentence now links in as much as it is what gives flesh' (*Future of Image* 47). What it gives 'flesh' to are precisely the prose pictures themselves; the 'sentence-image' is one where 'words possess the weight of visible realities … It is the sentence of the novelist who, even if we cannot "see" anything in it, vouches by his ear that we are in the true, that the sentence-image is right', as Rancière puts it (58). Few writers have had a better ear than either Flaubert or Proust, and, as strange as this claim might seem – that a novelist needs to rely on his *ear* in order to affirm the effectiveness of his prose picturing – it only affirms the vital interdependence between hearing and seeing that is always at play when prose strives to be visual. In the above passage, Andrew Brown's translation preserves much of the writing's euphoniousness, but the original's alliteration, assonance and rhythm contribute to this sense of 'rightness' to an even greater degree. The French text reads with a sense of inevitability about its verbal aptness, and the flowing ease of the language, created by alliteration ('feu', 'flots', 'foncée', 'flamboyait') and the assonance of the concluding vowel sound that occurs in French in the third-person singular and plural imperfect ('rayonnait', 'flamboyait', 'commençait', 's'abaissait', 'remontaient') – all contribute to the *ease* with which the sentence is able to function ekphrastically. Additionally, consisting as this passage does of measured pauses, marked by semicolons, the prose seems to undulate aurally like the sea it seeks to depict.

In Proust, there is a multitude of these kinds of intermedially coloured passages where 'the sentence-image is right'. One such passage is Marcel's unforgettable description of first seeing Robert de Saint-Loup at Balbec:

> One afternoon of scorching heat I saw in the dining-room of the hotel, plunged in semi-darkness to shield it from the sun, which gilded the drawn curtains through the gaps between which twinkled the blue of the sea, when along the central gangway leading from the beach to the road I saw approaching, tall, slim, bare-necked, his head held proudly erect, a young man with penetrating eyes whose skin was as fair and his hair as golden as if they had absorbed all the rays of the sun. Dressed in a suit of soft, whitish material ['Vêtu d'un étoffe

souple et blanchâtre'] ... the thinness of which suggested no less vividly than the coolness of the dining-room the heat and brightness of the glorious day outside, he was walking fast. His eyes, from one of which a monocle kept dropping, were the colour of the sea. ... He strode rapidly across the whole width of the hotel, seeming to be in pursuit of his monocle, which kept darting away in front of him like a butterfly. He was coming from the beach, and the sea which filled the lower half of the glass front of the hall made a background against which he stood out full-length, as in certain portraits whose painters attempt, without in any way falsifying the most accurate observation of contemporary life, but by choosing for their sitter an appropriate setting – a polo ground, golf links, a race-course, the bridge of a yacht – to furnish a modern equivalent of those canvases on which the old masters used to present the human figure in the foreground of a landscape ['donner un équivalent moderne de ces toiles où les primitifs faisaient apparaître la figure humaine au premier plan d'un paysage'].

(*Within a Budding Grove* 356–357; *À la recherche* 729)

As in the bedroom scene in Flaubert's text, the rhythm of this passage is distinct from earlier paragraphs, where Marcel summarily relates his conversation with his grandmother, following their drive about Balbec in the company of the grandmother's friend, Mme de Villeparisis:

Mme de Villeparisis gave us warning that presently she would not be able to see so much of us. A young nephew [Saint-Loup] ... was coming to spend a few weeks' leave with her. ... In the course of our drives together she had spoken highly of his intelligence and above all his kind-heartedness, and already I imagined that he would take a liking to me, that I would be his best friend.

(355)

Marcel's narrational commentary here acts as backstory, *preceding* the prose picture of Saint-Loup framed against the glass doorway. His anticipation of meeting the praised nephew (who will indeed become his best friend) thus becomes a kind of signal to the reader of the verbal frame to come.

Proustian description is more overtly painterly than Flaubert's (invoking 'certain portraits', 'the old masters'), and its ekphrastic frame is also more capacious, capturing Saint-Loup's movements but without upsetting the scene's stilled quality. Saint-Loup's prose picture blends motion and stillness, and the following 'sentence-image' portrays rightly, balancing stillness, conveyed by the lengthy metaphor-driven opening description, and movement, indicated by the closing clause: 'Dressed in a suit of soft, whitish material ... the thinness of which suggested no less vividly than the coolness of the dining-room the heat and brightness of the glorious day outside, he was walking fast.' Here, the airy thinness of the whitish suit is used as a metaphor for the seeing of the day's 'brightness', illustrating the synaesthetic quality of Proustian metaphors, where the opening analogy is used to render *more immediately* other kinds of sensations. The invocations of modern portrait settings with their scenery suggestive of wealth ('a polo ground, golf-links, a race-course, the bridge of a yacht') also facilitate the scene's slowdown, 'stressing by rhythm, tone, timbre and visual devices a picture highly intensified' (Caws 22).

Mnemonic ekphrases in Proust

In *Swann's Way*, when young Marcel describes his infatuation with Bergotte's prose, he reveals an attachment to just this kind of memorable description. He relates how he would always try to write with his favourite writer's clarity of vision, anxious lest his writing should fail to 'exactly reproduce what I had perceived in my mind's eye' (113). What most impresses Marcel about Bergotte's writing is its ability to picture beauty:

> Whenever he spoke of something whose beauty remained hidden from me, of pine-forests or of hailstorms, of Notre-Dame Cathedral, of *Athalie* or of *Phèdre*, by some piece of *imagery* he would make their beauty explode into my consciousness. And so, realising that the universe contained innumerable elements which my feeble senses would be powerless to discern did he not bring them within my reach, I longed to have some opinion, some *metaphor* of his, upon everything in the world, and especially upon such things as I might some day have an opportunity of *seeing* for myself.
>
> (my emphasis 112)

Marcel is magnetized precisely by those moments in Bergotte's books when the writer would break off his narrative and indulge descriptive fancy. It is the striking images, accurately conveyed by Bergotte's metaphors, that linger in Marcel's memory; as he says of such passages, 'I knew all of them by heart' (112). Whenever Bergotte 'resumed the thread of his narrative' – once narration took over from description – Marcel says that he was left disappointed (112). Now, I do not want to suggest that while reading Proust readers are similarly left disappointed whenever narration resumes and delight only in description. Rather, to quote Marcel's verdict on Bergotte, Proustian description is the kind of prose 'invocation, an apostrophe, a long prayer' (112) that is most *memorable* about his writing.

In this respect, a suggestive comparison can be made between the indelible impression made by Proustian description on the memory of the reader and a particular function of ekphrasis in antiquity that Webb traces in 'The Model Ekphraseis of Nikolaos the Sophist as Memory Images'. Nikolaos's ekphrases depict, in painstaking detail, statues of characters from the tragic stage, such as Medea, Antigone and Prometheus; 'the author of the ekphrasis', Webb writes, 'creates in his audience's mind the memorable image of a figure that bears the signs of her story and can therefore serve as a permanent reminder of that story in all its details' (473). Nikolaos's detailed descriptions served, in effect, as a kind of aide-memoire of the stories of classical literature, and the same can be said about mnemonic ekphrases in Proust, which also act 'as a permanent reminder' of the narrator's recounted past.

Description in Proust is arresting not only in the sense that it slows narration, but in that it *captivates* our attention, often surprising us with unexpected analogies. Once the narrator sees Combray emerge before his mind's eye out of the cup of tea, the prose presents his memories via lingering, memorable metaphors.[20] Marcel's descriptions of the streets and environs of Combray act like visual pauses, at times evocative of Impressionist landscapes:

> And on one of the longest walks we used to take from Combray there was a spot where the narrow road emerged suddenly on to an immense plain, closed at the horizon by a jagged ridge of forest above which rose the solitary point of Saint-Hilaire's steeple, so slender and so pink that it seemed to be no more than scratched on the sky by the finger nail of a painter anxious to give to such a landscape, to so pure a piece of nature, this little sign of art, this single indication of human existence.
>
> (*Swann's Way* 73–74)

There is a sense in this passage of nature imitating art, as a remembered scene is being compared to the *thereness* of a painted canvas, with the steeple of Saint-Hilaire rendered so strikingly tangible by the metaphor 'scratched on the sky by the finger nail of a painter'. These kinds of painterly analogies recur throughout

---

[20] Mnemonic ekphrasis seeks to make present what is absent, and metaphor, in Fredric Jameson's sense, enables it to do so most effectively; as Jameson puts it, 'what is inescapable is the function of metaphor to detemporalize existence, to dechronologize and denarrativize the present, indeed, to construct or reconstruct a new temporal present which we are so oddly tempted to call eternal ... consistent with the "eternity" of individual consciousness itself as long as it lasts' (26). Description, that is, de-narrativizes the narrative's present whenever it deploys metaphor, thus constructing 'a new present' – in Proust's case, a past moment that is fleetingly presenced before us.

the 'Combray' section of the novel. Another example is a memory of the walk Marcel would take with his parents along the Méséglise way, as he recalls

> a landscape in which all life appeared to be suspended, while the little village of Roussainville carved its white gables in relief upon the sky with an overpowering precision and finish. A gust of wind put up a solitary crow, which flapped away and settled in the distance, while against a greying sky the woods on the horizon assumed a deeper tone of blue, as though *painted in one of those monochromes that still decorate the overmantels of old houses* ['comme *peint dans ses camaïeux qui décorent les trumeaux des anciennes demeures*'].
>
> (my emphasis, Swann's Way 179–180; À la recherche 150)

Here, Proust's description not only invokes the visual but also displays its own artfulness. We see, that is, not only the images it presents but also the *manner* of their presentation: the revitalizing metaphors evoking them, comparing sights inwardly seen to objects and artworks externally perceived.

Later in the novel, when Marcel reconstructs the walk along the Guermantes way, he talks about memory itself in the language of a visual artist:

> And for such reconstruction memory furnishes me with more detailed guidance than is generally at the disposal of restorers: the pictures which it has preserved ['quelques images conservées par ma mémoire'] … of what Combray looked like in my childhood days; pictures which, because it was the old Combray that traced their outlines upon my mind before it vanished, are as moving – if I may compare a humble landscape with those glorious works, reproductions of which my grandmother was so fond of bestowing on me – as those old engravings of the Last Supper or that painting by Gentile Bellini, in which one sees, in a state in which they no longer exist, the masterpiece of Leonardo and the portico of Saint Mark's.
>
> (199; 166)

The Proustian conception of memory, as these passages illustrate, is one where memory is said to contain its own 'pictures', and it is up to the writer to turn his or her reader into spectator, verbally present-ing these recollected sights. It is thus not surprising that in narratives which share this conception, memory's verbal evocation often either invokes actual pictures or resorts to pictorial allusion. Liliane Louvel suggests that 'pictorial allusion realizes the link between memory, vision and representation … intimately; it solicits memory, yet, contrary to reference, it does not freeze it' (*Pictorial Third* 174). If pictorial allusion 'solicits' memory in this way, as it clearly does in Proust's novel, then this kind of solicitation is exemplified by mnemonic ekphrasis. The way pictorial allusion differs from intertextual citation, Louvel argues, is in the exchange of medium, an exchange that has implications for one's phenomenological experience of ekphrasis:

> [T]he image and its force of *evidence* interposes a 'something', an 'other thing' that cannot be pinpointed exactly, the visual, the *instantaneous* (in perception). The reader turns into spectator. In other words, while allusion to a work of literature consists in a concentric (centripetal) evocation, allusion to a painting performs an eccentric (centrifugal) movement.
>
> (174)

Unlike intertextual allusion, which operates centripetally in drawing us towards the hidden heart of a text, the sense-generating movement of ekphrasis produces a centrifugal semantic pulse that propels the mind's eye off the page and towards a picture that is the text's 'other thing'. Indeed, even when it depicts a *mnemonic* image, 'ekphrasis', in Webb's phrase, 'is haunted by the *idea* of the work of art' (*Ekphrasis, Imagination* 83).

The 'force of evidence', 'the instantaneous' and 'the idea of the work of art' that Louvel and Webb emphasize, I am suggesting, are all characteristic elements of the depicted memory image in Proust. Throughout the *Search*, the narrator's memory is evoked via intermedial allusions. Aside from painting, photography is another medium that helps Marcel to make sense of his past. When Marcel talks about pleasure (and pleasure, in Proust, is invariably retrospective), he likens its recollection to a photograph: 'What we take, in the presence of the beloved object, is merely a negative, which we develop later, when we are back home, and have once again found at our disposal that inner darkroom the entrance to which is barred to us so long as we are with other people' (*Within a Budding Grove* 522).[21] But it is painterly associations that dominate Marcel's meditations on memory. Indeed, the importance of painting for Proust's aesthetic sensibility can hardly be overstated, prompting Eric Karpeles to remark, 'writing is the way Proust painted' (20).[22]

---

[21] See Chapter 6. See also Emily Setina's recent essay 'Proust's Darkroom' (1081–1082). For a comprehensive account of how Proust relied on photographic reproductions of artworks as creative prompts, see Mary Bergstein 27–45. For an overview of scholarship on Proust and photography, see ibid. 14–22.

[22] See Eric Karpeles, *Paintings in Proust*. Karpeles's book compiles every passage invoking a painting in the *Search* with the painting's reproduction, counting one hundred artists named in the novel (10). Turning the pages of *Paintings in Proust*, the reader's eye jumps back and forth between two kinds of seeing: the vivid textual descriptions and the paintings arising between their lines. Where my reading of the novel departs from Karpeles's approach is in arguing that ekphrasis in Proust is also informed by mnemonic images lacking an *explicit* painterly referent. For an overview of Proust's knowledge of visual art, and how 'paintings stimulate memory' (86) in the *Search*, see Gabrielle Townsend.

In *Within a Budding Grove*, Marcel recounts his meeting with Elstir, a painter whom he admires and whose artistic vision instructs his own. What strikes Marcel's eye about Elstir's canvases are their pictorial 'metaphors'. For instance, Elstir's much-commented-upon painting of a harbour, *Le Port de Carquethuit*, defamiliarizes ordinary perspective 'by employing, for the little town, only marine terms, and urban terms for the sea' (480). Marcel presents us with an ekphrasis of this painting – over several pages – celebrating the way it, like all art, 'takes us out of our cocoon of habit' (482). Elstir's painting blurs the boundaries between sea and sky, showing how the expanse and ambience of the one reflects and comments upon the other; because of the unusual perspective, 'a ship actually at sea, half-hidden by the projecting works of the arsenal, seemed to be sailing through the middle of the town … A party of holiday makers were putting gaily out to sea in a boat that tossed like a jaunting-car on a rough road' (481). His eye thus tutored by Elstir's art, Marcel finds himself grasping for what he saw in it in his everyday surroundings. While sitting at table after breakfast, for example, he tries to apprehend the objects around him as if they were painted by Elstir: 'the broken *gestures* of the knives still *lying across one another* … the half-empty glass which thus *showed to greater advantage the noble sweep* of its curved sides and, in the heart of its translucent crystal, *clear as frozen daylight*, some dregs of wine, dark but glittering with reflected lights' (my emphasis 519). In staging this act of looking for art within the everyday, Marcel's description does to the reader what Elstir's canvases did to him – it strikes us with the poetry of its images, notably that unexpected metaphor, 'clear as frozen daylight', perfectly imaging the translucence of a wine glass.

We can discern both the distinctness of prose picturing and the kind of 'seeing' made possible via ekphrasis by examining this kind of acting out of recalled visual perception by verbal means. One of the defining characteristics of ekphrasis is that it presents us with a parataxis of detail artfully strung together to compose a scene. However, a paratactic arrangement is not sufficient to realize ekphrasis' aim: to make the reader seem to *see* the object of description. To *emulate* visual perception, description requires the support of metaphor. In a fittingly titled essay, 'The Function of Fiction in Shaping Reality', Paul Ricoeur captures the quintessence of literary description when he writes: 'The seeing created by language is … not a seeing of this or that, it is a "seeing-as"' (133). From this perspective, the function of ekphrasis is the verbal 'shaping' of visual perception, its enrichment; and the function of mnemonic ekphrasis in Proust and after is a verbal 'seeing-as' of memory images as if they were tangibly present before the mind's eye. In Marcel's description, the surface of the wine glass is rendered perfectly by the figure 'clear as frozen daylight': the phrase confers to the reader a sense of seeing the crystalline surface of a wine glass, as if for the first time, precisely *by solidifying* that which is diffuse and diaphanous (the Balbec daylight caught within the glass). The metaphor, by refracting visual recall verbally, enriches the memory being conveyed; in doing so, it also tutors our eye to see anew, without our eyes having seen anything other than words.[23]

Proust's conception of aesthetic value is captured in the following remark Marcel makes about Elstir, and it reflects on this function: 'if God the Father had created things by naming them, it was by taking away their names or giving them other names that Elstir created them anew. The names which designate things correspond invariably to an intellectual notion, alien to our true impressions, and compelling us to eliminate from them everything that is not in keeping with that notion' (479).[24] Proust elsewhere talks about art 'shattering … the ice of the habitual and the rational which instantly congeals over reality and keeps us from ever *seeing* it' (my emphasis, *Contre Sainte-Beuve* 267). Russian literary theorist Viktor Shklovsky characterizes aesthetic experience in terms surprisingly close to Proust's, and his account of art's effects on consciousness is instructive here. In Shklovsky – as in Bergson – habit reigns supreme over perception, producing what he calls 'an algebraic way of thinking' (79). In everyday life, we do not really notice things but see only their most accessible, superficial features; as Shklovsky puts it: 'A thing passes us as if packaged; we know of its existence by the space it takes up, but we only see its surface' (79). This kind of blinkered noticing is produced by prosaic speech, the verbal shorthand we use to get by with practical affairs – what Proust would call our referring to things by their *designated* names. Shklovsky writes:

> what we call art exists in order to give back the sensation of life, in order to make us feel things, in order to make the stone stony. The goal of art is *to create the sensation of seeing*, and not merely recognizing, things; the device of art is the '*ostranenie*' of things and the complication of the form, which increases the

---

[23] Cf. Ricoeur: 'the "seeing-as" activated in reading ensures the joining of verbal meaning with imagistic fullness … it joins the light of sense with the fullness of the image. In this way, the non-verbal and the verbal are firmly united at the core of the image-ing function of language' (*Rule of Metaphor* 252–253).

[24] See also Prendergast 153–154. Prendergast argues that when it comes to the defamiliarization at work in Proustian metaphors, 'there is probably very little to be added to this topic in critical discussion' (154). Prendergast's claim is hasty, however, not least because he does not mention the work of Viktor Shklovsky and the insights it imparts for a more complete understanding of Proustian metaphor – in particular, metaphor's intimate ties with the visual (and not only with painting).

duration and complexity of perception, as the process of perception is its own end in art and must be prolonged.[25]

(my emphasis 80)

Although Shklovsky is sensitive, like Proust, to the multisensory nature of aesthetic experience, his remarks emphasize 'seeing' life freshly. Verbal art creates 'the sensation of seeing' by 'de-automatizing perception' (93), Shklovsky adds, and it does so in large part by *describing* anew – by assigning things with names (metaphors) with which we (and they) are unacquainted.

Ekphrastic description with its metaphorical refraction of the real and Shklovskian *ostranenie* are, clearly, implicated devices. Ekphrasis in Proust is precisely where 'the sensation of seeing' is created, and there are particularly striking instances of this in *The Guermantes Way*. Early in the volume, Marcel is enchanted (though not without retrospective irony) by the magical, because so far inaccessible, world of the Faubourg Saint-Germain. His family has relocated to the Hôtel de Guermantes, a townhouse in Paris where, across the courtyard, resides Mme de Guermantes. Pondering the Guermantes's hidden riches, with their famed salon where the socially distinguished gather, Marcel muses: 'I should never be permitted to set my feet among them. And I must content myself with a shiver of excitement as I sighted from the open sea … like a prominent minaret, like the first palm, like the first signs of some exotic industry or vegetation, the well-trodden doormat of its shore' (27). Like the sea-tossed sailor who beholds the threshold of the minaret or palm that marks dry land, after many months at sea, Marcel, after years of dreaming, here sees a literal threshold – and never did a shabby doormat seem imbued with more significance than in this description. Or consider the following instance of ekphrastic *ostranenie*. While attending a theatrical performance, Marcel scans the boxes in quest of a glimpse of Princess de Guermantes. Gradually, he can see figures emerging before his gaze out of the darkened interior:

> [A]s the performance went on, their vaguely human forms detached themselves languidly one after the other from the depths of the night which they embroidered, and, raising themselves towards the light, allowed their half-naked bodies to emerge into the chiaroscuro of the surface where their gleaming faces appeared behind the playful, frothy undulations of their ostrich-feather fans, beneath their hyacinthine, pearl-studded headdresses which seemed to

---

[25] Shklovsky's translator Alexandra Berlina (58–62) stresses that *ostranenie* (остранение) is not quite the same as defamiliarization, as it has sometimes been translated.

bend with the motion of the waves. Beyond began the orchestra stalls, abode of mortals for ever separated from the sombre, transparent realm to which here and there, in their smooth liquid surface, the limpid, reflecting eyes of the water-goddesses served as frontier ...

Like a tall goddess presiding from afar over the frolics of the lesser deities, the Princess had deliberately remained somewhat in the background on a sofa placed sideways in the box, red as a coral reef, beside a large vitreous expanse which was probably a mirror and suggested a section, perpendicular, opaque and liquid, cut by a ray of sunlight in the dazzling crystal of the sea. At once plume and corolla, like certain subaqueous growths, a great white flower, downy as the wing of a bird, hung down the Princess's forehead along one of her cheeks, the curve of which it followed with coquettish, amorous, vibrant suppleness, as if half enclosing it like a pink egg in the softness of a halcyon's nest.

(37–39)

This description is packed with visual cues to the reader's imagination, in phrases such as 'raising themselves towards the light', 'the chiaroscuro of the surface', 'gleaming faces', 'a large vitreous expanse', and 'cut by a ray of sunlight in the dazzling crystal of the sea'. What Marcel the *character* saw in the theatre years ago, together with the attendant, if misguided, adoration he then felt for this garish world of the socially distinguished, Marcel the *narrator* evokes by means of colourful marine, avian and floral imagery. The prose picture of the theatre's interior space verbally reproduces a moment of recollected vision, recapturing the younger Marcel's romanticization of a person whom, years later, he will find to be mundane.[26] Encountering passages such as these in Proust's novel and contemplating their imagery, we can appreciate the fittingness of Shklovsky's words: 'Vision is the artist's goal; the artistic is "artificially" created in such a way that perception lingers and reaches its greatest strength and length' (93).

In one of his final interviews, Shklovsky thus summed up the purpose of art: 'we struggle with the world, but we don't see it ... [Art] looks at the things outside with wonder. Art is continuous astonishment' (Vitale 91). Art, that is, restores our apprehension of the world by re-presenting it in a way that surprises an intellect dulled by habit. We find an echoing conception in *Time Regained*, the closing volume of the *Search*. This is where Marcel presents us with his revelation about Time gifted to him by involuntary memory, and, in sketching his plans for

---

[26] See *Sodom and Gomorrah* 45 and 68–69, where an older Marcel realizes that he and the Princess have nothing in common, nothing meaningful to say to one another.

the book that he hopes to write, he retrospectively accounts for the *Search*'s own aesthetic principles. Marcel reflects: 'we have to rediscover, to reapprehend, to make ourselves fully aware of that reality, remote from our daily preoccupations, from which we separate ourselves by an ever greater gulf as the conventional knowledge we substitute for it grows thicker and more impermeable' (*Time Regained* 253). Ordinary life is encrusted with a layer of clichés, both perceptual and verbal. Marcel, we have seen, blames habits – Proust's shorthand for sensory sluggishness – which 'smother our true impressions, so as entirely to conceal them from us, beneath a whole heap of verbal concepts and practical goals which we falsely call life' (254).[27] Metaphor-effected *ostranenie* is art's redress of this kind of sensory deadening, and it is a key ingredient of Proust's prose pictures, waking perception from habit-induced slumber by means of verbal artistry.

Proust's novel features extensive depictions of the sights disclosed to Marcel by involuntary recall, producing textual loci of ekphrastic *ostranenie*. He experiences several instances of involuntary memory in *Time Regained*, and they all occur during his visit to the Guermantes's mansion. The Princess de Guermantes is hosting a musical soirée and Marcel, having been away for a long period of time at a sanatorium, memorably describes the spectacle of age staged by Time on the guests' familiar yet uncannily altered faces (286–292). When he first enters the Guermantes's courtyard, he is lost in thought and does not see a car coming towards him; stepping out of the way, he trips over a paving stone. Upon recovering his balance, he steps on 'a stone which was slightly lower than its neighbour' (216) and a sensation of great happiness overwhelms him – the same sensation he'd felt when tasting the madeleine cake soaked in tea, all those years ago. Note that the immediate recollection itself, here spurred on by the sense of touch, is intensely visual: 'a profound azure intoxicated my eyes, impressions of coolness, of dazzling light' (217). He realizes that the forgotten memory thus heralded is of the time he spent in Venice, when, in the baptistery of St. Mark's cathedral, he had similarly felt an uneven cobblestone underfoot (225–226).

Having arrived late to the soirée, he is directed to the library to wait for the musical performance to end. The Prince de Guermantes, seeing him there, asks a servant to offer him a drink and some petits fours. Marcel wipes his mouth

---

[27] See also Zwicky: 'the positive assertion in a metaphor is always an act of overcoming – as though "calcified" uses [of language] must in fact precede metaphorical gestures; as though it were characteristic of language that it first conceal the world – be non-metaphorical – before the metaphor reveals it to us' (11).

with the napkin that the servant brings him, and another vision from the past intervenes his present perception: 'a new vision of azure passed before my eyes, but an azure that this time was pure and saline and swelled into blue and bosomy undulations, and so strong was this impression that the moment to which I was transported seemed to me to be the present moment' (219). Here, the saline smell of the sea fuses with the sea's blue 'bosomy undulations', underscoring the way visual recollection ('a new vision of azure passed before my eyes') first follows on the heels of the other senses, and is subsequently itself enriched by them. This time, the memory hoisted out of the depths is of his stay on the Normandy coast at Balbec, where the towel he'd once used to dry his face had 'the same degree of stiffness and starchedness' as the napkin (219).[28] These chance mnemonic promptings are not at all like ordinary recollection, and what makes them unique is that they enable Marcel to experience a sense of timelessness. He realizes that the only way to convey to the reader this sense of being 'freed from the order of time' is by means of what he calls 'the miracle of an analogy' (223) coalescing past and present.

> And in this case as in all the others, the sensation common to past and present had sought to re-create the former scene around itself, while the actual scene which had taken the former one's place opposed with all the resistance of material inertia this incursion into a house in Paris of a Normandy beach or a railway embankment. ... I had remained in a state of ecstasy on the uneven paving-stones or before the cup of tea, endeavouring to prolong or to reproduce the momentary appearances of the Combray or the Balbec or the Venice which invaded only to be driven back, which rose up only at once to abandon me in the midst of the new scene which somehow, nevertheless, the past had been able to permeate ... so complete are these resurrections of the past during the second that they last, that they not only oblige our eyes to cease to see the room which is near to them in order to look instead at the railway bordered with trees or the rising tide ... they force our whole self to believe that it is surrounded by these places, or at least to waver doubtfully between them and the places where we now are, in a dazed uncertainty such as we feel sometimes when an indescribably beautiful vision presents itself to us at the moment of our falling asleep.[29]
>
> (226–227)

---

[28] See also Watt: 'A spoon knocking against a plate recalls the sound of a railwayman's hammer on the wheels of the train in which he sat and *observed, unmoved, the row of sunlit trees on his return to Paris*; wiping his mouth with a starched napkin *brings back the seascape at Balbec that he looked upon*, drying his face with a similarly textured towel, on his first morning there; the shrill sound of water in a pipe *recalls the pleasure-steamers at Balbec*' (my emphasis, *Cambridge Introduction* 100).

[29] See also Bergson: 'Memories, which we believed abolished, then reappear with striking completeness; we live over again, in all their detail forgotten scenes of childhood' (*Matter and Memory* 154).

Involuntary recall immerses Marcel into a contemplation of the past as though it had never ceased to be, and this immersion is ekphrastically represented, as if in a scene presently seen and presently felt.

In this sense, ekphrastic representation – when successful – mirrors involuntary memory's revitalizing effects. That is, whenever we encounter memory's visual description in Proust, we are not transported into the past. Instead, the past is brought back into the narrator's present and introduced *vicariously* into our own, as we find ourselves immersed in its prose-rendered contemplation. For the narrator, the senses of touch, sound, taste and smell function like recall's synapses, collapsing the gap between two sensorily corresponding moments separated in time, and what is thus restored is almost always a visual impression. These mnemonic visions gifted to the self are three-dimensional, unlike the two-dimensional picture postcards that the intellect shows us. For instance, this is how Marcel describes the vision prompted by the feel of the uneven cobblestones:

> [T]he unevenness of the two paving-stones had *extended in every direction and dimension the desiccated and insubstantial images* I normally had of Venice and St. Mark's and all of the sensations which I had felt there, reuniting the piazza to the cathedral, the landing-stage to the piazza, the canal to the landing-stage, and to all that the eyes see the world of desires [*sic*] which is seen only by the mind.
>
> (my emphasis 229)

It is as if a virtual space were gradually being created in this description, which can be seen as a blueprint for how mnemonic ekphrasis operates, unfolding a scene phrase by phrase, figure by figure.[30]

Remembering prose pictures

These kinds of descriptions are memorable precisely because of their visual framing, and this is significant in terms of the novel's themes. In the opening two volumes of the *Search*, we are presented with several prose pictures where Marcel captures the impressions that *exemplify* his recollection of key persons and places from his past. These prose pictures are then recalled by the older Marcel, reminding both himself and the reader of sights previously seen, as

---

[30] My sense of 'figure' here may be read alongside Rancière's wish to expand 'the concept of "figure", to make it signify not only the substitution of one term for another but the intertwining of several regimes of expression and the work of several arts and several media' (*Emancipated Spectator* 131).

well as of the distance (both temporal and affective) separating these sights from his older, narrating self (for the reader, this distance is felt in the sheer scope of the novel and the time it takes to read it). Thus, in the penultimate volume, Marcel recalls 'the day when I had seen Saint-Loup for the first time at Balbec, so fair-complexioned, fashioned of so rare and precious a substance, his monocle fluttering in from of him' (*The Fugitive* 792). Then, in the final volume, when Marcel mourns the death of his friend he remembers the same gloriously rendered sight of Saint-Loup at Balbec, calling up a prose picture not easily forgotten, despite its having appeared more than a thousand pages earlier: 'For several days I remained shut up in my room, thinking of him. I recalled his arrival the first time at Balbec, when, in an almost white suit, with his eyes greenish and mobile like the waves, he had crossed the hall adjoining the great dining-room whose windows gave on to the sea' (*Time Regained* 191–193).

Marcel's recollection of Saint-Loup's image, framed against the sea, calls up a related prose picture, one which we already encountered in the previous chapter. 'A few days after the day on which I had seen him pursuing his monocle and supposed him to be so haughty,' he continues, 'in that hall at Balbec, there was another living form which I had seen for the first time on the beach at Balbec and which now, like his, no longer existed except in the state of memory: Albertine, making her progress along the sand that first evening, indifferent to everybody around her, a marine creature, like a seagull' (193–194). The image of Albertine on the beach, silhouetted against the sea, is invoked repeatedly in the novel. In the concluding part of *The Fugitive*, for instance, when Marcel records his gradually waning stages of grief, following Albertine's untimely death, we are reminded of this image:

> Who would have told me at Combray, when I lay waiting for my mother's good-night with so heavy a heart, that those anxieties would be healed, and would then break out again one day, not for my mother, but for a girl who would at first be no more, against the horizon of the sea, than a flower upon which my eyes would daily be invited to gaze.
>
> (572–573)

In *The Captive*, Marcel refers to his most vivid recollections of Albertine as producing a kind of composite image of her, what he calls

> the superimposition not merely of the successive images which Albertine had been for me, but also of the great qualities of intelligence and heart, and of the defects of character, all alike unsuspected by me, which Albertine, in a germination, a multiplication of herself, a fleshy efflorescence in sombre colours,

had added to a nature that formerly could scarcely have been said to exist, but was now difficult to plumb. For other people, even those of whom we have dreamed so much that they have come to seem no more than pictures, figures by Benozzo Gozzoli against a greenish background … such people, while they change in relation to ourselves, change also in themselves, and there had been an enrichment, a solidification and an increase of volume in the figure once simply outlined against the sea.

(70–71)

Over the course of the novel, we encounter many prose pictures of Albertine that contribute to this 'superimposition' effect, fleshing out her image and solidifying a 'figure once simply outlined against the sea'.[31] One such descriptive 'efflorescence' is of Albertine sleeping. Marcel's description of (his memory of) Albertine asleep is filled, fittingly, with marine associations, such as his comparison of the sound of her breathing to 'nights of full moon on the bay of Balbec, calm as a lake upon which the branches barely stir, where … one could listen for hours on end to the surf breaking and receding' (72).[32] We are then presented with a lengthy ekphrasis of her sleeping figure, from which I quote a sample: 'Her hair, falling along her pink cheek, was spread out beside her on the bed, and here and there an isolated straight tress gave the same effect of perspective as those moonlit trees, lank and pale, which one sees standing erect and stiff in the backgrounds of Elstir's Raphaelesque pictures' (73). Here, we join the *narrated*-Marcel and look upon Albertine as focalized through his eyes. Focalization, in Mieke Bal's definition, designates 'the *vision* of the events', where 'the speech act of narrating is … different from the vision, the memories, the sense perceptions, and the thoughts that are being told' (*Narratology* 135). Thus, although the older Marcel is telling the story, whenever we encounter these kinds

---

[31] In Poulet's view, superimposition ultimately gives way to the juxtaposition of individual scenes in the *Search*, 'a universe where everything is juxtaposed' (100).

[32] Previously, in *Within a Budding Grove*, Marcel painted a similar verbal picture of Albertine lying in bed, contributing to the later superimposition effect. A younger Marcel here contemplates Albertine, before he tries to kiss her: 'I found Albertine in bed. Leaving her throat bare, her white nightdress altered the proportions of her face, which, flushed by being in bed … seemed pinker … her cheek was traversed by one of those long, dark, curling tresses which, to please me, she had undone altogether. She looked at me and smiled. Beyond her, through the window, the valley lay bright beneath the moon. … The sea, which was visible through the window as well as the valley, the swelling breasts of the first of the Maineville cliffs, the sky in which the moon had not yet climbed to the zenith … all the life-giving energy that nature could have brought me would have seemed to me all too meagre, the breathing of the sea all too short to express the immense aspiration that was swelling in my breast. I bent over Albertine to kiss her' (593).

of mnemonic ekphrases it is as if we, too, contemplate these images through his then-self's eyes. This kind of mediated contemplation is achieved by means of reinforcing metaphors – such as 'nights full of moon on the bay of Balbec, calm as a lake upon which branches barely stir' being echoed by 'those moonlit trees, lank and pale'.

There are several ekphrases of Albertine in the novel, including an extended prose picture of her playing the pianola, again reminding the reader of the earlier scenes at Balbec and again evoking painterly associations (*The Fugitive* 436–437). Their combined effect is to reflect both Marcel's grief at her death and his jealousy at her infidelity. For example, the description of sleeping Albertine reappears in Marcel's jealousy-induced imaginings of her affair with the 'laundry-girl'.[33] Marcel imagines the scene with the unwelcome aid of his memory of Elstir's painting of naked women in a wood:

> I had as it happened seen two paintings by Elstir showing naked women in a thickly wooded landscape. In one of them, a girl is raising her foot as Albertine must have raised hers when she offered it to the laundress. With her other foot she is pushing into the water another girl who gaily resists, her thigh raised, her foot barely dipping into the blue water. I remembered now that the raised thigh made the same swan's-neck curve with the angle of the knee as was made by the line of Albertine's thigh when she was lying by my side on the bed, and I had often meant to tell her that she reminded me of those paintings. … Remembering Albertine as she lay on my bed, I seemed to see the curve of her thigh, I saw it as a swan's neck, seeking the other girl's mouth.
>
> (*The Fugitive* 602–603)

When we first encountered the ekphrasis of sleeping Albertine, in the earlier volume, it was imbued with gentleness, the *then*-Marcel seeing in her 'the innocence and the grace of little children' (*The Captive* 74). When we reach the aptly named 'Grieving and Forgetting' chapter of *The Fugitive*, however, the earlier image is recalled in completely different emotional accents: Albertine's image is now presented in the tints of jealous suspicion, the curve in Albertine's thigh having metamorphosed into a 'swan's sneck, seeking the other girl's

---

[33] Karen Haddad argues that what we find in Proust are not only ekphrases of both real and imaginary artworks, but what she calls 'live images': descriptions of scenes that the narrator imagines, and because these (often jealousy induced) imaginings are vividly rendered, they come to 'exist as much for the reader as the memories "really lived"' (121). Although Haddad suggests that 'live images' fall outside the scope of ekphrasis, I propose that even these imaginary scenes are ekphrastic in this term's original, more capacious definition.

mouth'. Marcel then uses a visual analogy (one which also evokes, in the final metaphor, the sense of touch) to capture these vacillations between jealousy, tenderness and ultimately grief which jointly inform Albertine's composite image: 'As upon a beach where the tide recedes unevenly, I would be assailed by the onrush of one of my suspicions when the image of her tender presence had already withdrawn too far from me to be able to bring me its remedial balm' (*The Fugitive* 611). Reflecting on the 'many Albertines' into whom Albertine metamorphoses during the different stages of their romance, he discovers 'a truly objective truth … namely, that none of us is single, that each of us contains many persons who do not all have the same moral value, and that if a vicious Albertine had existed, it did not mean that there had not been others' (605). Ultimately, Marcel's variously coloured recollections of Albertine help him to discover the composite nature of his own self.[34]

A similar composite effect pertains to the narrator's memories of Gilberte. Young Marcel first sees Gilberte while taking a walk along the Méséglise way with his parents. This walk would take them past Swann's, where Marcel always yearned to catch a glimpse of Swann's daughter. Marcel recollects/depicts in detail the famous hedge of hawthorns and the description culminates in the following analogies:

> The hedge resembled a series of chapels, whose walls were no longer visible under the mountains of flowers that were heaped upon their altars … and their scent swept over me, as unctuous, as circumscribed in its range, as though I had been standing before the Lady-altar, and the flowers, themselves adorned also, held out each its little bunch of glittering stamen with an absent-minded air, delicate radiating veins in the flamboyant style like those which, in the church, framed the stairway to the rood-loft or the mullions of the windows and blossomed out into the fleshy whiteness of strawberry-flowers.
>
> (*Swann's Way* 165)

This description is synaesthetic, with the flowers' *smell* made tangible by visual imagery ('their scent swept over me, as unctuous, as circumscribed in its range, as though I had been standing before the Lady-altar'). The descriptive imagery is metaphorically elaborate – hawthorn hedge turning into chapel, flower stamens

---

[34] Joshua Landy suggests that the 'series' of retrospectively compiled scenes that makes up the novel also represents Marcel's several 'I's, in his quest to discover a 'total Self'; 'time breaks down into a series of discrete instants', Landy writes, 'and the Self fractures into a plurality of segregated *moi* … The apparently homogenous narrative of the *Recherche* in fact comprises several superimposed layers, each one deposited by a separate narrating instance, a separate diachronic *moi*' (132–133). See Landy 105–109 and 116–117.

becoming the mullions of windows – capturing the boy's burgeoning aesthetic sensibility by registering the romantic impressions he then experienced with these kinds of florid analogies. The description is followed by his meditations about perceiving beauty in nature, which, he says, always inspires him 'with that rapture which we feel on seeing a work by our favourite painter quite different from those we already know' (166). The boy continues to study the hedge and notices, higher up on the branches, newly opened pink buds. More analogies blossom on the page as the narrating-Marcel conveys to us the boy's impressions, this time via personification, anticipating the description of Gilberte that follows: 'Embedded in the hedge, but as different from it as a young girl in festal attire among a crowd of dowdy women in everyday clothes who are staying at home, all ready for the "Month of Mary" of which it seemed already to form a part, [the flower] glowed there, smiling in its fresh pink garments, deliciously demure and Catholic' (167–168). The boy who Marcel once was then sees Gilberte through a gap in the hedge: 'A little girl with fair, reddish hair, who appeared to be returning from a walk, and held a spade in her hand, was looking towards us, raising towards us a face powdered with pinkish freckles' (168).

Gilberte has 'black eyes' that gleam and yet, Marcel tells us, 'for a long time afterwards, whenever I thought of her, the memory of those bright eyes would present itself to me as a vivid azure' (168). This early revelation of memory's fallibility, its falling prey to desire's distortions, anticipates Marcel's *later* realization that he misread the look in little Gilberte's eyes as a sign of her contempt, whereas it was, in fact, an expression of affection. In the opening pages of *Time Regained*, the older Marcel revisits Combray. He takes a familiar walk along the Méséglise way, this time in the company of Gilberte from whom he learns the truth when she tells him, 'Why didn't you tell me? I had no idea. I loved you too' (4). It turns out that Gilberte had herself misread the look in the boy Marcel's eyes as disapproval of *her* desire to be seen *by him*. Having learnt this, Marcel ironically recalls us to that earlier scene among the hawthorn blossoms, as well as his memory of Albertine at Balbec: 'suddenly I thought to myself that the true Gilberte, the true Albertine, were perhaps those who had at the first moment yielded themselves with their eyes, one through the hedge of pink hawthorn, the other on the beach' (4). The childhood memory takes on a new meaning once it is brought back before our mind's eye as we recollect (that is, re-visualize) the scene alongside Marcel, when he reflects:

> I pictured Gilberte again in my memory. I could have drawn the rectangle of light which the sun cast through the hawthorns, the spade which the little girl

was holding in her hand, the slow gaze that she fastened on me. Only I had supposed, because of the coarse gesture that accompanied it, that it was a contemptuous gaze. ... And so I was obliged, after an interval of so many years, to touch up a picture which I recalled so well.

(7)

The earlier prose picture is reintroduced, but this time it is looked upon from the perspective of a self even more distant in time from this memory – the perspective of a narrator compelled to 'touch up' what had for so long seemed to be a true 'picture' of the past.[35]

In the 'Sojourn in Venice' chapter of *The Fugitive*, the previously encountered ekphrases of the Combray of Marcel's childhood are recalled in similar fashion, as another composite image is formed. Marcel here recounts his trip to Venice with his mother, commemorating their precious time together: 'I received impressions analogous to those which I had felt so often in the past at Combray,' he begins, 'but transposed into a wholly different and far richer key. When, at ten o'clock in the morning, my shutters were thrown open, I saw blazing there, instead of the gleaming black marble into which the slates of Saint-Hilaire used to turn, the golden angel of the Campanile of St Mark's' (715). This opening image exemplifies the rest of the chapter, which is a kind of mnemonic fugue where the memories of Combray and the other environs from Marcel's past (preserved, like the gleaming steeples of Saint-Hilaire, in the form of framed images in the reader's memory) reverberate alongside his depictions of Venice, producing a coalescence of remembered sights. To cite just one example:

> On the Piazza, the shadow that would have been produced at Combray by the awning over the draper's and the barber's pole was a carpet of little blue flowers strewn at its feet upon the desert of sun-scorched flagstones by the relief of Renaissance façade, which is not to say that, when the sun beat down, one was not obliged, in Venice as at Combray, to pull down the blinds, even beside the canal.
>
> (716)

---

[35] It is undeniable that Marcel the narrator is the one whose voice we hear throughout the novel; however, the focalization shifts between the perspectives of the narrated and narrating selves, and these shifts are reflected precisely in the kind of language used to describe the scenes in question (for instance, the florid metaphors used to depict the child Marcel's impressions of little Gilberte, as opposed to the plainer, more self-conscious redescription of the *same* memory from the perspective of the older narrating self). See also Landy: 'the narrator may acknowledge the importance of his or her former selves simply because they are also his or her *present* selves, synchronic-diachronic sediments remaining within the mind as deposed leaders waiting, perhaps, to return to power. The various *moi*, in other words, function ... as integral and persisting aspects of who the narrator is today' (119). I return to this point in the next Chapter.

In Caws's reading of Proust, the effect of these allusions to previously encountered scenes is that

> instead of being read in an ordinary linear movement, the episodes are seen to work in cumulative and progressively more significant superpositioning, one scene easily pictured as placed directly above the preceding one, to which it looks back in a retrospective reframing ... a *mise-en-abyme* by which Proust rivets our attention upon his work as recapture of time and self.
>
> (28)

I share Caws's view where the narrating-self is concerned: the narrating-Marcel, by his own admission, experiences a 'superimposition' of scenes from his past. His changing attitude towards the places and people depicted in these scenes, as we have seen, is reflected by means of a verbally enacted 'retrospective reframing'. But, for the narrated-Marcel, the self he *then* was, the depicted scenes retain their affective distinctness. For when we *first* encounter the kinds of mnemonic ekphrases that have been examined in this chapter, we seem to gaze upon these retrieved moments through younger, less-disillusioned eyes.

*

This chapter has argued that description remains in productive tension with narrational progress in Proust's novel, as ekphrastic visualization seeks to delay the flow of time and bring a memory to the forefront of attention. When reading Proust and his successors, as subsequent chapters will argue, we experience the spatiality of such descriptions, even as these stilled scenes are carried along and animated by the flow of narrative – the whole wherein they find *retrospectively-doubled* sense. In this way, the Proustian narrative gifts its reader with two perspectives on memory and, of necessity, time: one horizontal, another vertical. The horizontal view is seen from the perspective of the character (narrated-) Marcel, where the scenes happen as if in the present, because rendered in arrestingly descriptive prose. From this perspective, the places and persons depicted are either framed against the horizon (Saint-Loup; Albertine) or captured by a painterly or still more fanciful framing effect (the pictorial sights of the two walks in Combray; the Princess de Guermantes in her aquatic theatre box; young Gilberte framed by pink hawthorn blossoms). The vertical perspective, on the other hand, is the prerogative of the narrating-Marcel, whose views on memory and time are disclosed to us via the analogies he uses to image the 'superimposition' of the successive impressions of all the significant others, including his own younger self, whom he has lost to Time.[36]

The next chapter will examine more closely this bifocal gaze on the past, as well as the ironized nostalgia that is Proust's legacy for those seeking to capture the work of memory within the confines of a book's covers.

---

[36] See also Deleuze: 'Such is time, the dimension of the narrator, which has the power to be the whole *of* these parts without totalizing them, the unity *of* these parts without unifying them' (*Proust and Signs* 169).

2

After Proust: By way of ironized nostalgia

'The trueness of the whole picture'

In the second volume of the three-part *Time and Narrative*, Paul Ricoeur proposes three modernist novels that refigure our understanding of time in the complex ways they plot the protagonists' experience: Woolf's *Mrs Dalloway*, Mann's *The Magic Mountain* and Proust's *Search*. The *forms* of these fictional narratives, Ricoeur contends, tell us something unsayable about time outside of narrative because only here do we get to experience shifting temporalities alongside the protagonists while we read, vicariously sensing the difference between lived time and clock time.[1] Less ambitiously but in similar spirit, I want to suggest in this chapter that Proust's *Search* tells us something about memory (and how mnemonic prose pictures compel the mind) which is unsayable outside of novelistic form. An encounter with a literary text such as Proust's novel refigures our understanding of memory and enlarges the scope of the creative possibilities for new efforts of writing about the past.[2]

In the final pages of *Time Regained*, Proust's narrator unveils his philosophical reflections on time and memory, informing the reader of what the novel has already made actual: namely '[the] notion of Time embodied, of years past but not separated from us' (449). Marcel here echoes Bergson's idea of the past's coexistence with the present, where all the (forgotten) past accompanies every present moment, the present moment being the apex of the widening 'cone' of

---

[1] 'The originality of *Remembrance* lies in its having concealed', Ricoeur argues, 'both the problem and its solution up to the end of the hero's course, thus keeping for a second reading the intelligibility of the work as a whole' (*Time and Narrative* 2, 132).

[2] The idea that literature may 'tell' us something about life is explored by Michael Wood in *Literature and the Taste of Knowledge*, where we re-encounter the idea that the knowledge that literature imparts comes to us via the route of 'as if': 'Literature frames knowledge with visible or invisible sentences, saying, "If I were to say this … "' (59).

the virtual past.³ Bergson's memory cone metaphor intends to show how the demands of present experience always 'touch' memory at its inverted apex, the narrowest point containing so-called quasi-instantaneous memory, and the further one travels into memory's ever-widening cone, the deeper one enters into the past (*Matter and Memory* 152–154). In Proust's terms, involuntary memory is what prompts a forgotten recollection, to borrow Bergson's eloquent phrasing, '[to] descend from the heights of pure memory down to the precise point where *action* is taking place … it is from the present that comes the appeal to which memory responds, and it is from … present action that a memory borrows the warmth which gives it life' (153).

I suggest that we can apply Bergson's schema to describe the working of our own memory while reading Proust (see Figure 2).

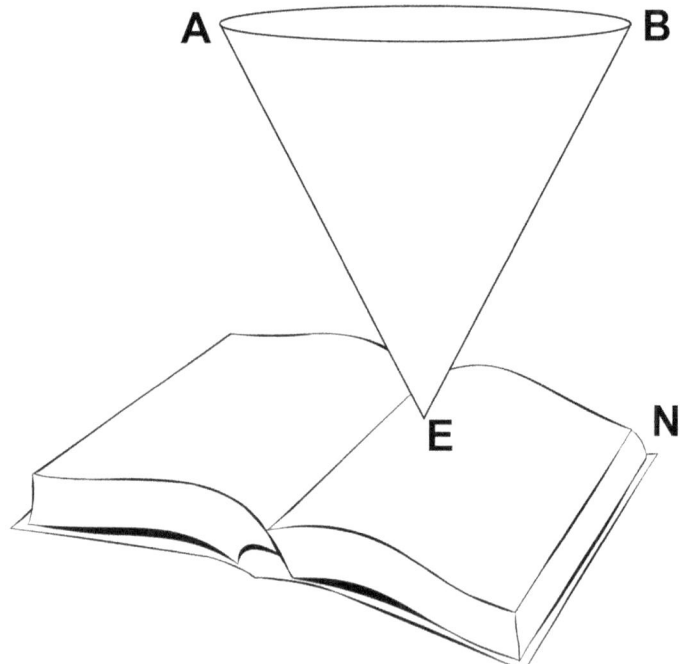

Figure 2 Adapted from Bergson's original diagram.

---

³ Bergson pictures the so-called virtual past as follows: 'Duration is the continuous progress of a past which gnaws into the future and which swells as it advances. And as the past grows without ceasing, so also there is no limit to its preservation. Memory … is not a faculty of putting away recollections in a drawer, or of inscribing them in a register. … In its entirety, probably, it follows us at every instant; all that we have felt, thought and willed from our earliest infancy is there, leaning over the present which is about to join it, pressing against the portals of consciousness that would fain leave it outside' (*Creative Evolution* 7).

In Bergson's original diagram, the plane over which memory's cone is suspended is 'my actual representation of the universe' (152), so in this case it would stand for the narrative (N) we are presently reading, traversing its represented world. Ekphrasis in Proust is a textual locus (E) of great density, attracting images out of the narrator's past. The further we read on, the deeper our memory (AB) of the novel becomes. Then, whenever Marcel experiences the mnemonic jolts triggered by a taste, smell, touch or sound and describes the scenes they unveil, our own memory responds to the appeal of these textual prompts, as we try to recall the resurrected moment (the mnemonic ekphrasis) alongside the narrator. When we finally arrive at the concluding pages of *Time Regained*, we are able to share Marcel's wonder at the elapsed years (for us, the elapsed pages recounting them, over months, perhaps even years of reading the novel) as the prose pictures we encountered *earlier* in the novel resurface within us, like involuntary memories resurfaced within the narrator.

Marcel realizes that the only way he can communicate to the reader his newly discovered sense of 'timelessness' is via metaphor.[4] Reality, he contends, 'is a certain connexion between these immediate sensations and the memories which envelop us simultaneously with them' (246). The writer's difficult task is to *image* this connection 'in the necessary links of a well-wrought style … by comparing a quality common to two sensations, we succeed in extracting their common essence and in reuniting them to each other, liberated from the contingencies of time, within a metaphor' (246). In the final pages of the novel, while waiting in the library at the mansion of the Princess de Guermantes for the end of the musical performance, Marcel hears the pealing of a bell, a pealing, he is convinced, that is reaching him out of the past, when, as a child, he would hear it every time his mother opened the garden gate on her way back from saying farewell to their guests:

> [U]nmistakably I heard these very sounds, situated though they were in a remote past. And as I cast my mind over all the events which were *ranged in an unbroken series* between the moment of my childhood when I had first heard its sound and the Guermantes party, I was terrified to think that it was indeed the same bell which rang within me.
>
> (my emphasis 449)

---

[4] On the philosophical significance of metaphor in Proust, particularly on the way it critically reflects on Aristotle's theory of metaphor, see Miguel de Beistegui 66–96. On the ways in which Proust also uses metaphors to expose 'the trick played by tropes' in the novel, see David R. Ellison 9–29.

The recollection of the ringing of the garden bell at Combray is the final instance of involuntary memory in the novel, and, like a forgotten scene kindled by a touch, taste or smell it too evokes within Marcel a visual impression.

However, this time what is evoked within is not an impression of a particular moment, but a kind of synoptic view of the narratively traversed past, captured in the narrator's crowning metaphor (anticipated by that telling phrase 'ranged in an unbroken series') of standing upon tall stilts and looking down at the expanse of recollected events. Having past the Dantean milestone of life's span, Marcel finds himself looking down from Time's height:

> In this vast dimension which I had not known myself to possess, the date on which I had heard the noise of the garden gate bell at Combray – the far-distant noise which nevertheless was within me – was a point from which I might start to make measurements. And I felt ... a sensation of weariness and almost of terror at the thought that all this length of Time had not only ... been lived, experienced, secreted by me ... was in fact me ['qu'il était moi-même'], but also that I was compelled so long as I was alive to keep it attached to me, that it supported me and that, perched on its giddy summit, I could not myself make a movement without displacing it. A feeling of vertigo seized me as I looked down *beneath* me, yet *within* me ['J'avais le vertige de voir *au-dessous* de moi, *en* moi pourtant'], as though from a height, which was my own height, of many leagues, *at the long series of the years.*
>
> (my emphasis, Time Regained 451; Le Temps retrouvé 352)

A curious thing is happening in this passage: it is as if Marcel is failing to keep at a distance the subjective and the objective views of time. In fact, it looks as though the two perspectives are mutually repellent, like magnets of equal polarity, requiring rhetorical muscle to hold together. Marcel must repeatedly qualify this metaphor – a metaphor that inevitably spatializes time – to indicate that when looking down from time's great height, he is also looking down from his *own* height, and when looking down *beneath* himself (*au-dessous* de moi) he is in fact looking *within* himself (*en* moi). Time must remain within for Marcel, but language fails to keep it there as the visual metaphor is reliant on a notion of exteriority: of finding oneself at the summit of (and thus being supported by) objective time, but as a subjective witness who embodies the summit.[5]

---

[5] Arnaud Dandieu's *Marcel Proust: Sa Révélation psychologique* (1930) is among the earliest studies of the *Search* to draw attention to the importance of metaphor in this novel's thinking about the past. Dandieu was possibly Proust's first reader to point out that Marcel's attempt to place himself within duration cannot avoid becoming contradictory: 'L'attitude du romancier classique ou naturaliste

I have emphasized 'at the long series of the years' because this phrase suggests less the notion of depth and more of breadth: of something spread out over space, like a great canvas seen from above. Indeed, Marcel earlier compares himself to 'a painter climbing a road high above a lake, a view of which is denied to him by a curtain of rocks and trees. Suddenly through a gap in the curtain he sees the lake, its whole expanse is before him, he takes up his brushes' (435). The Proustian philosophy of time, I am suggesting, is produced by Proust's *ekphrastic staging* of Marcel's memory: it is the conceptual child of the *form* of his novel and the mode of descriptive writing it elects for representing the past. In this sense, when Marcel speaks of 'the long series of the years' he can be said to be inadvertently commenting on the novel's structure, which consists of a long series of interpenetrating descriptive scenes of moments from his life – scenes resurrected within him by the miracle of contingently sparked recall. As readers, we retrospectively collate these ekphrastic images, superimpose them and thereby grasp the truth behind the philosophical reflections revealed to us at the novel's end. Hence, when Marcel reaches the end, he can gesture at the 'mosaic' of his life, the landscape of memory completed before him and which we, too, can now contemplate from 'above' – as the virtually visual shape of this novel.[6]

In this respect, Proust's novel departs from Bergson's philosophy by discussing time in spatial terms, which Bergson would reject because duration is for him dimensionless and only appears to consciousness to possess extension. As Ricoeur emphasizes, the *Search* 'is far from a Bergsonian vision of a duration free of all extension; instead, it confirms a *dimensional* character of time' (*Time and Narrative 1*, 151).[7] At the end of the *Search*, the phenomenological narrator without equal in effect becomes a philosopher of cosmological time: time ceases to be the ongoing past-becoming-present of Bergsonian duration and instead becomes a kind of *untensed landscape of one's prose pictured past*. Of course, the price of gaining this view of time is to cease writing (and reading): to gain it,

---

    est de se placer *au-dessus* du temps. Il s'en suppose maître. Proust, au contraire, renonçant à cette prestidigitation, se place dans la durée concrète. Il court ainsi le risque d'être confus et contradictoire [The manner of the classical or naturalist novelist is to place himself *above* time. He assumes that he is master over it. Proust, on the contrary, renouncing this prestidigitation, places himself within concrete duration. He thus runs the risk of being confusing and contradictory]' (my translation 20–21).

[6] In her reading of the *Search*, Caws also describes Marcel's story as 'the creation of the mosaic of memory and time' (233).

[7] See also Poulet 102. For a comparison of time in Proust and Bergson, see David Couzens Hoy 189–193 and Deleuze, *Proust and Signs* 58–61.

one must step back from the verbal canvas of life and outside narrative time, and this may only be done at narration's end. It is only then, in retrospect, that this kind of untensed landscape of the past appears, precisely because it has become 'concretized' in memory.

In this way, the novel's representation of memory foregrounds our dependence on narrative as a vital tool in understanding time's paradox. This paradox is deftly unpacked by Mark Currie in *About Time*, where Currie argues: 'The idea that moving forwards in time involves a backwards narration is more than just a novelistic structure, it might be thought of, with Proust, as the shape of time itself' (88). If one is a good reader (I use 'good' both with and without irony), then one begins a novel at the beginning and makes progress (a slow one with Proust) through the unknown alongside the novel's characters. A good reader forgets that he is reading a novel and pretends that the future is unknown and open to contingency, as it is in life outside of fiction. Reading the novel 'rightly', or beginning at the beginning, the reader experiences time as constant flow, as progress forward, and the consequent asymmetry between past and future that characterizes lived experience. As Currie explains:

> the present of the reading becomes a kind of gateway through which words, descriptions and events pass in their transition from the realm of possibility into the realm of actuality. The experience of reading, thus described, corresponds to a tensed conception of time and represents the egocentric, or subjective pole in the relation of the reading subject to the textual object.
>
> (16)

But we know that the future in fiction is not open: the book contains all of time for its characters; its future is pre-written, and the reader is free to make a journey forward in time – to skip ahead in the plot and find out how things end. This closed or block-view of time is represented by the book itself; the block-view of time, Currie argues, thus corresponds to the text's 'determinate number of pages, verbal structures and sequence of events from beginning to end' (16). Marcel's discovery of Time, in this sense, could only occur at the end of his narration, for it is only then that he can discover (or that his completed narrative allows him to recognize) that aspect of time which his own narration prevented him from seeing. In other words, Marcel the phenomenological narrator discovers, or regains, untensed time in the finished form of his narrative.

Tensed and untensed conceptions of time correspond, respectively, to 'A-theory' and 'B-theory' accounts of time, terms derived from Anglo-American philosophical discourse about temporality. Currie provides the following pertinent summary of their respective positions:

> The theory based on the A-series conception of time (A-theory) normally holds that the future and past do not exist, and that existence therefore is presence. It is possible to say only that the events of the past did exist, and that the events of the future will exist, but these events are *tensed* in relation to the present, to now, which is thought of as having special ontological properties. The A-theory is therefore a tensed theory of time, and goes by a variety of other names such as *presentism* and the *moving now* theory. B-theory, on the other hand, dispenses with the idea of the now, and therefore with the idea of events being past and future. Time, according to B-theory, is a sequence of events all of which are equally real, and between which the only relations are those of *earlier than* and *later than*, and the idea of 'now' or 'the present' is merely psychological. B-theory is therefore *untensed*, and is often thought of as an objective and essentially spatial way of understanding events, as if time were spread out like a landscape.
> (142)

All narratives negotiate between these opposing conceptions of temporality; tensed and untensed views of time are never mutually exclusive in a narrative (Currie 144). The value of this distinction for my own argument is that it captures the temporal drama at the heart of Proust's novel, and, by extension, all narratives possessed by the ekphrastic desire to render present the spaces of time past. Clearly, a memory narrative is a mimesis of subjective temporality and consequently subservient to the tensed view of time. Yet an ekphrastic memory narrative also seeks to be a 'storehouse' for the images of memory; having read such a narrative, one is able to recall its contents with the aid of visual descriptions and, potentially, conceive the novel as a spatially laid-out series of scenes. One might even test one's memory (never equal to the demands placed upon it) and list the descriptive scenes that constitute the narrated memory of the protagonist whose life one has completed reading. Conceiving the novel in these terms is thinking it through the *untensed* theory of time: the scenes of memory now assume 'earlier than' and 'later than' relations, no longer dependent on the present of the narrator from whom they originated. For Currie, the untensed view of time is the tangible book itself, so that 'the fictional narrative represents, artificially, a B-theory of time in the sense that its time sequence is laid out spatially as a book, and that all moments of that sequence exist equally, co-temporaneously as written words' (143). I would only add that our own memory also enables us to view the contents of the book – as it were, the virtual imagery corresponding to the written words – in this 'untensed' manner.[8]

Reading memory, like personal memory, is forgetful, and one could never hold the entire contents of a narrative before the mind's eye (certainly not with Proust). Nonetheless, this is, I believe, the import of Marcel's crowning metaphor; age makes us grow taller in Time, and he finds himself sick with the vertigo of the years as he imagines himself 'perched upon living stilts which never cease to grow', adding, 'it seemed to me that quite soon now I might be too weak to maintain my hold upon a past which already went down too far' (*Time Regained* 451). The vertiginous sense imparted by this image is that as one grows upwards upon Time's 'living stilts', so the landscape beneath one broadens in scope, as still more territory of the past becomes visible. When, earlier in the volume, Marcel reflects on the wondrous workings of involuntary memory, he adopts a similar figure to describe his apprehension of the past:

> It was precisely the fortuitous and inevitable fashion in which this [the feel of uneven paving stones] and other sensations had been encountered that proved the trueness of the past which they brought back to life, of the images which they released, since we feel, with these sensations, the effort they make to climb back towards the light ... And here too was the proof of the trueness of the whole picture formed out of those contemporaneous impressions which the first sensations bring back in its train, with those unerring proportions of light and shade, emphasis and omission, memory and forgetfulness to which conscious recollection and conscious observation will never know how to attain.
>
> (233)

Currie prefers the metaphor of the 'landscape' to describe the untensed theory of time; having read Proust, though, we could also picture it as a collage: 'the whole picture', illuminated throughout the novel by metaphorical descriptions of the images released from the darkness of forgetting.

Writing memory ekphrastically, as the novels considered by the chapters ahead all exemplify, issues from the hope that descriptive language is sufficient to restore to presence absent moments. But this hope is always complicated by its

---

[8] See also Poulet: 'Thus everything depends on a memory that is not the involuntary memory: memory of the total work, memory total in itself, which conserves and reproduces the mass of episodes. ... Intact, always similar to themselves, always enclosed, and as if localized in the interior of their frameworks, the episodes of the Proustian novel present themselves in an order which is not temporal, since it is anachronistic, but which cannot be other than spatial, since, like an array of jars of jam in the cupboards of our childhood, it arranges a series of closed vases in the caverns of the mind' (104–105).

double: the fear that words are insufficient and lack the immediacy of the visual. Mnemonic ekphrasis epitomizes this precarious prospect that conditions every effort of describing memory's images. When Marcel likens his authorial role to that of a painter contemplating an expanse of nature, taking up his brushes to paint pictures of the past, he adds: 'The mind has landscapes which it is allowed to contemplate only for a certain space of time … But already the night is at hand, the night which will put an end to his painting and which no dawn will follow ["et sur laquelle le jour ne se relèvera pas"]' (*Time Regained* 435; *Le Temps retrouvé* 340). Marcel is here voicing his intimation of mortality – the fear that he will not have enough time to complete his novelistic painting.[9] But this statement invoking darkness could also be read as a writer's fear of the limitations of his own medium of expression. Seen in this light, it is as though the prospect of *writing itself*, its difficulty and uncertainty of success, comes to darken the bright spectacle of memory that Marcel presents to his reader – and, fearfully, before his future self.

On irony and nostalgia

Proustian narratives are quests for origins that insist on loss, the kind of loss captured in Svetlana Boym's definition of nostalgia:

> Nostalgia (from *nostos* – return home, and *algia* – longing) is a longing for a home that no longer exists. … Nostalgia is a sentiment of loss and displacement, but it is also a romance with one's own fantasy. … A cinematic image of nostalgia is a double exposure; or a superimposition of two images – of home and abroad, past and present, dream and everyday life. The moment we try to force it into a single image, it breaks the frame or burns the surface.
>
> (xiv)

Boym's use of a visual metaphor is pertinent, suggesting, once again, that the image we have of the past is a kind of 'superimposition' – this time of memory and imagination. This is because memory images come to be narrated as palimpsests of fantasy and fact, where the outlines of fact (the past recalled) are traced by imagination's line (metaphor-shaped ekphrasis). Proust is certainly aware of imagination's agency, writing in *Contre Sainte-Beuve*: 'The stuff of our

---

[9] Proust once described his novel using the metaphor 'painting' in a letter to Jean Cocteau, when he wrote: 'mon volume est un tableau' (qtd. in Boyer 19).

books, the substance of our sentences, should be drawn from our imaginations, not taken just as it comes from real life, but our actual style and the episodes too, should be made out of the transparent substance of our best moments, those in which we transcend reality and the present' (273). 'We are thus always trying to work back through time to that transcendent home', Peter Brooks writes of Flaubert, 'knowing, of course, that we cannot. All we can do is subvert or, perhaps better, pervert time: which is what narrative does' (*Reading for Plot* 111). Brooks's comment on Flaubert's legacy for modern fiction is perhaps even more fitting for Proust's: in Proust, it is precisely *because* the past is unobtainable and ungraspable that it must be recounted. Narrativizing memory cannot but 'pervert' phenomenological time (time as becoming), and the *Search*, I have argued, seeks to bring together two opposing conceptions of temporality: the open time of becoming and the closed time of fate. Because of this, a Proustian narrative is a nostalgic quest to re-enter the world of the past, through the measure of 'as if', where the shadow of one's present self remains superimposed over the past's visions.[10]

In Proust, an ironic spectatorship takes place in the narrator's retrospective depictions. This happens because the narrated-I becomes the *object* of the nostalgic gaze of the narrating-I. Christopher Prendergast has noticed that the split of the self into narrating subject and narrated object already occurs in the first sentence of Proust's novel, where the original reads: 'Longtemps, je me suis couché de bonne heure' (*À la recherche* 3). The revised Scott Moncrieff translation renders this sentence as follows: 'For a long time I would go to bed early' (*Swann's Way* 1). However, if we transposed French grammar into its English equivalent, we would have the grammatically awkward sentence, 'For a long time, I put *me* to bed early.' The self-reflexive verb form in French, which requires the splitting of the first-person pronoun into nominative and accusative cases, *je/me*, announces the very form of this novel, as

---

[10] This notion of arriving at knowledge through the measure of 'as if' is the subject of Hans Vaihinger's *The Philosophy of 'As If'*, which draws on Immanuel Kant's philosophical method. Vaihinger argues that Kant employs the conjunction 'as if' in order to formulate a principle founded on an impossible epistemological assumption, such as the demand of the categorical imperative: 'man' must act 'as if' he were free (suggesting that he is not totally free), and live in such a way 'as if' his behaviour were governed by natural laws, and 'as if' he could discern these laws through his own use of reason (256–260). My own argument restricts the function of 'as if' to the kind of knowledge that fiction imparts, and it is closer in spirit to Ricoeur's claim that fiction gives us knowledge, but through its 'kingdom of the *as if*' (*Time and Narrative 1*, 64). Fiction gives us knowledge by immersing us in a narratively constructed world, whereas philosophy occasionally has to resort to hypothetical assumptions to frame its tenets. I am grateful to Mark Currie for directing me to Vaihinger's book in this connection.

Prendergast eloquently suggests: 'Proust's grammar thus gives us a subject split into nominative and accusative, both speaker and spoken, and the book this sentence inaugurates is a many-thousand-page detour through this gap' (164). Proust thus has his narrator, right at the outset, present himself as a past subject he no longer is, but one whom he continually tries to re-join: *as if* he were again a self he once was.[11]

Proust's *Search* is about Marcel's quest to rescue his past self (or selves) from the darkening of forgetting. His past self is an inhabitant of a different temporal realm, one imperilled by oblivion. In *Time Regained*, Marcel reflects:

> In the past the fear of being no longer myself was something that had terrified me, and this had made me dread the end of each new love that I had experienced … because I could not bear the idea that the 'I' who loved them would one day cease to exist, since this in itself would be a kind of death. … For I realized that dying was not something new, but that on the contrary since my childhood I had already died many times. To take a comparatively recent period, had I not clung to Albertine more tenaciously than to my own life? Could I at the time when I loved her conceive my personality without the continued existence within it of my love for her? Yet I no longer loved her, I was no longer the person who loved her but a different person who did not love her.
>
> (437–438)

This recurring experience of the loss of his past self, of becoming a different self over the course of time, illustrates a fundamental feature of Proustian narration: namely it is a commemoration of the death of that 'other' person who one once was. Involuntary memory is what enables Marcel to resurrect his past self, however fleetingly. In a key scene at the Guermantes library, Marcel casually pages through *François le Champi*, the novel by George Sand that he had loved as a child, when, suddenly, he encounters a stranger:

> My first reaction had been to ask myself, angrily, who this stranger was who was coming to trouble me. The stranger was none other than myself ['Cet étranger, c'était moi-même'], the child I had been at the time, brought to life within me by the book … wanting to be seen only by his eyes, to be loved only by his heart, to speak only to him.
>
> (*Time Regained* 240; *Le Temps retrouvé* 191)

---

[11] In the *Poetics*, Aristotle's description of the importance of visualization for the playwright's craft is certainly applicable to Proust's novel. 'When constructing plots', Aristotle observes, 'one should as far as possible visualize what is happening. By envisaging things very vividly in this way, *as if one were actually present* at the events themselves, one can find what is appropriate' (my emphasis 27).

Having re-encountered this 'stranger', Marcel mourns the childhood self he once was, and his only recourse is to narratively imagine what it was like to have been this child, to have read this book with a child's eyes, and involuntary memory provides him with the impressions needed to achieve this approximation.

In his lecture on *Swann's Way*, Nabokov, drawing on Dandieu's (still untranslated) study of Proust's novel, writes that Proust's 'whole enormous work … is but an extended comparison revolving on the words *as if*' (*Lectures on Literature* 208). In other words, the narrating self, time-riven from the narrated self, can bridge the gap in time only by imaginatively writing about the past *as if* it again found itself there. In writing memory, to write as mimetically as possible about one's past self, one therefore writes a kind of biography about that 'other' who is no longer present. Proust conceives identity as being narratively inflected, where the narrator *authors* his earlier self as a character in a story.[12] Hence, to write a Proustian narrative is to approach one's non-identical past self by figuring it as 'other', a fact that Proust's novel repeatedly underscores.[13] For instance, this is what Marcel says about his waning affection for Gilberte:

> [W]e can never be certain that the happiness which comes to us too late, when we can no longer enjoy it, when we are no longer in love, is altogether the same as that same happiness the lack of which made us at one time so unhappy. There is only one person who could decide this – our then self; it is no longer with us, and were it to reappear, no doubt our happiness – identical or not – would vanish.
>
> (*Within a Budding Grove* 237–238)

And, in the following sentence from *Time Regained*, time's passage compels Marcel to dress his past-I in the garb of quotation marks;[14] having re-encountered his child-self in the Guermantes' library, Marcel describes his effort to locate the earliest memory, the 'primary image' of first reading this book that he once so loved: 'I am no longer the "I" who first beheld it, even though I must make way for the "I" that I then was if that "I" summons the thing that it once knew and that the "I" of today does not know' (*Time Regained* 244).

---

[12] On the self-othering aspect of retrospective first-person narration, where the self's relation to its own past mirrors metaphorical signification, see my chapter 'Oneself as Character'.

[13] See also Hägglund: 'The experience of involuntary memory does not yield an identity that is exempt from time. On the contrary, it highlights a constitutive temporal difference at the heart of the self. While a past self is retrieved through involuntary memory, the one who remembers can never be identical to the one who is remembered' (23). For a discussion of identity in Proust, and a cogent argument in favour of rejecting the notion of a unified 'Self' in the *Search*, see ibid. 44–48.

[14] In *Le Temps retrouvé*, the quotation marks around the first-person disjunctive pronoun are absent, but the sense of self-estrangement conveyed by the writing seems to justify their inclusion in the Scott Moncrieff-Kilmartin revised translation: 'pour pouvoir retrouver la première [image], moi qui ne suis pas le moi qui l'ai vue et qui dois céder la place au moi que j'étais alors, s'il appelle la chose qu'il connut et que mon moi d'aujourd'hui ne connaît point' (194).

It is precisely this self-othering aspect of Proustian narration that distinguishes it from the mode of confessional literature. The premise of confessional writing is the self's transparency; for confessional writing to take place, there first must be a belief in the possibility of disclosing one's innermost, constant self to another. This premise is foregrounded by Rousseau in the *Confessions*, as he opens Book I by addressing, like Augustine before him, the figure of the 'Supreme Judge': 'I have shown myself as I was ... I have disclosed my innermost self as you alone know it to be' (5). Allied to this faith in being able to disclose his innermost self is Rousseau's conviction of the constancy of his self through time; as he states at the conclusion of Book IV: 'I never promised to offer the public a grand personage; what I did promise was to portray myself as I am; and if the reader is to know me as I am in my later years, he must have known me well in my youth' (170). As we shall see in the chapters ahead, *both* assumptions – the possibility of fully disclosing one's innermost self as well as the notion of a uniform identity – are undermined in Proustian memory writing.

On the formal level, every act of writing about oneself requires a 'split' of the narrator's identity into writing 'subject' and observed 'object'. Superficially, Rousseau performed a kind of self-othering in writing his trilogy of confessional texts – *Confessions*, *Dialogues* and *Reveries of a Solitary Walker* – for in all of these he regularly refers to himself in the third person. James Olney, one of Rousseau's most perceptive readers, observes that in the *Dialogues* 'Rousseau was frequently to speak of himself in the third person, as if he were acting and at the same time standing off observing himself acting, as if he were subject and object' (*Memory and Narrative* 169). However, Olney argues that this ostensible splitting of the self 'not only does not mitigate against singleness of being but on the contrary ... positively reinforces the *integral oneness* of [Rousseau's] own being and his writing' (my emphasis 168). Rousseau's figuring of his subjectivity into narrative personae is merely a rhetorical effect, intended to strengthen the core assumption of Rousseauan confession: one's self remains constant from birth, and identity is fully recoverable through narration. Indeed, this effect of Rousseauan narration, what Olney also refers to as the 'all too near sameness between the *I* then and the *I* now' (235), is perhaps the main reason why today we are left suspicious of many of Rousseau's disclosures.[15]

---

[15] See Olney's account, in *Memory and Narrative* 130–149, of the difficulties Rousseau runs into in his desire both to tell the truth and to portray himself as the victim of circumstance – a contradiction that results in the most implausible excuses for his misdeeds, particularly the reasons he gives for having abandoned all five of his children to a grim fate in a foundlings' hospital. See also Rousseau, *Confessions* 347–349.

For Proust, the 'other' is no longer seen as the figure of the judging 'Reader', who so persecuted the imagination of Rousseau. Instead, the 'other' has become *internalized* as the narrated-I supplants the figure of the uniform self as a recreated character self. In other words, in Proustian narration the past self is figured as an-Other, whom the narrating self tries to resurrect from its resting place in forgetting. Writing memory after Proust has become much more self-conscious, precisely because, having read Proust, uniform identification with one's past self cannot but be deemed naive.[16] Another way of saying this is that in Proust we have self-narration not as self-revelation, as we have it in Rousseau, but as self-creation.

In this respect, Bernard Stiegler rightly includes Proust in his comment on modernity's sabotaging of a stable sense of identity: 'It is precisely this fissuring of consciousness that we hear in Schoenberg's music – Schoenberg who came after Nietzsche who discovered (uncovered) what Freud, at practically the same time, made into a clinic subject [*sic*], and Proust into a subject for literature: the non-unity of the I' (*Symbolic Misery 2*, 54). In Proust, I have argued, the 'non-unity of the I' is enacted by the form of the novel, where the narrating-Marcel represents the narrated-Marcel as though a character in a story, in full acknowledgement of the inescapable artifice (both contrivance and artfulness) of this act. We thus experience in Proust the sense of creative *authorship* of one's past, as the narrative enacts the process of telling about oneself-as-if-about-another to a much more radical degree than earlier autobiographical modes.[17]

Proust is an exemplary practitioner of a self-reflexive memory-telling, and the mode of narrative discourse informing his novel is a kind of ironized nostalgia. If, as Hayden White has memorably claimed, 'the symbolic content of narrative history, the content of its form, is the tragic vision itself' (*Content of Form* 181), then the content of the form of Proust's *Search* is the nostalgic vision instructed by irony. I merge these quite different but not unrelated orientations towards life to convey both the perceived distance from one's past self (irony) and the desire to merge with it (nostalgia) that inform, in equal measure, Proustian narration.

---

[16] As Emerson and Morson argue, 'Overcoming naivete is part of a novel's generic "task" … Faced with such behaviour, other genres must adapt. If they do not, they come to sound hopelessly anachronistic and unsophisticated, or even un-intended self-parodies' (304).

[17] While Proustian memory narration is characterized by its penchant for ekphrasis, I do not wish to suggest that Proust is unique in this second characteristic, namely fictioning himself as a story-character. Samuel Beckett, for instance, is another notable practitioner of this mode of writing the autobiographical self, albeit in ever more radical forms, through the mediation of fiction. See Olney, *Memory and Narrative* 229–270, and Boxall, '"The Existence I ascribe"'.

A seminal and perhaps unsurprising precursor of the ironic autobiographical approach is Charles Baudelaire.[18] Baudelaire's essay 'Of the Essence of Laughter' illuminates the inherent split in modern subjectivity noted by Stiegler and the irony that, in Baudelaire's view, always accompanies it. Baudelaire sees laughter as a kind of safety valve that releases pent-up frustration, and he posits that laughter often 'comes from a man's idea of his own superiority' (145). For those capable of *self*-irony, however, laughter does not only come about from the spectacle of others' misfortune; it can also be turned inward at oneself as the object of one's own laughter, and here we gain further insight into the duality of narrative self-consciousness as it is expressed in Proust. 'It is not the man who falls down who laughs at his own fall', Baudelaire writes, 'unless he is a philosopher, a man who has acquired, by force of habit, the power of getting outside himself quickly, *and watching, as a disinterested spectator, the phenomenon of his ego*' (my emphasis 148). We have seen that becoming this kind of spectator of oneself is constitutive of ekphrastically evoking the past; this contention might now be stretched further, adding that the more distance (intellectual, moral, psychological) that one can create between one's present and past selves, *pace* Proust, the more authentic will such representation become.

The duality required of one capable of laughter at himself may thus be seen as a mirror image of the duality required of an ekphrastic writer of memory. '[I]n order for the comic … to exist', Baudelaire continues, 'there must be two beings in the presence of each other … the existence in the human being of a permanent dualism, the capacity of being both himself and someone else at one and the same time' (160). Self-directed irony means becoming an actor playing oneself in a kind of tableau vivant from one's past.[19] In memory's ekphrasis, the

---

[18] See Katherine Elkins, 'Middling Memories and Dreams of Oblivion'. Elkins's essay is unique in comparing memory's conception in Baudelaire and Proust, arguing that the poet and novelist reject the notion of 'archival memory', in that both view the process of remembering as entirely contingent and continually prey to oblivion: 'Isolated, different selves are actually punctuated by gaps of forgetfulness, gaps that it is memory's purpose to bridge. Between an initial impression of an event and its subsequent recollection lies a stretch of forgetfulness … Baudelaire's speaker and Proust's narrator remember themselves only indirectly, by remembering others' (54–55).

[19] Walter Benjamin, in a justly celebrated essay on Baudelaire, captures the method of Baudelairean *correspondances* (correspondences) by citing Proust's own comments on the poet: 'When Proust in the last volume of his work reverts to the sensation that suffused him at the taste of the *madeleine*, he imagines the years which appear on the balcony as being loving sisters of the years of Combray. "In Baudelaire … these reminiscences are even more numerous … There is no one else who pursues the interconnected *correspondances* with such leisurely care … – in a woman's spell, for instance, in the fragrance of her hair or her breasts – *correspondances* which then yield him lines like "the azure of the vast, vaulted sky" or "a harbor full of flames and masts." These words are a confessional motto for Proust's work' (*Illuminations* 183). In *The Threshold of the Visible World*, Kaja Silverman also singles out this passage from Benjamin's essay, suggesting 'that Baudelaire and Proust, like all authors who know how to "light up" the objects about which they write, do so by synthetically producing in the reader the effects of unconscious memories' (100).

one who writes similarly becomes 'both himself and someone else at one and the same time': I depict myself knowing that the I *who is describing me* is distinct from the self I once was. In ekphrastic description, the self is thus divided: it is both the self who is remembering (narrating) and the narrated self who is being remembered (described).

Irony illuminates the method of mnemonic ekphrasis, for, like ekphrasis, irony deals with a *single* moment, a single image of oneself as if divided. As Paul de Man comments on Baudelaire's essay:

> irony comes closer to the pattern of factual experience and recaptures some of the factitiousness of human existence as a succession of isolated moments lived by a divided self. Essentially the mode of the present, it knows neither memory nor prefigurative duration, whereas allegory appears as a successive mode capable of engendering duration as the illusion of continuity that it knows to be illusionary. Yet the two models, for all their profound distinctions in mood and structure, are two faces of the same fundamental experience of time.
>
> (*Blindness and Insight* 226)

I lack the space to traverse de Man's account of allegory, and only wish to draw attention to his distinction between irony and allegory as two 'models' for representing time in narrative, because this distinction corresponds to my own between the depicted self-image (the textual site of the temporally distant self) and narrational progress (the unfolding of the story that expresses the self's continuity). Memory narratives, in short, encompass both prose pictures and their plotting, which, approximately, correspond to de Man's distinction between irony and allegory. What de Man calls the novel's 'truly perverse assignment', at the conclusion of his essay, I prefer to call its *techne*: 'the novel is caught in the truly perverse assignment of using both the narrative duration of the diachronic allegory and the instantaneity of the narrative present; to try for less than the combination of the two is to betray the inherent *gageure* of the genre' (227). In the Proustian novel, the synchronicity of the memory image is always caught up in the diachronicity of narrative temporality. The image, rendered in ekphrastic prose, is that individual slice of time, that moment of presence that seeks to become 'untensed' – to escape the ceaseless displacement of the self by itself over time, so that a sense of self-presence, however illusory it may be, can be prolonged.

In ironic self-address, the narrator separates her present self from her past self: the narrated-I is depicted as an alienated self, figured as object. In nostalgic self-address, on the other hand, a narrator seeks to blend with her narrated-I in a longing to reinhabit a lost home. Recall Boym's definition of nostalgia: to try to reinhabit the past in this way is to engage in 'a romance with one's own fantasy'. The closing sentences of *Swann's Way* speak this very romance:

> The places we have known do not belong only to the world of space on which we map them for our convenience. They were only a thin slice, held between the contiguous impressions that composed our life at that time; *the memory of a particular image is but regret for a particular moment*; and houses, roads, avenues are as fugitive, alas, as the years.
>
> (my emphasis 513)

The nostalgic narrator seeks to step across the temporal gulf separating her from these spaces lost in time to become the I of one's past, as if one could forget the I of one's present. If we reconcile these two positions, though, we discover the mode of ironized nostalgia, where the writer of memory acknowledges that she is – in the very act of narration – both the other she once was (described character) and the self she currently is (narrator).

Herein lies Proust's legacy for writing memory. The tone of such writing is inescapably nostalgic because the past is acknowledged to be irretrievable from the outset. But this is exactly what impels the writer to create, by an ekphrastic transposing of memory's images, the mimetic illusion of their presence. As Genette suggests, 'no narrative can "show" or "imitate" the story it tells. All it can do is tell it in a manner which is detailed, precise, "alive", and in that way give more or less the *illusion of mimesis*' (*Narrative Discourse* 164). In Proust and after, mimetic illusion is maximized at the textual site of ekphrasis, where narrative progression is delayed, and the reader's gaze is fixed upon a memorable, though fleeting, moment.

*

In conclusion, let us consider two such moments, both taken from Nabokov's *Speak, Memory*, an autobiography that can be said to have adapted the blueprint of Proust's novel. In the opening chapter, Nabokov describes an indelible memory from his childhood, in pre-Revolution Russia, when his father was called away from the living room by a group of workers from the Nabokov estate. When thus called upon to mediate in a local dispute of some sort, Nabokov's father – should he grant the workers' request – would be 'put through the national ordeal of being rocked and tossed up and securely caught by a score or so of strong arms' (*Speak, Memory* 15). Nabokov remembers:

> From my place at table I would suddenly see through one of the west windows a marvellous case of levitation. There, for an instant, the figure of my father in his wind-rippled white summer suit would be displayed, gloriously sprawling in midair … reclining, as if for good, against the cobalt blue of the summer noon, like one of those paradisiac personages who comfortably soar, with such a wealth of folds in their garments, on the vaulted ceiling of a church while below, one by one, the wax tapers in mortal hands light up to make a swarm of minute flames in the mist of incense, and the priest chants of eternal repose, and funeral lilies conceal the face of whoever lies there, among the swimming lights, in the open coffin.
>
> (15)

This is a memorable description which, via metaphoric imagery, both encapsulates the boy's valorization of his father and foreshadows the father's death in the not-too-distant future. Memory and imagination work jointly, as the recollection of the father's 'levitation' gets displaced by the image of an 'open coffin', awaiting its implied occupant. The memory of the sprawling figure 'in his wind-rippled white summer suit' calls up images derived from painting ('one of those paradisiacal personages'), and the ekphrasis then expands to include a church, shifting the opening ecstasy into melancholy as our gaze descends to the lily-covered figure, lying in the coffin below.[20] The scene is momentarily static, as time is stilled for that single instant that Nabokov's father remains aloft against 'the cobalt blue' of sky in his memory, and yet mention of the coffin introduces *time* into this stillness. The coffin acts as an arrow pointing forwards in our reading, hinting of the end to come – the father's approaching death, recounted later in the autobiography. The levitation thereby corresponds to the delay of ekphrasis, while the open coffin corresponds to endings, which demand narration and time. In this way, Nabokov's description acts as a reminder to the reader that even those scenes that have most to do with life – and that also seem most alive before the reader's eye – can only temporarily forestall endings, endings both narrational and literal.

---

[20] Just these kinds of 'paradisiacal personages' are captured in Marcel's prose picturing of Giotto's frescoes on the walls and ceiling of the Arena Chapel in Padua (*The Fugitive* 744).

The essential illusion of ekphrastic writing is that while we read and contemplate such descriptions the past does *seem* to be restored.[21] But then the narrator is compelled to admit that he hasn't quite got there – that past presence remains absent; veiled. In chapter 5 of the autobiography, dedicated to fond memories of his governess, Nabokov, while imaginatively accompanying her on a lonely sleigh journey across the Russian steppe, catches himself in a moment of becoming-one with his child-self and then finds himself rudely catapulted back into the present – sixty years later – of his narrating-I.

> But what am I doing in this stereoscopic [because both memory and imagination are at work] dreamland? How did I get here? Somehow, the two sleighs have slipped away, leaving behind a passportless spy on the blue-white road in his New England snowboots and stormcoat. The vibration in my ears is no longer their receding bells, but only my old blood singing. All is still, spellbound, enthralled by the moon, fancy's rear-vision mirror. The snow is real, though, and as I bend to it and scoop up a handful, sixty years crumble to glittering frost-dust between my fingers.
>
> (*Speak, Memory* 70)

This spellbinding instance of ekphrastic *ostranenie*, picturing how the present dissolves the evoked past, like a handful of quickly melting snow, shows that the recovery of past presence is an impossibility that all self-recounting faces. Memory's prose picturing is an ideal that melts away each time, in its ultimate aim, because such are the very tenets of representation.

What Derrida says of the faith necessary for drawing – and for every act of ma(r)king a trait – is equally applicable to the faith necessary for creating prose pictures: 'faith, in the moment proper to it, is blind. It sacrifices sight, even if it does so with an eye to seeing at last' (*Memoirs of the Blind* 30). The mimetic illusion of the verbally evoked past proves sufficient despite its blindness – a blindness in the guise of black ink that, somehow, makes ekphrastic sights possible.

---

[21] See also Elizabeth Bruss 149. Bruss describes Nabokov's autobiographical stance as follows: the author adopts 'the role of an observer and an auditor, a member of memory's audience' (161). As in Proust, the narrating-I of *Speak, Memory* observes his own narrated world as if he, too, was a member of the audience of readers contemplating these textually imparted visions.

3

Description and narration in Vladimir Nabokov's *Ada or Ardor*

Metaphor clings to memory: in its quest for it, a discussion of memory soon finds itself covered in figures. Memory is often figured as a series of snapshots of the past; as affective tableaux; as a kind of film; or, in cognitive science, as information stored in the brain in something akin to binary code. The common denominator in all these metaphors is the notion of the trace, the imprint, the *mark* left by the present on the tissue of the past, and this notion has come down to us from ancient Greece. During antiquity, memory was commonly thought to resemble a wax tablet: impressions on the mind were likened to impressions made by a signet ring or stylus upon the soft clear surface of the tablet (Yates 35–36).[1] For Mitchell, memory is 'a double-coded system of mental storage and retrieval', and 'the composite imagetext structure of memory seems to be a deep feature that endures all the way from Cicero to Lacan to the organization of computer memory' (*Picture Theory* 192–193). Of course, describing memory either as a 'wax tablet' or a 'composite imagetext' does not explain how memory functions neurologically. However, that kind of description would have little use for an exploration of how memory is *experienced* while reading ekphrastic literature. In the present chapter I approach this issue from the phenomenological base: that is, what visual description makes happen when we read such narratives, and the understanding of our own memory that we might derive from this reading experience. In this regard, Mitchell's notion of imagetext is particularly fitting as a description both of memory's writing and reading, where neither image nor text is primary but always their suture, precisely because of memory's interdependence with narrative and visual media. As we will see throughout this chapter's reading of Vladimir Nabokov's *Ada or Ardor*, though, there is a

---

[1] For a survey of the wax tablet metaphor and its uses in Aristotle and Plato, see David Farrell Krell 13–47.

tension between the two words that make up imagetext, and it is their repulsion–attraction that produces this philosophically rich novel.

There is, however, another figuring of memory that evinces the long-standing alignment of memory with images, and one I want to use in this chapter as a model for ekphrastic description after Proust: the fabled memory theatre. The memory theatre is a mnemonic device first developed, according to legend, by the pre-Socratic poet Simonides, and its story is recounted by Frances Yates in *The Art of Memory*. A banquet was once held by a nobleman from Thessaly, where Simonides was hired to sing a panegyric praising said nobleman, Scopas. Sometime during the banquet, a messenger arrives and tells Simonides that two men are waiting for him outside. Just as Simonides leaves the building to attend to them, the roof of the hall collapses, killing everybody inside. When the relatives come to bury their dead, they cannot identify the 'mangled corpses', but, as Yates writes, 'Simonides remembered the places at which they had been sitting at the table and was therefore able to indicate to the relatives which were their dead … this experience suggested to the poet the principles of the art of memory' (1–2). Thus was born the idea of the memory theatre, the principles of which are here spelled out by Cicero: '[Simonides] inferred that persons desiring to train this faculty (of memory) must select places and form mental images of the things they wish to remember and store those images in the places, so that the order of the places will preserve the order of the things' (qtd. in Yates 2). The only extant textbook of rhetoric which outlines 'the art of memory' is the so-called *Ad Herennium* (Yates 6). The mnemonics may be summed up as follows: one begins by selecting an actual building of moderate size with a well-lit interior – in Quintilian's version, the building may also be imagined – and proceeding to memorize it as vividly as possible. This done, one then assigns to each specific place inside this virtual space the information or words to be remembered. It is important that the mnemonic images for the relevant information should be of an unusual, singular nature; as the anonymous author of the *Ad Herennium* puts it, 'We ought … to set up images of a kind that can adhere longest in memory. And we shall do so if we establish similitudes as striking as possible. … The things we easily remember when they are real we likewise remember without difficulty when they are figments. But this will be essential – again and again to run over rapidly in the mind all the original places in order to refresh the images' (qtd. in Yates 10).

Yates's book examines how the classical principles of 'the art of memory' metamorphosed into new constellations of ideas during the Middle Ages and the Renaissance. I want to discuss, briefly, an actual memory theatre built by the Italian philosopher Giulio Camillo (1480–1544) and suggest that this model may be used as a figure for the ekphrastic novel's structure, as we find it in both Proust and Nabokov. Camillo's 'Memory Theatre' was built according to the mnemonics inherited from classical rhetors, but he also channelled into its design diverse currents of Renaissance thought, including Jewish Cabbala and Hermetism (Yates 150–151). Camillo built two versions during his lifetime; however, by 1550 the fabled theatre was destroyed, and no visual reproductions of it survive (Yates 135). To picture it, then, we must rely on the testimony (or description) of those who saw it and on Camillo's own writing explaining the theatre's design. Yates relates that Viglius – a friend of Erasmus – once visited Camillo's theatre in Venice and described it in a letter to the eminent scholar. The theatre was evidently big enough to accommodate two people, and what Viglius would have seen, Yates explains, is a classical Vitruvian amphitheatre, but 'in Camillo's Theatre the normal function of the theatre is reversed. There is no audience sitting in the seats … The solitary "spectator" of the Theatre stands where the stage would be and looks towards the auditorium, gazing at the images [illustrations]' (137). What the visitor would have seen were seven sections for each of the seven planets of Hermetic thought, the lowest level of which (the places traditionally assigned to the *highest* in social rank) corresponding to the 'seven essential measures on which, according to magico-mystical theory, all things here below depend' (Yates 138). Camillo's construction thus represents a complex, cosmic world view, acting more than a mnemonic device.[2]

At this point, let us recall Marcel's two metaphors of having reached a great height upon Time's 'stilts' from which he can survey the spectacle of the past below him and comparing himself to a painter arduously climbing a wooded hill and contemplating the view through the tress. And this is how Camillo describes the vision he wanted to impart to those who visited his 'Memory Theatre':

> If we were to find ourselves in a vast forest and desired to see its whole extent we should not be able to do this from our position within it for our view would be limited to only a small part of it by the immediately surrounding trees which would prevent us from seeing the distant view. But if, near to this forest, there was a slope leading up to a high hill, on coming out of the forest and ascending the slope we should begin to see a large part of the form of the forest, and from the top of the hill we should see the whole of it. The wood is our inferior world; the slope is the heavens; the hill is the supercelestial world.
>
> (qtd. in Yates 143)

---

[2] See also Yates's (144–145) diagram reconstructing Camillo's theatre.

Camillo's theatre is a microcosm that would, he believed, enable the visitor to gain this kind of 'distant view' from above and thus come to understand the divine macrocosm (Yates 147–148). In the above passage, Camillo is using a visual analogy to depict the Neoplatonic conception of the world, but he may as well be describing Proustian narration, where past moments ('the wood') are captured by Marcel as he matures as an artist ('the slope'), until he reaches the moment when he can contemplate the spectacle of his journey through Time ('the supercelestial world').

I want to suggest that, like Camillo's 'Theatre' of the macrocosm with its seven planetary sections, Proust's novel may be conceived in similar fashion (coincidentally, it also happens to be divided into seven volumes).[3] Each of this imagined theatre's sections would represent a volume of the *Search*, and we would move up the grades of the amphitheatre towards greater and greater levels of scenic detail. Such a construction – to indulge this fantasy – would also include visual illustrations of representative scenes from each volume. Considering the plenitude of visual detail in Proust, one would need to be selective, but they may well include the impressionistic prose picturing of Combray's environs along the Méséglise and Guermantes ways (*Swann's Way* 73–75; 198–224); descriptions of the 'little band' of girls and Elstir's canvases (*Within a Budding Grove* 425–437; 479–488); the ekphrases of theatre boxes with their aquatic occupants (*Guermantes Way* 35–42); the botanical and entomological imagery used to depict Charlus's encounter with Jupien in the Guermantes's courtyard (*Sodom and Gomorrah* 1–38); the ekphrases of sleeping Albertine and Bergotte seeing the *View of Delft* (*The Captive* 71–74; 207–209);[4] the reflections upon memory, jealousy and grief after Albertine's death, and the sights seen in Venice with Mamma (*The Fugitive* 546–637; 741–754); and, finally, the 'puppet-show' staged by Time with the faces and bodies of old friends at the Guermantes's soirée (*Time Regained* 290–326).

In Camillo's model, under each of the pictorial illustrations upon the auditorium's receding grades there were 'coffers' containing philosophical texts,

---

[3] In a fortuitous yet satisfying coincidence, I have discovered that Victoria Nelson has also drawn this comparison. In *The Secret Life of Puppets*, Nelson devotes a chapter to the 'art of memory', exploring the philosophies of Giordano Bruno and Giulio Camillo and their enduring legacy for generations of writers; she cites 'two great early twentieth-century memory palaces, Proust's *In Search of Lost Time* and Joyce's *Finnegans Wake*, but particularly the former, that "vast structure of recollection" and secular cathedral whose dogma is an elaborate metaphysics of memory ... in a way analogues to Bruno's memory wheel or Camillo's theatre' (194).

[4] Karpeles thinks that the dying Bergotte's parting encounter with Vermeer's painting 'presents the single most palpable collaboration of word and image in the novel – arguably in any novel' (16). Karpeles's *Paintings in Proust* would be an invaluable resource for any such model-building exercise.

making Camillo's theatre, in Yates's phrase, 'look like a highly ornamental filing cabinet' (145). Given technical acumen and sufficient financial resources, an enterprising Proust scholar might well build a similar model representing the *Search*, with extracts from the novel filed in drawers next to accompanying illustrations for each volume. These extracts could then be used to compare the illustrations (e.g. paintings, photographs, even film stills taken from cinematic adaptations of the *Search*) with the text's imaging of them. Exploring the model-theatre, the student of Proust would thereby not only gain insight into this novel's complex structure, but also more readily apprehend that the scenes recalled from narrated memory are inseparable palimpsests of text-and-image. What the student of Proust would see during her *retrospection* of the read text are not only the pictures displayed above the drawers, but also the *images elicited within* by ekphrasis' sites. (Whenever we reread a novel and return to its sites of description, new images are invariably superimposed over the fading watermarks of remembered scenes.) And this means that our hypothetical scholar's construction would need to be continually painted over, refurbished and updated with new illustrations – like the process of rereading itself, only much more laborious and costly.

I want to keep this figure of a virtual memory theatre in the wings of this chapter, as we examine Vladimir Nabokov's most ekphrastic novel, *Ada or Ardor*. Nabokov's conception of authorship is nothing if not visual. In *Lectures on Literature*, for instance, he observes:

> The pages are still blank, but there is a miraculous feeling of the words all being there, written in invisible ink and clamouring to become visible. You might if you choose develop any part of the picture, for the idea of sequence does not really exist as far as the author is concerned. ... If the mind were constructed on optional lines and if a book could be read as a painting is taken in by the eye, that is without the bother of working from left to right and without the absurdity of beginnings and ends, this would be the ideal way of appreciating a novel, for thus the author saw it at the moment of its conception.
>
> (380)

Amalgamating Nabokov's authorial tropes with Camillo's model, we can think of narratives such as *The Gift, Speak, Memory* and certainly *Ada* as virtual memory theatres containing images of the depicted past. Describing how the rhetors conceived the relationship between mnemonic images and words upon which the memory theatre was founded, Webb notes: 'What lies behind vivid speech is the gallery of mental images ... The souls of both speaker and listener are stocked with internal images of absent things, and these provide the raw material with which each party can "paint" the images that ekphrasis puts into words' (*Ekphrasis, Imagination* 113). Webb's description of rhetorical practice perfectly fits Nabokov's authorial vision; as in the classical model of 'the art of memory', his prose pictures are arranged according to the ordered sequence of their topoi, the ekphrastic 'places', within the novel, composed and configured by its plot. Nabokov the ekphratic dreamer believed that the novel-painting pre-existed its telling; regardless of the veracity of this belief, his novel trusts in his readers' capacity to respond to the images his prose presents before them, with their own culturally acquired material.

On contemplative description

Ada is narrated by Van Veen – philosopher, psychologist, writer – who records the story of his lifelong love affair with his sister, Ada. Van is a nonagenarian at the time of writing, and, while the novel is divided into five parts, the first two parts, chronicling Van and Ada's childhood and adolescence, make up its bulk. Nabokov scholar and biographer Brian Boyd eloquently captures its structure: '*Ada* records rhythms that are common to us all: the seemingly endless expanse of childhood time, the accelerating collapse of the years, the steadily swelling stores of memory' (*Nabokov's Ada* 260). Indeed, this novel is engrossed with the passing of time, and both Van and Ada suffer from what Martin Hägglund calls 'chronophobia': their fear of losing each other to the passing of Time.[5] The gradually shorter lengths of the succeeding parts dividing the narrative are indicative of time speeding up as one ages, and this structure points to the tension between delay and motion that is one of the novel's central themes.

The novel's 'swelling stores of memory', in Boyd's apt phrase, are given expression by means of ekphrastic description, and, in order to shed light on the significance of visual detail in *Ada*, I want to return to Genette's conception of narrative as consisting of two kinds of representations, 'which', he writes, 'are closely intermingled and in variable proportions: on the one hand, those of actions and events, which constitute the narration in the strict sense and,

---

[5] In *Dying for Time*, Hägglund persuasively argues that *Ada* is concerned with the spacing of time as writing and that '[t]his spacing of time – and the interdependence of love and loss that follows from it – is the cause of the chronophobia that haunts chronophilia from beginning to end' (109). I return to Hägglund's reading of the novel at the end of this chapter.

on the other hand, those of objects or characters that are the result of what we now call description' (Genette, *Figures* 133). Description attempts to defer story time, and this implies (certainly for ekphrastic narratives) that if memory is representable via a prose picturing of the past, then it seems that memory itself seeks to slow down time's flow.[6] Every narrative, clearly, involves change, displacement, development. If a narrative consisted solely of description, it would cease being a narrative; we would then be left with a text that represents 'objects simply and solely in their spatial existence, outside any event and even outside any temporal dimension' (Genette 133). Genette's discussion of narration and description culminates in the following passage: 'These two types of discourse may, then, appear to express two antithetical attitudes to the world and to existence, one more *active*, the other more *contemplative*, and therefore, following a traditional equivalence, more "poetic"' (136). Genette's distinction between 'active' narration and 'contemplative' description corresponds to the two roles of memory identified by Bergson. According to Bergson, we recall, there are two kinds of memories: 'contemplative' memory and 'action' memory, which he also defines, respectively, as 'the plane of pure memory, where our mind retains in all its details the picture of our past life', and 'the plane of action – the plane in which our body has condensed its past into motor habits' (*Matter and Memory* 241). Both the narratologist and the philosopher use similar language to express a distinction between a life governed by the needs of memory, the *contemplative* existence, and a life governed by useful 'motor habits', the *active* existence. By extension, these opposing attitudes might be said to be characteristic of two broad types of narrative fiction: the descriptively dense, contemplative novel about memory filled with visual detail, and the narrationally speedier page-turner, where peripeteia is the norm rather than the exception.

Ada is patently an example of the contemplative narrative, where description – while it can never become master – seeks to slow the progress of events. Mitchell makes the following helpful observation that relates to Genette's distinction above:

> Memory, like description, is a technique which should be subordinate to free temporality: if memory becomes dominant, we find ourselves locked in

---

[6] Genette argues that in Proust descriptive pauses remain anchored in temporality because we view them from the perspective of the narrating self, 'and thus the descriptive piece never evades the temporality of the story' (*Narrative Discourse* 100). The only thing I would add is that Proust's descriptions alter our phenomenological grasp of the *narrated* self's time, precisely by *prolonging* the depicted moment and slowing down narration.

the past; if description takes over, narrative temporality, progress towards an end, is endangered, and we become paralyzed in an endless proliferation of descriptive detail.

(*Picture Theory* 194)

By associating memory with description, Mitchell inadvertently provides an accurate diagnosis of the malaise of *Ada* qua narrative: this novel, that is, suffers from too much memory, the paralysis caused by too much description. If memory and, consequently, description become dominant, as Mitchell warns, then the narrator becomes stuck in the past; more importantly, he or she is then also apt to *neglect the future*. (I return to this point at the end of this chapter.)

Nabokov's novel asks for extensive visualization on the part of the reader. The baroque prose, though it often draws attention to its own ornamentation, gradually seduces the imagination into seeing the scenes of Van's memory. In Parts I and II especially, the descriptions of Van and Ada's trysts and games in Ardis Hall are excessively detailed – they are like verbal paintings of the past that wrestle with time itself. Reading these pages, it seems as though Van wishes to remain in these idylls of childhood and resist the onward march of narration. Genette, we have seen, argues that description spreads the narrative in space, bringing to mind an image of a canvas. However, description relies on language and language is itself temporal (its grammar speaks of time). As James Heffernan has argued, 'ekphrasis cannot be simply equated with spatialization … the history of ekphrasis suggests that language releases a narrative impulse which graphic art restricts' (302). No matter how much written language may seek to dwell on the past, it is towards the future that it is directing the reader's eye. If a writer seeks, as Nabokov clearly does, to become a verbal painter, then he must contend with language's temporality. As D. Barton Johnson and Gerard de Vries argue, in *Nabokov and the Art of Painting*, 'As a storyteller, Nabokov relied heavily on images. The course of a story is frequently *interrupted* by pictorial interludes … when creating a plot which engenders fine images or pictures assembled into a story … a writer, unlike a painter, has to attend to what precedes his images and what follows from them' (my emphasis 31–32). Pictorial details certainly do get 'assembled into a story' in *Ada*, but they still retain their function as interruptions of narrative temporality: temporary suspensions of narrative development.

The literary device that Nabokov employs to accrete textual islands of descriptive detail amidst the flow of story is, of course, ekphrasis. The following passage is a typical example of ekphrastic description in the novel. Van is here remembering his first summer at Ardis Hall: he is on his way for a dip in the garden brook, when in

> a corner room he found, standing at a tall window, a young chambermaid ... a tortoiseshell comb in her chestnut hair caught the amber light; the French window was open, and she was holding one hand, starred with a tiny aquamarine, rather high on the jamb. ... Her cameo profile, her cute pink nostril, her long, French, lily-white neck, the outline, both full and frail, of her figure ... moved Van so robustly that he could not resist clasping the wrist of her raised tight-sleeved arm.
>
> (48)

This is an extended description of a very minor character in the novel, and it is a typical instance of the proliferating visual detail adorning many of its pages. It also reminds us of the fact that even the most detailed description emits traces of narrativity: Van 'could not resist clasping the wrist', and this action may be seen as a kind of metaphor of Van's character (his impetuousness and 'clasping' after beauty and pleasure, which ultimately result in tragedy). A few pages further on, our memory as readers – one should actually say, following Nabokov's own prescription, *rereaders* – gets tested.[7] Van 'stooped to pick up a tortoiseshell comb ... he had seen one, exactly like that, quite recently, but when, in whose hairdo?' (53). If we were reading attentively and visualized the earlier description of the chambermaid, then we would likely recognize this detail of the 'tortoiseshell comb'. There are several such 'memory tests' in Van's narration, and they all serve to emphasize narrative's ability to retain (as in a memory theatre) the recounted past in memorable images.

Regarding this novel's painterly aspirations, J. E. Rivers argues that *Ada* is 'the most serious attempt since *À la recherche* to combine the aesthetics of painting and the aesthetics of literature' (144). Proust's novel, as we saw in Chapter 1, is filled with meditations on painting and alludes to both actual painters and fictional artists. *Ada* likewise makes repeated reference both to real and imaginary artworks. Early in the novel, Van discovers a volume called 'Forbidden Masterpieces' that contains various imaginary works by real Renaissance artists, and, during his recollection of an amorous scene with Ada, he refers to one of these paintings: 'Van could not recollect whose picture it was that he had in mind, but thought it might have been attributed to Michelangelo da Caravaggio

---

[7] See Nabokov, *Lectures on Literature* 1–6.

in his youth. It was an oil on unframed canvas depicting two misbehaving nudes, boy and girl, in an ivied or vined grotto or near a small waterfall' (140–141). The allusion here is fictitious – no such painting by Caravaggio exists (Barton Johnson 129). However, the reader of this passage can imagine this scene well enough, despite the lack of a precise visual referent; we might say that we have a general notion of the meaning of a 'Caravaggesque' painting to imagine one. Tamar Yacobi suggests that in these cases, an understanding of ekphrases of artworks is further refined by what she calls 'pictorial models', where writers 'are not alluding to any specific picture or statue but to a pictorial model, a common denominator, a generalized visual image' (601). This is precisely what happens here: by offering possible titles for this verbal painting – 'Faun Exhausted by Nymph? Swooning Satyr?' (141) – Van is triggering the reader's imagination into visualizing familiar painterly scenes. This stimulation of the imagination by 'pictorial models' serves as a descriptive aid, making the depicted image easier to visualize. (Note that Van also seems *anxious* about the descriptive powers of his language; as if verbal description by itself were insufficient and required the mediation of a visual model to succeed in capturing this scene of the recollected past.)

Another example of description in *Ada* is even more painterly. Van and Ada have been reunited after a long separation, and this scene describes their seduction of Lucette (their younger half-sister, smitten with Van):

> Thus seen from above … we have the large island of the bed illumined from our left (Lucette's right) by a lamp burning with a murmuring incandescence on the west-side bedtable. The top sheet and quilt are tumbled at the footboardless south of the island where the newly landed eye starts on its northern trip, up the younger Miss Veen's pried-open legs. A dewdrop on russet moss eventually finds a stylistic response in the aquamarine tear on her flaming cheekbone. Another trip from the port to the interior reveals the central girl's long white left thigh. … The scarred male nude on the island's east coast is half-shaded, and, on the whole, less interesting. … The recently repapered wall immediately west of the now louder-murmuring (*et pour cause*) dorocene lamp is ornamented in the central girl's honor with Peruvian 'honeysuckle' being visited … by marvellous Lodigesia Hummingbirds, while the bedtable on that side bears a lowly box of matches, a *karavanchik* of cigarettes, a Monaco ashtray … The companion piece on Van's side supports a similar superstrong but unlit lamp, a dorophone, a box of Wipex, a reading loupe … Ten eager, evil, loving, long fingers belonging to two different young demons caress their helpless bed pet. Ada's loose black hair

accidentally tickles the local curio she holds in her left fist, magnanimously demonstrating her acquisition. Unsigned and unframed.

(419–420)

The concluding epithet is unnecessary, as the reader is hardly in doubt that this is a verbal portrait. The narrator instructs us to move our gaze in various directions over the 'island' of the bed, and my ellipses eliding several descriptive sentences accentuate the compulsive proliferation of visual detail in this passage. Yacobi's definition of ekphrasis is apt here: 'literature's alleged yearning for imagelike simultaneity, roundness, permanence, eternal return – in short, deliverance from time – finds its quintessential expression in the "still moment" or "stopped moment" captured by ekphrasis' (615). Indeed, the above passage compels us to hold this verbal canvas before the mind's eye and linger over this slice of spaced time. However, no ekphrasis can *stop* time in narrative; it can only delay it, as the caressing movements of the 'eager, evil, loving, long fingers' already gesture towards description's limit, its submissiveness to narration. Narrative progression always reasserts itself, as we read on: 'for the magical gewgaw liquefied all at once, and Lucette, snatching up her nightdress, escaped to her room' (420). What is restaged here is precisely the description versus narration tussle identified by Genette, where narration always has the upper hand over memory's need to pause over its images. Before moving on from this example, though, it should be kept in mind that, while Van is claiming to be remembering this scene, his memory of the illicit-love-triangle is portrayed from *above*, as though the one remembering could see himself – his past self – as a figure spread on a 'canvas' before his memory's eye. This is not what one would call a straightforward description of what happened, but a highly imaginative *staging* of a past occurrence with narrative significance. By evoking the memory in this stilled fashion, and by mentioning Lucette's subsequent escape from the room, the passage foregrounds, respectively, both the narrator's desire to slow time and preserve the happy moment, and his acknowledgment that this is ultimately unattainable – that such stilled moments 'liquefy' all too soon in time.

Ekphrasis, as it is practised here, underscores role of the imagination in visual memory writing. Edward Casey, in *Remembering: A Phenomenological Study*, makes a distinction between what he calls the passivist and activist conceptions of memory. The passivist conception of memory, traced back to Aristotle, is defined as follows: 'It is the view that all memories necessarily repeat the past in a strictly replicative manner. The contribution of the remembering subject is nugatory – if not outright distortive or destructive. ... Memories should take the form of images that are isomorphic with what they are images *of*' (269).[8] The passivist paradigm conceives of the past as perfectly reproducible, and the most suggestive metaphor for this conception is the photograph: 'If recollection is indeed a matter of depicting the past in a crisp, visualized format, a format modelled on that of photographic likeness, it will be deprived of any effective autonomy of its own' (Casey 270). 'Autonomy' is the key word here: Casey maintains that any act of remembering is an essentially autonomous act; there is a freedom (and frailty) to memory that passivism fails to acknowledge. Nabokovian memory, in one sense, is precisely about the 'matter of depicting the past in a crisp, visualized format', yet one would not call it 'passivist'. This is where we can appreciate the usefulness of the metaphor of painting rather than of photography for Nabokovian memory. Painting grants memory far more scope for autonomy, and memory as painting is a good metaphor of the 'activist' model of remembering. Activism 'involves the active transformation of experience rather than its internalized reduplication in images or traces construed as copies' (Casey 15). In the activist paradigm, Casey argues, 'I am not merely picturing my memories; I am bringing them forth in a concerted, and often a quite *constructive*, manner. Every reproduction, therefore, has a productive aspect' (my emphasis 271). Casey does not quite spell this out, but the implication of his argument is that 'activist' memory involves the *narrative* imagination in the presentation of its contents.

'If memory is not a matter of pictographic transparency', Casey continues, 'if it is an active affair of dense interinvolvement with a massive past – it will not bring any particular past experience back in a pristine format' (285). The fact that memory cannot promise transparency implies that whatever story we tell about the past is a story we ourselves have, at least in part, created. That is not to say that we have merely imagined it, but that telling a story about life involves turning the episodic images of memory into a cohesive whole – which is to say, into a story. And it is in the narrativization of memory where we find the imagination playing its most active role. For instance, Van's description of his mother, Marina, points precisely to the *absence* of imagination and its consequences

---

[8] Aristotle gives the following account of what it means to have a 'memory image' of something: 'one must conceive the image in us to be something in its own right and to be of another thing. In so far, then, as it is something in its own right, it is an object of contemplation or an image. But in so far as it is of another thing, it is a sort of copy and a reminder' ('De Memoria' 51). In Aristotle's account, there is also a distinction between a memory image, *mneme*, which spontaneously arrives before consciousness, and *anamnesis*, defined as a purposeful seeking out of the past (59).

for memory: 'lacking as she did that *third sight* (individual, magically detailed imagination) which many otherwise ordinary and conformant people may also possess, but without which memory ... is, let us face it, a stereotype or a tear-sheet' (252). Van's calling unimaginative memory a 'stereotype' is revealing: a stereotype, in the OED definition, is 'a method of replicating a relief printing surface', something 'reproduced in an unchanging manner' ('stereotype'). To lack imagination is to reproduce the same past in each telling, as if the past came ready-made and all that it required is a replication of its originary tale. Moreover, to claim that one produces the past in each act of remembrance is also to suggest that memory itself is non-narrational in nature.

Memory can, of course, sometimes seem to possess a quasi-narrational structure, when certain memories fall spontaneously into a story sequence. One crucial thing that memory lacks though, as Casey emphasizes, 'is a proper *narrative voice*, the voice of an authoritative narrator who spins out the tale. Whether actually spoken or present in written form, this voice commands the course of the tale in story-telling, reflecting the fact that the narrator knows the entire story in advance' (44). Memory, one might say, is tellingly silent – it shows us its images but cannot by itself tell us a story that would be meaningful. This is another reason why it is useful to think about narrative form in relation to memory as a kind of technics: it provides the narrator with the necessary tools to emplot memory into a story about the past. Memory supplies the verbal artist with images that then need to be transposed via the technics of narrative; to grant memory a *voice* – to let memory 'speak', in Nabokov's sense – is to conjoin image to text within a particular emplotted configuration. Mitchell's notion of memory as an imagetext can thus be elaborated slightly to suggest: only once memory becomes *narrativized* does it fully form the compound imagetext. The point of contact of these two concepts is also the point where memory and imagination flow over each other, become imbricated. This is because the narrator must not only choose what remembered images to form into a narrative sequence but also determine how best to use his language to articulate (describe) the individual memories themselves.

Memory and imagination thus work in unison at the level of the depiction of individual memory images. Casey explores the overlap of these two seemingly separate mental functions in his essay, 'Imagining and Remembering'. He is concerned with finding examples where 'imagining-*and*-remembering functions as a single (though often internally complex) unit of mental activity' (194). The use of 'pictorial models' in the past's description is one instance of this imbrication; we recall how Van relies on painterly allusions to aid the reader in visualizing the scene he is describing. Describing the past in terms of visual models clearly involves imagining-and-remembering as a complex form of mental activity. Casey argues that imagination and memory often display this kind of 'cooperativeness', adding: 'On many occasions, moreover, one act seems designed to solicit the other – to call the other to its aid' (195). An example from the novel that illustrates this is Van's memory of walking away from Ada once he learns of her infidelity, thus beginning their first period of separation:

> He could swear he did no look back, could not – by any optical chance, or in any prism – have seen her physically as he walked away; and yet, with dreadful distinction, he retained forever a *composite picture* of her standing where he left her. The picture – which penetrated him, through an eye in the back of his head, through his vitreous spinal canal, and could never be lived down, never – consisted of a selection and blend of such random images and expressions of hers that had affected him with a pang of intolerable remorse at various moments in the past.
>
> (my emphasis 297)

Van then lists these various images 'of intolerable remorse' that together make up Ada's 'composite picture'. The important point here is that he sees this 'picture' of Ada only with the eye of narrativized memory, something that he never actually *saw* in the past (he had his back turned to her), and that can only be formed retrospectively in the compilation of his memories. Van continues: 'and the girl in yellow slacks and black jacket, standing with her hands behind her back, slightly rocking her shoulders, leaning her back now closer now less closely against the tree trunk, and tossing her hair – a definite picture that he knew he had never seen in reality – remained within him more real than any actual memory' (298). Clearly, one cannot accuse Van of merely 'imagining' Ada, since this narrated vision is a composite of images of her he had seen in the past, and this prose picture becomes, as he puts it, 'more real than any actual memory'. Equally, one cannot exactly say that Van is remembering Ada and the way she stood with her back against the tree, rocking her shoulders. Casey notes that there are instances in our remembering when memory and imagination are fused together in this way, and neither is eliminable: 'each act is indispensable *in its collaboration with the other*. Each is not just essential but *co*-essential, essential in its very co-ordination with the other' (196). As Van's image of Ada demonstrates, this entanglement is most evident in the past's prose picturing, when imagination and memory *converge* in an image of a significant person or place. The importance of the imagination here is that it fills in a gap in memory for the purpose of memory's telling: it is vital to Van that he can visualize Ada as she (must have) looked when he left her in order to *plot* their future reunion more effectively and in order for this story event to be more affecting. Any narrative about the past thus relies on the resources of both imagination and memory, and the imagetext ekphrasis is the locus of their inextricability.

Invoking (and deriding) painting

I have suggested that one strategy Van adopts in his narration is using 'pictorial models' as aids to the reader's imagination. However, there is an important scene in the novel that invokes a specific picture, and it is especially helpful in unpacking the tension within the imagetext compound. The picture in question is *Divan Japonais*, a poster by Henri de Toulouse-Lautrec that is associated in Van's imagination with Lucette (see Figure 3).

Figure 3 Poster for *Divan Japonais*, by Henri de Toulouse-Lautrec (1864–1901). Courtesy DeAgostini Getty Images.

The image of a woman in black sitting at a bar recurs three times in the novel, and we are given several clues about its provenance. First, adolescent Van is at a railway station tea-room with Ada, where he notices 'a slender lady in black velvet, wearing a beautiful black picture hat, who sat with her back to them at a "tonic bar" and never once turned her head, but the thought brushed him that she was a cocotte from Toulouse' (169). The reference to 'Toulouse' is the first hint to the reader of the picture and artist being referred to. A second occurrence takes place at a restaurant, later in the story: 'At the end of the room, on one of the red stools of the burning bar, a graceful harlot in black – tight bodice, wide skirt, long black gloves, black-velvet picture hat – was sucking a golden drink through a straw … he caught a glimpse of her russety blond beauty' (307). These initial descriptions act as primers for the imagination until we reach the following scene. Van is aboard a cruise ship and goes for a drink at the ship's bar, called 'Ovenman's', and he there unexpectedly encounters Lucette (who is soon to commit suicide, after Van refuses her amorous advances):

> For a minute he stood behind her, sideways to remembrance and reader (as she, too, was in regard to us and the bar), the crook of his silk-swathed cane lifted in profile almost up to his mouth. There she was, against the aureate backcloth of a sakarama screen next to the bar, toward which she was sliding, still upright, about to be seated, having already placed one white-gloved hand on the counter. She wore a high-necked, long-sleeved romantic black dress with an ample skirt, fitted bodice and ruffy collar, from the black soft corolla of which her long neck gracefully rose. With a rake's morose gaze we follow the pure proud line of that throat, of that tilted chin. The glossy red lips are parted, avid and fey, offering a side gleam of large upper teeth. We know, we love that high cheekbone (with an atom of powder puff sticking to the hot pink skin), and the forward upsweep of black lashes and the painted feline eye – all this in profile, we softly repeat. From under the wavy wide brim of her floppy hat of black faille, with a great black bow surmounting it, a spiral of intentionally disarranged, expertly curled bright copper descends her flaming cheek. … [She] must be seen, I hope, by the friends and admirers of my memories, as a natural masterpiece incomparably finer and younger than the portrait of the similarly postured lousy jade with her Parisian *gueule de guenon* on the vile poster painted by that wreck of an artist for Ovenman.
>
> (460–461)

In case we are still unclear about the 'vile poster'– and as further incentive for a curious reader to locate it – Van later tells Lucette: 'Your hat … is positively lautreamontesque – I mean, lautrecaquesque' (461). Reading this description, it is clear that the narrator is striving to depict the scene very closely to the way it is shown on Toulouse-Lautrec's poster. As he is describing a scene that he is remembering, it is also clear that the Toulouse-Lautrec poster serves as a 'pictorial model' for the reader's *own* imagination – assuming, of course, that the (ideal) implied reader recognizes this lithograph, which then functions as a kind of aide-memoire or aide-imagination.[9]

What we see when we read Nabokov's prose painting, however, is not only the Toulouse-Lautrec picture (even if we happen to visualize it while we read the text). In addition to whatever we phenomenologically visualize, we also see language acting out this picture, performing it verbally. The only way that language can conjure the visual is indirectly, by way of 'seeing-as' – the detour of metaphorically loaded expressions. For instance, only metaphorical language allows us to grasp the sense of looking at someone 'sideways from remembrance' – to see someone simultaneously 'sliding' towards the bar and 'about to be seated' – and apprehend how a 'powder puff' on a pink cheek can be imaged as an 'atom'. For Jas Elsner, the true subject of ekphrastic description is less 'the verbal depiction of a visual object, but rather the verbal enactment of the gaze that tries to merge with and penetrate the object' (68). What we see in the prose painting is exactly this kind of verbal-cum-perceptual enactment at work, and, because we may not favour some of the implications of Van's rhetorical moves in bringing this enactment about (such as the objectification of the female body expressed by the phrase 'with a rake's morose gaze'), we notice how ekphrasis allows us to gain a more critical sense of certain culturally inherited habits of seeing.[10] Baldwin, as we saw in Chapter 1, argues that whenever we read visual description in Proust we encounter a kind of 'picture plane', understood as 'the edge of the virtual space that the iconic object lives in', which 'acts as a foil to material contact' (137). Baldwin sees 'picturing' as a kind of '"modelling tool" for Proust' (135), one that draws our attention to the narrator's (and our own) perceptual limits. Proustian ekphrasis allows us to be especially attuned to errors in perception and judgment because these are, ultimately, errors of *seeing* – whether oneself or another as pictured by oneself. Nabokov's ekphrases, particularly in *Ada*, similarly foreground a 'picture plane' making the reader all

---

[9] Karpeles thinks that what we discern in Proust's creative method is an 'art-assisted memory' (22), and the same may be said of Nabokov's fiction.
[10] For a discussion of the 'male gaze' in its relation to ekphrastic representation, and how ekphrasis as literary mode can help create a female aesthetic, see Jane Hedley. On how ekphrasis encourages readers to 'question ways of seeing and showing' (407), see Brosch, 'Ekphrasis in Recent Popular Novels'.

the more aware of the artifice involved in these kinds of pictorial conjurations by the narrator. A significant effect of this is that ekphrasis' 'picture plane' also makes language well up on the page before our gaze. In Nabokov as in Proust, we 'encounter a text that designates itself as something that is meant to be seen rather than (or as well as) read' (Baldwin 141).

Boyd, in analysing the Lucette ekphrasis, makes the following claim: 'Van's attention to the finest detail, the most delicate glints of light, *stands in marked contrast* to Toulouse-Lautrec's bold but flat colouring and his vigorous but crude handling of line' (my emphasis, *Nabokov's Ada* 130).[11] Boyd finds Nabokov's colourful prose much more impressive than Toulouse-Lautrec's (intentionally) 'flat colouring', but the way in which he expresses this preference is peculiar. His statement would seem to imply that there is an unproblematic transparency in a verbal description, as though words themselves could register – like dishes in Dutch *stilleven* – 'the most delicate glints of light'. It is as if the two media, writing and painting, despite working with different matter, may nonetheless achieve the *same* results, if only used appropriately. But this way of comparing words and pictures leaves quite unresolved the question of the mutual *dependence–opposition* of the verbal and the visual as it manifests in an imagetext. Brosch has suggested that 'one can conceive of ekphrasis as a complex interactive process of cooperation. Supplementing the ideas of opposites and competition with one of collaboration can help us to update Mitchell's unfinished project' ('Ekphrasis in the Digital Age' 234). My own argument in this chapter is attempting to do just this, by arguing for the usefulness of 'Mitchell's unfinished project' to a better understanding of ekphrastic memory writing. Contrary to Boyd, then, we might see Nabokov's ekphrasis as encapsulating the compounding repulsion–attraction between image (both tangible and mnemonic) and text that is at the heart of Proustian narration.

Van claims that his verbal description 'must be seen' by fans of his memories as a 'masterpiece incomparably finer' than the poster. The question Van's claim raises is: If verbal description is that much more superior and evocative than visual art, then why resort to visual art as a *source* for this description in the first place? One response would be, as Boyd suggests, that Van refers to the Toulouse-Lautrec poster with the intention of topping it by artful description. Another

---

[11] Boyd (31) points out that Nabokov also had in mind a Barton & Guestier wine advertisement for the description of Lucette; appearing in the *New Yorker* issue of 23 March 1963, it restaged the Toulouse-Lautrec lithograph photographically, with similarly positioned models displayed in the foreground and the original poster hanging on the wall in the background. See also Barton Johnson and de Vries 115–118.

possibility, however, is that Van's angry dismissal of 'the vile poster painted by that wreck of an artist' betrays his *dependence* on visual art for his (Nabokov's) prose effects. Considering how often both 'pictorial models' and actual paintings are invoked over the course of this novel, it is evident that visual art aids this verbal artist by launching him into ekphrastic evocations of his memories. Marina Grishakova suggests that 'the failure of the verbal to reach the state of the visual is used as a constructive principle in Nabokov's fiction' (283); I want to suggest that it is less the failure of language to depict than the foreknowledge about descriptive language's dependence on the visual that informs Nabokov's writing. The device of ekphrasis is employed so regularly and to such magnificent effects in his novel precisely because he appreciates the *inseparability* of the verbal and the visual. In Nabokov and Proust, each medium of representation 'corroborates the other', to borrow Heffernan's phrase (311).[12] Yet, because Nabokov is a verbal artist (as is his erudite fictional narrator), he wishes to retain for words their ostensible supremacy over visual art. On the one hand, the images of memory depend on writerly language for their verbal picturing; on the other hand, verbal description must itself rely on visual cues in order, paradoxically, to assert its superiority over the visual. But in asserting its own superiority, description risks reneging its function – for then we only see black marks upon a white page.

Depicting memory for another

The narration of memory is always an address to another, even if the 'other' happens to be one's own future self. In Nabokov's work, this aspect of narrated memory extending beyond the self, of memory being *for* some significant other, is a defining feature of his writing about the past.[13] In *Ada*, Van's addressee is, of course, Ada. In several instances in the novel, Van includes parentheses recording his conversations with Ada, reminiscing about their shared past:

> (I wonder, Van, *why* you are doing your best to transform our poetical and unique past into a dirty farce? Honestly, Van! Oh, I *am* honest, that's how it went. I wasn't sure of my ground, hence the sauciness and simper ... Sorry, no – if

---

[12] See also Marshall McLuhan 51–61 for a discussion of the ways in which artists are the first to discover how one medium often harnesses the expressive powers of another.
[13] For instance, in *Speak, Memory*, Nabokov repeatedly uses the second person pronoun to refer to his wife, Vera Nabokov, while in the autobiographical novel *The Gift*, the protagonist-narrator, Fyodor, addresses himself both to his partner Zina and to his own future self, when he proclaims: 'And one day we shall recall all this ... ' (364).

people remembered the same they would not be different people. That's-how-it-went. But we are not 'different'! Think and dream are the same in French. Think of the *douceur*, Van! Oh, I am thinking of it, of course I am – it was all *douceur*, my child, my rhyme. That's better, said Ada.) (120)

In other instances, Ada interjects as 'editor' of the narrative, alternately making corrections or giving compliments to Van's writing. For this reason, Van's story takes on the characteristics of reminiscence, rather than plain recollection. Casey suggests that reminiscing is a distinct mode of remembering, and it is distinguished by being 'much more consistently social in origin and operation. … It is a matter, in short, of remembering *with others*' (*Remembering* 105). This means that the significant other with whom one is reminiscing – or for whom one is writing one's memories – acts as a kind of force in-forming memory's narration.

This informing role of the other in Nabokov's work recalls Derrida's remarks on the 'finitude' of memory:

> [T]his finitude can only take that form through the trace of the other in us, the other's irreducible precedence; in other words, simply the trace, which is always the trace of the other, the finitude of memory, and thus the approach or remembrance of the future. If there is a finitude of memory, it is because there is something of the other, and of memory as a memory of the other, which comes from the other and comes back to the other.
>
> (*Memoires for Paul de Man* 29)

Derrida's remarks elucidate his conception of memory as mourning (he is here discussing de Man's reflections on prosopopoeia, where the dead are given voice to speak).[14] The 'finitude of memory', expressible as 'the trace of the other in us', is also a helpful way of characterizing the sine qua non of reminiscing. Thus, Van's most vividly depicted scenes are those involving the 'trace' of Ada in him. Ada, as the significant other who shapes Van's narration by means of her presence in his memories, thereby limits and focuses his recollection of the past to their shared moments of pleasure (and, as we will shortly see, their shared moments of pain). This is why it makes sense to speak of the *finitude* of memory: the significant other sharpens one's recollection of the past by acting as a kind of telescope for remembering.

---

[14] De Man discusses prosopopoeia in his classic essay, 'Autobiography as Defacement', and my argument in this book is on the whole in sympathy with his (slightly morbid) claim that autobiography is 'the fiction of the voice-from-beyond-the-grave' (*Rhetoric of Romanticism* 77) – in the sense that autobiography is a requiem commemorating one's departed self.

This social aspect of reminiscence also shows why the most common metaphors of memory tend to be communicative media; as Mitchell argues: 'The reason, in my view, why accounts of memory inevitably appeal to models of writing, painting, photography, sculpture, printing, etc. is that memory is an intersubjective phenomenon, a practice not only of recollection *of* a past *by* a subject, but of recollection *for* another subject' (*Picture Theory* 193). Indeed, it is improbable that one would choose to write about one's past in the complete absence of significant others acting as guiding 'informants' for reminiscence. Casey, however, suggests that 'reminiscing seems to involve a certain *ingrained egocentrism*, a tendency to recount only what concerns one's own being, one's own fate (even if this is a fate shared with others)' (*Remembering* 109). Having read Nabokov's novel, though, we might amend Casey's definition by adding, '*especially* if this is a fate shared with others'. The 'ingrained egocentrism' that Casey refers to is most often dependent on others for its gratification, since it is other people who are ultimately the biggest source of all our pleasures and pains – or both, as Van and Ada discover. The fact that a memory narrative is narrative written *for* another situates memory on an intersubjective plane. In striving to depict the past in words, the memoirist places great faith in the communicative power of his prose; his ekphrastic hope is that the images of his solitary self will become *visible* to another. From this perspective, the other is not only the implied addressee of one's memoir: the other (or, in Proust's case, oneself as another) is a presence in the very act of narrativizing memory.

On future remembrance

In Part IV of the novel, we are presented with Van's philosophical discussion, titled 'The Texture of Time' – a treatise that seeks, above all, to negate the future. 'The future', as Van quips, 'is but a quack at the court of Chronos' (560). In the remainder of this chapter, I examine how Van's ekphrastic narration of memory predisposes him to adopt this peculiar philosophical position and show that Van the character-self is able to think the future in less radical and more productive terms than Van the narrating-self.

'The Texture of Time' begins with the commonplace that the future is indeterminate. Unlike the contents of the past, which can be verbalized as visual descriptions, the future is a tabula rasa to consciousness; as Van reasons, 'At best, the "future" is the idea of a hypothetical present based on our experience of succession, on our faith in logic and habit. Actually, of course, our hopes can no more bring it into existence than our regrets change the Past' (560). However, Van then makes a more radical suggestion:

> Time is anything but the popular triptych: a no-longer existing Past, the durationless point of the Present, and a 'not-yet' that may never come. No. There are only two panels. The Past (ever-existing in my mind) and the Present (to which my mind gives duration and, therefore, reality). If we make a third compartment of fulfilled expectation, the foreseen, the foreordained, the faculty of prevision, perfect forecast, we are still applying our mind to the Present.
>
> (559–560)

What is really being denied here is not the future as such – not futurity – but a deterministic understanding of temporality; hence Van's emphasis on 'fulfilled expectation, the foreseen, the foreordained'. Nonetheless, the implication of his argument is that the future is itself an illusory concept.[15] The irony is that the 'spectre' of the future remains an all-too-real presence in his treatise, as Van's argument trips over its own paradoxes. This is most apparent in the fact that, while he is mentally composing his tract about time, Van is driving on his way to a reunion with Ada at a hotel in Switzerland. Ideas of progress and motion continue to haunt his philosophizing, despite his dismissals of them: 'We reject without qualms the artificial concept of space-tainted, space-parasited time, the space-time of relativist literature' (541). Space, however, proves to be recalcitrant: 'To give myself time to time Time I must move my mind in the direction opposite to that in which I am moving, as one does when one is driving past a long row of poplars and wishes to isolate and stop one of them, thus making the green blur reveal … its every leaf' (549). Moving either forwards or backwards in space indicates not only directionality but duration – the duration of motion – and this, in turn, affirms the horizon of the future as that towards which the moment is tending. A meditation about time inevitably relies on spatial metaphors to describe it, and, despite Van's ingenuity and metaphorical flights, he cannot rid his time of space.

What Van is really contending against is not the open future of phenomenological time, but the closed future of what is known in philosophy as the untensed view of time. According to the untensed view, Currie notes, '[T]he future exists, and … the ontological priority of the present is an error produced by the mere psychological experience of time' (*About Time* 15). This

---

[15] The narrator of Nabokov's *Transparent Things* similarly proclaims, '[T]he future has no such reality (as the pictured past and the perceived present possess); the future is but a figure of speech, a spectre of thought' (1).

is the kind of perspective propounded by the fatalist – Van's ultimate nemesis. Yet we should also bear in mind that Van is a writer and, therefore, someone who is quite ready to view life itself as story. If life is thought of as a story, then its ending must already be written: life becomes construed as a destiny already written down in the Book of Fate. As Currie expands on this point:

> a written narrative … clearly imports into an understanding of temporality elements of predetermination, predestination and fate that cannot be uncritically assumed for the description of human time, since the 'now' of a reading moves forward into a future which is already there, unalterable by efforts of will. If we accept the reading of a narrative as a model of temporal experience it seems to represent human action in its most passive mode in relation to a future that is not open, the arrival of which we simply await. The future, in a written narrative, is accessible to us, as readers, in a way that seems to render it ontologically distinct from the open future of life: a false future which is, in fact, the past, since it is already written.
>
> (*The Unexpected* 66)

This is precisely the kind of future that Van refuses to accept: a future already complete but towards which he appears to be ignorantly moving. Van denies the future because he construes it, quite literally, in *narrative terms*: he applies the model of narrative time to his own life. In imaging time as a 'triptych', moreover, Van is imagining his own life's course in ways not dissimilar to the principles of the memory theatre: he suspects that the unseen *topoi* (places) where his future experiences will become fossilized as memories might already pre-exist him.

This is not to suggest, however, that narrative temporality does not provide us with a more productive relation to futurity; it does so, by allowing us to think of the future not as what will happen, but in the future anterior mode as what will have happened. First, though, let us examine further Van's philosophical position with its inherent contradictions. This is how Van defines the present: 'Our modest Present is, then, the time span that one is actually and directly aware of, with the lingering freshness of the past still perceived as part of the nowness' (550). The 'lingering freshness of the past' is reminiscent of Husserlian phenomenology. For Edmund Husserl, every present moment consists of what he calls 'retentions' – our immediate awareness of the past – and 'protentions' – our immediate anticipations of the future (41). Husserl's own metaphor for passing time is the trail left in the wake of a comet; he defines 'primary memory or retention as a comet's tail that attaches itself to the perception of the moment' (37). Describing time in these terms spatializes it: a stationary comet is a contradiction in terms, and a moving comet can only move forward in space, and hence over a period of time. Husserl's comet metaphor thus expresses the ever-impending future, and awareness of the future is called protention. Casey describes Husserlian protention as giving the present 'its aura of immediate futurity … consciousness of flow, of intercepting the future in the making' (*Remembering* 201). If we now return to Van's treatise, we discover a very similar conception of the consciousness of time. Van observes: 'we may say that conscious human life lasts only one moment, for at any moment of deliberate attention to our own *flow* of consciousness we cannot know if that moment will be followed by another' (my emphasis 550). Van acknowledges impending futurity by describing consciousness as flowing, as moving towards the unknown. Similarly, he describes time as a sense of continuous becoming and memory in the making: 'In every individual life there goes on from cradle to deathbed the gradual shaping and strengthening of that backbone of consciousness, which is the Time of the strong. "To be" means to know one "has been". "Not to be" implies the only "new" kind of (sham) time: the future. I dismiss it' (559). This passage encapsulates Van's paradoxical reasoning: having admitted temporal progression into his scheme ('from cradle to deathbed'), he subsequently denies futurity as 'sham' time.

It is clear that when Van claims to be denying the future, he is in fact denouncing a deterministic conception of temporality. He comes close to admitting this much: 'the future remains aloof from our fancies and feelings. At every moment it is an infinity of branching possibilities … The unknown, the not yet experienced and the unexpected, all the glorious "x" intersections, are the inherent parts of human life. The determinate scheme by stripping the sunrise of its surprise would erase all sunrays' (560–561). The question that this virtuosic rhetoric poses is *why* Van should insist on conceiving the future as being predetermined, while admitting that 'the unexpected' is inherent to human life. The reason for this is, perhaps, to be found in Van's conception of the past. Recall Van's proclamation that '[t]ime is anything but the popular triptych': the metaphor indicates that only *two* 'panels' of time, the past and the present, are visible to consciousness. Van's objection is to the 'block-view' of time, which would state that the third triptych also contains its 'pictures': the future is 'pre-painted' but we cannot yet see it, immersed as we are in phenomenological duration. This is what Van means by the 'determinate scheme': visualizing what the third triptych of time contains in advance of experiencing it. The import of Van's metaphor is that our notion of futurity is *grounded* on our conception of the past. That is to say, we project onto the future the image we have already formed of our past; futurity carries the germ of pastness within. Van is aware of this, and, in order to preserve surprise, the unexpected and the indeterminable as apposite characteristics of the future, he must deny the 'picture' of the future that his own figuration of the past creates within him. Casey describes both memory and expectation in the following suggestively visual terms: 'These regions, the past and the future proper, are never experienced in their entirety, but only in fragmentary form, through partial perspectives. Such perspectives are opened up and maintained by secondary memory when we seek to reillumine already expired experiences, and by secondary imagination, when we attempt *to light up* possible experiences to come' (my emphasis, *Remembering* 204). Van's treatise on time, from this perspective, wants to foreclose this impulse to 'light up' future experiences – he wishes to preserve the element of surprise in his life by only directing his gaze backwards, rather than forwards in protensive guesses at future eventuality. Indeed, Van's denial of the future grows out of his fear that the future 'panel' of time might already contain its 'pictures', which would reflect back the light produced by the beams of his expectation.

In the foregoing analysis of Van's treatise, I have not mentioned death, and death's shadow is the primeval harbinger that harasses any meditation on time. Nabokov scholars tend to view death in his fiction as a moment of transcendence to a higher plane of being; as Boyd suggests, 'Death could offer us a completely new relation to time: freedom from our being pegged to the present, freedom of access to the whole of the past' (*Nabokov's Ada* 92). Boyd even argues that death in Nabokov promises 'consciousness without the degradation of loss' (84).[16] However, attending closely to Van's argument and to this narrative as a whole, it is questionable whether we ought to accept such a positive interpretation of death's epilogue. There are two important allusions to death in Part IV of the novel. After concluding his ambulatory peroration about time and arriving at the hotel room, Van's sedative pill starts to work and he falls asleep. He dreams that he is delivering a lecture about time, when a member of the audience asks him, '[H]ow did the lecturer explain that in our dreams we know we shall awake, is not that analogous to the certainty of death and if so, the future – ' (561). The thought ends in a dash, but the syllogism's conclusion is clear: contrary to Van's propositions, the certainty of death *guarantees* the future, certifying it beyond the flailing reaches of argument. The second invocation of death occurs during Van and Ada's reunion in her hotel room: 'Van, kneeling and clearing his throat,

---

[16] See also Vladimir Alexandrov 3–6 and *passim*, for a similar reading of Nabokov's fiction.

was kissing her dear cold hands, gratefully, gratefully, in full defiance of death' (562). Death is an all too real aspect of Van's being, we might even say of his being-towards-death. If Van thought of death as the bringer of 'consciousness without the degradation of loss', as Boyd argues, then he would hardly oppose death's approach with such fierceness.

Van the philosopher describes himself as 'an epicure of duration. I delight sensually in Time, in its stuff and spread, in the fall of its folds, in the very impalpability of its greyish gauze, in the coolness of its continuum' (537). Yet this ardent passion for Bergsonian *la durée* (duration) has its converse side: a fear of time. In Part V of the novel, the nonagenarian Van describes his fear of dying in the following, almost Beckettian passage: he relates how he would sleep only on one side, 'so as not to hear his heart: he had made the mistake one night in 1920 of calculating the maximal number of its remaining beats (allowing for another half-century), and now the preposterous hurry of the countdown irritated him and increased the rate at which he could hear himself dying' (569–570). Throughout his narration, Van is concerned to preserve his time with Ada; he seeks to give permanence to the images of his memory via ekphrastic description, which expresses his desire to arrest the flow of time and delay the future's imminence. Description provides a hiatus, a brief suspension in the progression of diegetic events towards the end of the book (and, in Van's case, the end of his life). The fact that this novel is so rich in description evinces Van's struggle with time: his desire to *preserve* moments of happiness and in so doing to *postpone* the impending future that he fears. The future, as uncertainty itself, is the source of all our pain and bliss, and pain and bliss are at the heart of *Ada*. Near the conclusion of his narrative, Van muses: 'One can even surmise that if our time-racked, flat-lying couple ever intended to die they would die, as it were, into the finished book, into Eden or Hades, into the prose of the book or the poetry of its blurb' (587). Van's understanding of Ada as the source of all of his pleasure (Eden) and all of his pain (Hades) mirrors his understanding of time itself: his love of the past and his fear (and unsuccessful denial) of the future.[17] Both coexist in his mind, and their interrelation is expressed by the opposing forces of description versus narration (as the past-made-present opposing the future) that jointly make up the structure of this novel.

The very precariousness of temporal existence motivates Van to record the story of his life. Contrary to Boyd's suggestion that Van's goal is to repose in the

---

[17] The name 'Ada' is a bilingual pun: in Russian 'ahd' (ад) means hell, 'iz ahda' (из ада) means from hell. Hence, Ada is both Van's hell and heaven (*ardor*).

timeless folds of immortality, it is apparent that Van is invested in a project of survival in time. This contention is at the core of Hägglund's *Dying for Time*, where Hägglund introduces the notion of 'chronolibido'. 'Chronolibido' involves a co-implication of chronophobia and chronophilia:

> If one removes the fear of what may happen to a temporal being (chronophobia) one removes the attachment to the same temporal being (chronophilia), since one no longer cares if what happens to it is vital or lethal … attachment to a temporal being means that every affirmation is inhabited by negation from the start and even the most active embrace of life cannot be immune from the reactive mourning of death.
>
> (Hägglund 111)

The temporal logic of 'chronolibido' is that it binds one to finitude. The idea that life and death are interdependent realities which define each other by their difference is Van's reason for writing his autobiography. As he states it near the end: 'The strange mirage-shimmer standing in for death should not appear too soon in the chronicle and yet it should permeate the first amorous scenes' (584). Death haunts narration from the start, and the act of writing memory is driven by the desire to live on as a temporal being, as well as to preserve memory for the future. The import of Hägglund's argument is that without the possibility of death, without its 'strange mirage-shimmer' permeating remembrance, there would be no need to preserve memory. Moreover, writing itself acts as a metaphor for the 'chronolibidinal' purchase on life, as Hägglund argues:

> This necessity of writing – of inscribing the present as a memory for the future – follows from the negativity of time. Every moment immediately negates itself – it ceases to be as soon as it comes to be – and must therefore be inscribed as a memory in order to be apprehended at all. Without the inscription of memory nothing would survive, since nothing would remain from the passage of time. The passion for writing that is displayed by Nabokov and his protagonists is thus a passion for survival. Writing is here not limited to the physical act of writing but is a figure for the chronolibidinal investment in living on that resists the negativity of time while being bound to it.
>
> (84)

Writing, in Hägglund's sense, may thus be read as a figure for the working of narrative form over memory. In my own account of the novel, ekphrasis attempts to *oppose* this logic of survival, by seeking to delay time and linger over treasured remembered scenes, to prevent the rest of the narrative from continuing. Yet, with Hägglund's help, we can see that the structure of narrative mirrors the logic of survival, in that every narrative has its own death on its horizon, because every narrative *ceaselessly* approaches its own end. The difference between life and narrative is that narrative does allow us temporary reprieves from time's passage – we may, if we so wish, dwell on select passages of our choosing and resist reading on. We only go wrong, as Van's paradoxical treatise on time evinces, whenever we suspect that life itself is prewritten – like an already completed triptych.

In his treatise on time, Van seeks to negate the future because he equates it with determinism: he sees the future as what *will* happen. However, this fatalistic conception belies the understanding of the future of Van the character. In a key passage from Part II, Van and Ada are looking at photographs of themselves and reminiscing about the early stages of their romance. Describing the following photograph, Van remembers how his past self, all those years ago when the photograph was taken, *anticipated* one day having this future memory:

> Another photograph ... at a tripod table, Ada sat reading, her half-clenched hand covering the lower part of the page. A very rare, radiant, seemingly uncalled-for smile shone on her practically Moorish lips. Her hair flowed partly across her collarbone and partly down her back. Van stood inclining his head above her and looked, unseeing, at the opened book. In full, deliberate consciousness, at the moment of the hooded click, he bunched the recent past with the imminent future and thought to himself that this would remain an objective perception of the real present and that he must remember the flavor, the flash, the flesh of the present (as he, indeed, remembered it half a dozen years later – and now, in the second half of the next century).
>
> (402)

At the moment the photograph is taken, Van is thinking of the future as what will have happened: he envisages himself *looking back* on this moment from the future.[18] This shows that Van thinks of the future here not as a predetermined sequence of events; instead, he sees the future as the ground of possibility for future memory, for future acts of recalling the past. Thinking of the future as what will have happened may be described, in Heideggerian fashion, as historicizing ourselves out of the future. As Casey argues, 'To historicize *out* of such a future is to realise a genuinely autonomous action, one that requires us to come to terms with the virtuality of the past itself. Rather than awaiting the future – e.g. by "expectation", through which we make the future determinate

---

[18] On the significance of the future anterior tense in this passage, see also Hägglund 97–98. Hägglund reads this scene as a singular illustration of 'the negativity of time' fully discernible only in writing.

beforehand, a form of inauthenticity – we *make it possible*' (*Remembering* 278). This kind of understanding of temporality enables one to sidestep the problem of determinism, since the future becomes *what will have been remembered*, and not that which can be foreseen; the emphasis shifts from predicting what could happen, to anticipating one day remembering what does happen. '[T]he basic structure of narrative', Currie suggests, 'is one that blends what has not yet happened with what has already taken place, or which fuses together two apparently incompatible ideas of the future – the future which is to come and the future which is already there' (*The Unexpected* 13). The reason that Van the philosopher contests the future is that he sees it *only* as 'the future which is already there'. Yet Van the character (before he begins philosophizing) sees the future differently: he sees it as the moment-to-come of future remembrance of whatever the future brings. He conceives his future in the mode of anticipated retrospect, and Currie contends that this is the crucial tool offered by narrative to our negotiation with time:

> We might regard narrative as part of our memory of the present, in the sense that it is one of the cognitive resources that we have at our disposal to anticipate what is to come, not only because we anticipate when we read, but perhaps more significantly because we anticipate in the mode of retrospect, as if we already know how to look back upon the present.[19]
>
> (*About Time* 66)

The future certainly exists, Van's narration is saying, but it exists only as the possibility when the writer looks back on the future moment as it turned out to be with the help of his words.[20]

In terms of Van's penchant for ekphrasis, we might say that the future is the time for further remembering-cum-describing, when newly remembered scenes will become newly depicted in words. Although ekphrasis seeks to delay the flow of time, description remains the submissive servant of narration, as the scenes of memory are doggedly displaced by the progression of narrative events. The narrator prone to dwell on the image – the extended scene seen by the eye of memory – may stray into conceiving the future as already containing its own

---

[19] Cf. Wolfgang Iser: 'during the process of reading, there is an active interweaving of anticipation and retrospection, which on a second reading may turn into a kind of advance retrospection' (287).
[20] Jacques Lacan, albeit in a different context, has also expressed this insight into a futurally retrospective understanding of identity: 'What is realised in my history is not the past definite of what was, since it is no more, nor even the present perfect of what has been in what I am, but the future anterior of what I shall have been for what I am in the process of becoming' (247).

'pictures' (of what has not yet occurred). Yet if the narrator is a good learner of the lessons taught by narrative, he will realize that the third panel of time's triptych is only the space reserved for *virtual* memory or future recollection. In life, it is the space still in darkness to memory's eye, whereas in literature it is like an illumined memory theatre with its places where visions are already stored. In Bergson's striking metaphor, memory is somewhat like perception's shadow: 'Step by step, as perception is created, the memory of it is projected beside it, as the shadow falls beside the body. But, in the normal condition, there is no consciousness of it, just as we should be unconscious of our shadow were our eyes to throw light on it each time they turn in that direction' (*Key Writings* 177). In the same way that we cannot gaze at our own shadow and continue moving without accident, we are constitutively unable to recall all that has happened, and future perceptions of particular events may or may not themselves become memories. Nabokov's novel instructs us that the future is the time for further remembering, when future memories *might* be recalled.

In *Ada*, the future is presented as the hope in one day remembering what is and has been, and also as the wish to prose picture memories of what will have happened. If Nabokov's novel were modelled after Camillo's 'Theatre', then it would be a complex interior full of places with their images located at ekphrasis' sites – and it would be a space that, on each visit, we will have seen anew. The novel is a textual memory theatre where we can make some kind of sense, in Marcel's haunting phrase, '[of] that incomprehensible contradiction between memory and non-existence' (*Sodom and Gomorrah* 194).

4

Narration's looming of the archive in W. G. Sebald's *Austerlitz*

In *The Emigrants*, W. G. Sebald's narrator evokes the following prose picture:

> Behind the perpendicular frame of a loom sit three young women, perhaps aged twenty. ... The light falls on them from a window in the background, so I cannot make out their eyes clearly, but I sense that all three of them are looking across at me, since I am standing on the very spot Genewein the accountant stood with his camera. The young woman in the middle is blonde and has the air of a bride about her. The weaver to her left has inclined her head a little to one side, whilst the woman on the right is looking at me with so steady and relentless a gaze that I cannot meet it for long. I wonder what the three women's names were – Roza, Luisa and Lea, or Nona, Decuma and Morta, the daughters of night, with spindle, scissors and thread.
>
> (237)

This passage concludes this haunted narrative, and, upon coming across a reproduction of the original photograph – in Carol Jacobs's *Sebald's Vision* (37) – I was convinced that I had seen this very photograph in the novel. But, when I picked it up again and turned to the last page, I only found the photograph's absence. I have discovered that I was not alone in this experience of misremembering photographs in Sebald's prose. Here is Carole Angier: 'The book ends with a description of three young women sitting at a carpet loom in the Lodz ghetto in 1940. ... I am convinced that I have seen their photograph on the last page; I remember the loom, their hands, their faces. But it isn't there' (Schwartz 75). What does this tell us about Sebald's prose? First, that memory, both of life and narratives we have read, is fallible. Second, and more importantly, that Sebald's writing compels our imagination to *remember* these three women *as if* we had seen their photograph in the text. Sebald – like Nabokov and Proust before him – commemorates the past ekphrastically. Russell Kilbourn and Eleanor Ty observe that 'together with more contemporary authors, such as Vladimir Nabokov and W. G. Sebald, Marcel Proust stands as a bona fide theorist of memory, despite his decision to explore these questions through fictional narrative discourse' (5). Sebald, this chapter argues, is indeed a 'bona fide theorist of memory' like Proust and Nabokov, but his singular narratives alternately adopt a critical and kindred stance towards his predecessors' manner of writing the past.

W. G. Sebald was an émigré from Bavaria who spent most of his adult life as a lecturer in Britain, first at Manchester University and then at the University of East Anglia.[1] His writing is concerned with history, in particular with unearthing traumas that seek to stay buried. Sebald's narrators are often auto-fictional stand-ins of their author, and his prose presents a kind of metaphysics of historical sense-making, showing the way such sense-making often resists the writer's engagement. Sebald's books are truly protean in form: part fiction, historiography, memoir, essay – an entrancing amalgam of genres. With his final publication, *Austerlitz* (2001), Sebald wrote a book that sits more comfortably on the fiction shelf because its protagonist Jacques Austerlitz – unlike the personages in earlier novels – is a purely fictional character. However, Austerlitz's fictionality does nothing to lighten the heaviness of the questions that he poses to the archive in his quest to re-member what time has sundered.

Sebald's novel shares not only Proust's celebration of descriptive language's capacity to revive memories of the forgotten but also certain key thematic aspects of the *Search*. The following passage-in-homage, for example, echoes the famous instance of involuntary memory in *Time Regained*:

> As I walked through the labyrinth of alleyways, thoroughfares and courtyards between the Vlasska and Nerudova, and still more so when I felt the uneven paving of the Sporkova underfoot as step by step I climbed uphill, it was as if I had already been this way before and memories were revealing themselves to me not by means of any mental effort but through my senses, so long numbed and now coming back to life.
>
> (212–213)

Like Proust's novel, Sebald's fiction places emphasis on vision and features visual description whenever his narrators thus re-encounter their forgotten memories. The importance of vision for Sebald's poetics is most apparent in his use of

---

[1] See Carole Angier's excellent biography, *Speak, Silence: In Search of W.G. Sebald*, chapters 13–18.

photographs, so that we might call his works quite literally intermedial.² They are singular narrative constructs of words and photographs, but, as will become apparent in this chapter, the relationship between these particular modes of representation is not unproblematic.

Jacques Austerlitz adopts an 'as if' relation to his past, as though his past self is a character whom he first needs to observe and whose story he can subsequently narrate. During one of his conversations with the narrator, Austerlitz, like Marcel, recognizes the unbridgeable gap separating his present and past selves: 'As I speak of it now, said Austerlitz, it is *as if* I had been sitting in the south-facing drawing-room of Andromeda Lodge among the mourners only yesterday, *as if* I could still hear their quiet murmuring' (my emphasis 156). In another passage, Austerlitz has an explicitly visual experience of his young self re-emerging from oblivion. This takes place in a disused waiting room at Liverpool Street Station, and it heralds the beginning of Austerlitz's rediscovery of his forgotten past:

> [I]n the gloomy light of the waiting room, I also *saw* two middle-aged people in the style of the thirties, a woman in a light gabardine coat with a hat at an angle on her head, and a thin man beside her wearing a dark suit and dog collar. And I not only *saw* the minister and his wife, said Austerlitz, I also *saw* the boy they had come to meet. He was sitting by himself on a bench over to one side … but for the small rucksack he was holding on his lap I don't think I would have known him, said Austerlitz. As it was I recognized him by that rucksack of his, and for the first time in as far back as I can remember I recollected myself as a small child, at the moment when I realized that it must have been to this waiting room I had come on my arrival in England over half a century ago.
>
> (my emphasis, 193)

With respect to memory's narrative remediation, what Sebald most shares with Proust, I am suggesting, is his conception of himself as a 'visual writer'. Orphan Pamuk explores what it means to be a 'visual writer' in a series of lectures, *The Naïve and the Sentimental Novelist*. 'Some writers are better addressing our verbal imagination', he argues, 'while others speak more powerfully to our visual imagination. I will call the first kind "verbal writers" and the second kind "visual writers"' (90). And then, perhaps more contentiously, Pamuk adds: 'novels are essentially *visual* literary fictions. A novel exerts its influence on us mostly by addressing our visual intelligence – our ability to see things in our

---

² See also Lauren Walsh 113–124 for a reading of ekphrasis in *Austerlitz* as being emblematic of a kind of 'photo-textual memory', and the ways in which Sebald's novel, more so than Proust's, reminds its reader 'of a great degree of ultimate unknowability of the past, even one's own' (124).

mind's eye and to turn words into mental pictures' (92). (In Chapters 6 and 7, we will consider how a 'visual' novel equally addresses our sense of hearing, the sense that ekphrasis often tries to silence.) Pamuk shares Nabokov's painterly metaphor in defining the prose artist's task: 'Writing a novel means painting with words, and reading a novel means visualizing images through someone else's words' (93). This conception of writing construed as painting echoes Sebald's own essay on Nabokov. In 'Dream Textures', an essay on *Speak, Memory*, Sebald notes: 'writing, as Nabokov practiced it, is raised on high by the hope that, given sufficient concentration, the landscapes of time that have already sunk below the horizon can be seen once again in a synoptic view' (*Campo Santo* 151). We are also here reminded of Marcel's metaphor of looking beneath himself at the 'synoptic view' of the landscape of receding years below.

The dream to see the past with words is the very essence of ekphrastic hope, and it is what Sebald himself sought in all writing, as he observes apropos of Nabokov's unforgettable descriptions: 'suddenly, with a few well-chosen words, the whole cosmos of childhood is conjured up before our eyes as if pulled out of a black top hat' (151). There is an anecdote from Sebald's life as teacher of creative writing which reveals this desire for seeing by means of language. Novelist Luke Williams, who attended Sebald's seminars at the University of East Anglia, recalls that the students were required one day to bring a passage of prose they admired. Williams, thinking he would impress Sebald by choosing a German writer, brought a story by Ingo Schulze: 'He seemed to hate it. He tore it apart (and by extension, my taste). The story was clumsy, artless, imprecise. Worse, he said, you just couldn't *see* what the author was talking about. ... I can't *see* it, Sebald kept on saying' (147).

This chapter begins with an examination of Sebald's poetics of picture and text, photograph and narrative. It argues that rather than performing an illustrative function of the text, the inserted photographs serve as reminders of forgetting, reminding readers of all that personal memory *fails* to remember. In doing so, they underscore ekphrastic desire leading on to ekphrastic fear; the photographs, that is, serve as reminders of language's lack, its inability to picture the past tangibly – only to figure it. The photographs also denote the archive as parataxis: the enumeration of historical traces before they come to wear narrative form. Archival memory narratives such as Sebald's fiction enact the move from paratactic reality to a hypotactic emplotment of that reality. Certain singular works of literature may both bear witness to the historical past and, in Derek Attridge's words, 'at the same time, as literary works, they stage the activity of witnessing' (97). Sebald's *Austerlitz*, this chapter suggests, may be read as a fictional model which bears witness to how the real – both one's own recollected past and the historical archive – can be memorably mediated via the tropological sense-making operation of narrative discourse.

Celluloid slices of time past

Sebald's fiction impels us to consider the role of the archive – exemplified by the grainy photographs that lodge in this prose – and the challenges that the archive poses for personal memory. In *Visions of Modernity*, a panoramic study of visual media's impact on memory, Scott McQuire argues that what we refer to as the 'archive' began its life, in its modern sense, with the dawn of the camera:

> As images created by cameras have increasingly constituted much of the 'evidence' from which we gain knowledge and draw inferences about the nature of reality, they have necessarily assumed greater importance in the production and legitimation of history. From the personalised visual history of the photo-album to public collections in museums and libraries, to commercial stockpiles in television stations and film studios, the result has been the unprecedented expansion of all that might constitute an archive.
>
> (108)

The photograph is the quintessential historical document because, by its very nature, it contains an actual trace of the past: reality's fingerprint in light left on celluloid. Unlike a painting, writes Susan Sontag, a photograph is 'something directly stencilled off the real, like a footprint or a death mask' (154). Sontag adds that while 'a painting, even one that meets photographic standards of resemblance, is never more than the stating of an interpretation, a photograph is never less than the registering of an emanation ... a material vestige of its subject in a way that no painting can be' (154). The unprecedented ability to hold 'slices' of reality, moments of time forever frozen before one's gaze in a picture-object held in one's hand, encouraged viewers to remember 'photographically'. McQuire suggests that the camera's impact on our understanding of memory was that it instigated the search for an *exact* image of the past: 'Objective memory demanded the reproduction of the past as it was, without mediation or alteration. According to this determination, remembering consists of preserving or restoring an original presence' (165). As a consequence, photography has promoted nostalgia in the modern subjectivity. Because photography captures the past so tangibly, it promotes the *longing* to recapture it and relive those vanished moments. Sontag, writing in the 1970s, noticed this elegiac mood that to some extent still pervades culture today:

> It is a nostalgic time right now, and photographs actively promote nostalgia. Photography is an elegiac art, a twilight art. Most subjects photographed are, just by virtue of being photographed, touched with pathos. ... All photographs are memento mori. To take a photograph is to participate in another person's (or thing's) mortality, vulnerability, mutability. Precisely by slicing out this moment and freezing it, all photographs testify to time's relentless melt.
>
> (15)

In an interview, Sebald echoes Sontag in his comment on photography's uncanny preservation of the departed that serves to promote this kind of nostalgic reverie: 'photographs are for me, as it were, one of the emanations of the dead, especially these older photographs of people no longer with us. Nevertheless, through these pictures, they do have what seems to me some sort of spectral presence' (Schwartz 40).[3]

A concomitant influence of photography on consciousness is that it has altered the way we speak about our own interiority and the way in which we conceptualize memory. For instance, in her study of Walter Benjamin's writings on photography, Esther Leslie argues:

> In modernity, memory cannot be thought of without recourse to the technologies that seem to usurp its role as archivist. ... Benjamin's is not a dismal view of how celluloid partners memory, replacing it or turning it toward death. For him, the new technologies of image making have entered into modern lives ... and they have made themselves indispensable. Photographs and film have seized our imaginations, which is to say they have made themselves part of our internal worlds.
>
> (31)

As Leslie suggests, Benjamin's thinking, and even his language, strove for the kind of visual immediacy captured by photography and, later, film. One often finds in Benjamin's writing photographic figures of memory such as the following example, where Benjamin explains why certain places become more memorable than others:

> It is not ... due to insufficient exposure time if no image appears on the plate of remembrance. More frequent, perhaps, are the cases when the half-light of habit

---

[3] See also McQuire's account of the climate of nostalgia in contemporary media culture, 173–181. For a genealogy of a distinctly modern nostalgia, one which defers 'homecoming' and opposes the teleological conception of history, see Svetlana Boym 19–32 and 49–55.

denies the plate necessary light for years, until one day, from an alien source it flashes as if from burning magnesium powder, and now a snapshot transfixes the room's image on the plate.

(*Reflections* 56)

We find a similar description of memory as (if) photography in *Austerlitz*, when Austerlitz states: 'In my photographic work I was always especially entranced, said Austerlitz, by the moment when the shadows of reality, so to speak, emerge out of nothing on the exposed paper, as memories do in the middle of the night, darkening again if you try to cling to them, just like a photographic print left in the developing bath too long' (109). However, these two metaphors, despite being highly suggestive of the *experience* of memory images resurfacing out of the pools of forgetting, risk misleading the writer by promising an objective ideal remaining out of remembrance's reach.

One of the ironies of history is that the invention of the camera, which seemed to guarantee the perdurance of the past, came at a time when a motley of ideological factors were working diligently to refute a certain inherited understanding of historical truth. The nineteenth century was a century of revolutions and historical revisions that needed to be free of the weight (in the revolutionists' view) of ideologically suspect 'historical memory', so that they could invent a new future and, as McQuire aptly puts it, 'pluck a new beginning from the wings of time itself' (113). The timing of photography's invention happened to coincide with the rise of a much more radical historicism in European intellectual thought, and Marx, Nietzsche and Freud are the outstanding figures of this shift in the understanding of historical memory. As Paul Hamilton writes,

> Marx, Nietzsche and Freud revive historicist doubts as to whether there can be a general subject of history. In contrast to what they see as an outmoded form of natural law, they insist on the particular interests powering any generalization or any claim disinterestedly to tell the truth. The history of modernity becomes the histories of ideology, power and the unconscious.
>
> (96)

The great enthusiasm for photography that gripped the second half of the nineteenth century may therefore be understood as a reaction against this promotion of forgetting the 'outmoded' forms of historical understanding.

Sebald was once asked by an interviewer about the purpose behind his use of photographs. I would like to focus, for the moment, on the first part of his response: 'The first and obvious notion is that of verification – we all tend to believe in pictures more than we do in letters. Once you bring up a photograph in proof of something, then people generally tend to accept that, well, this must have been so' (Schwartz 41). Note that Sebald says nothing about memory here – only that photography verifies what happened. Barthes, writing in *Camera Lucida* (a book which Sebald knew well), phrases it this way: 'in Photography, I can never deny that *the thing has been there*. There is superimposition here: of reality and of the past' (*Camera Lucida* 76).[4] This kind of indubitable proof, especially when it concerns one's *own* past, is often a challenge to memory, as Barthes himself well knew; for what happens when one does not remember the moment from one's life to which the photograph obstinately attests? 'One day I received from a photographer a picture of myself which I could not remember being taken,' Barthes writes, 'And yet, *because it was a photograph* I could not deny that I had been *there* (even if I did not know *where*). This distortion between certainty and oblivion gave me a kind of vertigo' (85). This sense of vertigo is certainly familiar to Sebald's narrators. We witness it in Austerlitz's reaction, for instance, when his aunt Vera shows him a photograph of himself as a boy wearing the costume of the Rose Queen's page: 'hard as I tried, both that evening and later, I could not recollect myself in that part. I did recognize the unusual hairline running at a slant over the forehead, but otherwise all memory was extinguished in me by an overwhelming sense of the long years that had past' (259). This sense of feeling overwhelmed when confronting the real that one does not remember may be read as a first intimation of the threat, or at least of the challenge, of photography to personal memory. After seeing the photograph of himself as that forgotten boy, Austerlitz reflects: 'As far back as I can remember, said Austerlitz, I have always felt as if I had no place in reality, as if I were not there at all, and I never had this impression more strongly than on that evening in the Sporkova when the eyes of the Rose Queen's page looked through me' (261).

Photography's objectivity calls memory to rise to the challenge, but memory falls short. As Sontag writes of Proust: 'by considering photographs only so far as he could use them, as an instrument of memory, Proust somewhat misconstrues what photographs are: not so much an instrument of memory as an invention of it or a replacement' (165). Perhaps, though, it would be more accurate to say that photography does not so much replace memory, as that it may usurp some of the *images* that are memory's rightful possession. In this sense, we could say that the archive, in the guise of photography, while it does come to invade the

---

[4] On Sebald's wide reading on photography, see also Clive Scott, 'Sebald's Photographic Annotations'.

'space' of memory, can never replace memory itself. The reason for this is that memory is always *my* memory, while the archive never belongs to me alone. Despite this reservation, the archive, as tangible image, may certainly supplant one's individual recollections of the distant past.

This is what happened to Henri Beyle, better known to the world as Stendhal. In Sebald's *Vertigo*, the narrator recounts Stendhal's reminiscences (as recounted in *The Life of Henry Brulard*) of his trek, in the year 1800, through the St. Bernard Pass with Napoleon's army. The narrator notes that Stendhal had for many years

> lived in the conviction that he could remember every detail of that ride, and particularly of the town of Ivrea. … It was a severe disappointment, Beyle writes, when some years ago, looking through old papers, he came across an engraving entitled *Prospetto d'Invrea* and was obliged to concede that his recollected picture of the town in the evening sun was nothing but a copy of that very engraving. This being so, Beyle's advice is not to purchase engravings of fine views and prospects seen on one's travels, since before long they will displace our memories completely, indeed one might say they destroy them. (8)[5]

Stendhal made these observations before the widespread use of photography, yet we can already discern in this admonition to travellers the threat posed by the visual archive to recollection.

A deep ambivalence, then, is discernible in Sebald's approach to the photograph. On the one hand, it is the elegiac art that promotes nostalgia, so that we might call photographs 'incitements to reverie' (Sontag 16). On the other hand, photography poses a threat to memory, for it may come to replace one's own unique but imperfect memory images with indubitable pictures of the real. *Austerlitz* is a novel that meditates on this power of tangible pictures over memory, specifically, how a particularly affecting picture can both shape and curtail our knowledge of history. This is what Austerlitz learns from Hilary, his gifted schoolteacher:

> Our concern with history, so Hilary's thesis ran, is a concern with pre-formed images already imprinted on our brains, images at which we keep staring while the truth lies elsewhere, away from it all, somewhere as yet undiscovered. I myself, added Austerlitz, in spite of all the accounts of it I have read remember only the picture of the final defeat of the Allies in the Battle of the Three Emperors. Every attempt to understand the course of events inevitably turns into that one

---

[5] See Stendhal, *Life of Henry Brulard*, chapter 45. In another manifestation of ekphrastic anxiety, Stendhal accompanies his autobiographical writing with sketches and drawings of the places he is describing – as if his words alone could not do the job well enough.

scene where the hosts of Russian and Austrian soldiers are fleeing on foot and horseback onto the frozen Satschen ponds. I see cannonballs suspended for an eternity in the air, I see others crashing into the ice, I see the unfortunate victims flinging up their arms as they slide from the toppling floes.

(101–102)

Austerlitz does not specify what painting or illustration he has in mind when referring to this battle (also called the Battle of Austerlitz), but it is clear that it remains dominant in his memory over everything else that he has learnt from Hilary about the Napoleonic Wars. It is difficult to *supplant* a picture (especially a photograph) of a historical event with a narrative about this event; it is as though they persist alongside each other, the picture remaining longest in memory while the narrative details become forgotten over time.

The photograph as reminder of forgetting

In the context of personal recollection, does photography promote memory? Barthes thinks not: 'Not only is the Photograph never, in essence, a memory (whose grammatical expression would be the perfect tense, whereas the tense of the Photograph is the aorist), but it actually blocks memory, quickly becomes a counter-memory' (*Camera Lucida* 91). McQuire provides an explanation of this 'blockage' of memory caused by photography:

> It is evident that the ideal memory, posited by nineteenth century history – so easily named photographic memory – obeys only one side of memory's double injunction. In valorising repetition without alteration, this ideal memory remembers to remember, but forgets the irreducibility of forgetting, and so risks becoming a fixation, a blockage, a form of cultural constipation; an ethnocentrism which abandons the memory of the other traced in the heart of the self. *Lapsus*, absence, transformation and loss have their own claim on memory.

(173)

In this sense, the photographs that invade the prose of Sebald's novel are less reminders of past events than they are reminders for both narrator and reader of the frailty of memory. They literally *show* us what memory does not and cannot show: namely reproductions of the past 'without alteration', without meditation. This is why the photographs seldom illustrate what either the narrator or

Austerlitz claims to remember; instead, they often show us places all too easily forgotten: decrepit buildings, grainy interiors, obscure architectural oddities, and, in Austerlitz's case, people whom he had once known but no longer *recognizes*. The photographs' function in Austerlitz's story is thus to disclose memory's darker twin – forgetting – and to remind the reader of memory's reliance, in McQuire's phrase, on 'the other traced in the heart of the self'. Photographs often compel the self to call on others for their interpretation, as Austerlitz discovers when Vera shows him a picture of himself in the costume of the page boy, a boy whom he does not recognize. Or as he learns after experiencing one of his lapses of memory, following a visit to the veterinary museum in Paris: 'Only when I developed the photographs I had taken that Sunday in September at Maisons-Alfort was I able, with their aid and guided by Marie's patient questioning, to reconstruct my buried experiences' (374).

Austerlitz's concluding phrase, 'my buried experiences', evinces the longevity of the Bergsonian notion of the virtual past that continues to inform discussions of recollection. In Chapter 2, we saw that Bergson's metaphor of memory as an inverted cone suggests that to reach the buried past, memory, activated by 'touching' present sensation with the tip of its cone, *expands*, taking one back into its distant regions (*Matter and Memory* 104–105). Deleuze, amplifying Bergson, thus observes: 'Not only does the past coexist with the present that has been, but, as it preserves itself in itself (while the present passes), it is the whole, integral past, it is *all* of our past which coexists with each present' (*Bergsonism* 58–59).[6] We are never conscious of this 'complete state of coexistence' because consciousness almost always operates in the mode of 'action', employing so-called habit memory. For Ricoeur, who also draws on Bergson's model, forgetting represents the past's 'coexistence' with the present and thereby expresses memory's potentiality:

> It is this hypothesis of the preservation by the self, constitutive of duration as such, that I will attempt to extend to other phenomena of latency, to the point that this latency can be considered a positive figure of forgetting, which I call the reserve of forgetting. It is indeed out of this treasure of forgetting that I draw when I have the pleasure of recalling what I once saw, heard, felt, learned, acquired.
>
> (*Memory* 417)

---

[6] For a reading of *Austerlitz* that relies on Deleuze's interpretation of Bergson, see also Mary Griffin Wilson.

Ricoeur's phrase 'the treasure of forgetting' echoes Benjamin's archaeological account of searching for memory's images in his metaphor-sprouting prose:

> Language shows clearly that memory is not an instrument for exploring the past but its theatre. It is the medium of past experience, as the ground is the medium in which dead cities lie interred. He who seeks to approach his own buried past must conduct himself like a man digging. ... He must not be afraid to return again and again to the same matter; to scatter it as one scatters earth, to turn it over as one turns over soil ... which yields only to the most meticulous examination what constitutes the real treasure hidden within the earth: the images, severed from all earlier associations, that stand – like precious fragments or torsos in a collector's gallery – in the prosaic rooms of our later understanding. ... Fruitless searching is as much a part of this as succeeding, and consequently remembrance must not proceed in the manner of a narrative or still less that of a report, but must, in the strictest epic and rhapsodic manner, assay its spade in ever-new places, and in the old ones delve to ever-deeper layers.
>
> (*Reflections* 26)

Benjamin's rhetorical excavation of memory's earthy depths risks leading us astray. It is true that *remembrance* does not proceed in the manner of a narrative sequence (as we saw in Chapter 3), but the moment remembrance becomes transposed into discourse, it inevitably takes on minimal narrative shape.

Like Benjamin, Austerlitz does eventually rediscover some of the buried treasures of his past in the loam of forgetting: 'these and other images, said Austerlitz, ranged themselves side by side, so that deeply buried and locked away within me as they had been, they now came luminously back to my mind' (221). Forgetting, observes Ricoeur, 'designates the *unperceived* character of the perseverance of memories, their removal from the vigilance of consciousness' (*Memory* 440). Sebald can be said to conceive memory as 'unperceived' visual impressions stored away in the depths of forgetting. Each writer has his own strategy for the retrieval of these hidden sights: for Proust, the greatest moments of illumination occur by chance, involuntarily, the visions triggered off by the senses; for Nabokov, the sights of memory return when they are imagined-cum-remembered as if painterly tableaux. Sebald, however, is more cautious, more questioning of memory and aware of its other self: forgetting. And his photographs are there to remind the reader of memory of precisely this: archival photography may furnish us with indexical proof of the past, yet this proof remains *external* to the self. Recall Barthes's dismay at seeing a photograph of himself whom he does not remember: that is a photograph *of* me, but it does not belong *in* my memory. Or rather: there is a 'space' in my memory where this picture of myself might lodge, but I cannot say that this picture is *mine*, as I can say of a mnemonic image of myself that I clearly recall. This is why a photograph, especially of oneself whom one does not remember, may be said to remember you, whereas you might not recognize it.[7] This is the sum of Austerlitz's experience when he sees himself as a boy in costume: when he sees his forgotten self returning his gaze, from the archive. This challenging gaze is precisely the question that the archive never ceases to pose – like a slice of time that disrupts its most artful, even its most truthful re-presentation.

Facing the archive

The novelty of *Austerlitz*, read as a singular iteration of the Proustian model, is that here personal memory confronts the archive. The novel is both an account of Austerlitz's painstaking recollection, as well as a detective quest into the historical past about which he is ignorant (or which he has forgotten). Austerlitz's attempt to recover his past belongs to that loose category of narratives called 'origin stories'. His story has its roots deep in the scars of twentieth-century history, as he is consumed by his search for documentary traces of his lost parents, both of whom almost certainly perished at Auschwitz.

Jacques Austerlitz is five years old when he is sent to Britain from Central Europe by the *Kindertransport* mission, in March 1939. He grows up with Calvinist adoptive parents in Bala, a little Welsh town. A gifted student, he becomes an erudite scholar of European architecture. Many years into his academic career, he suffers a nervous breakdown and, upon recovery, becomes obsessed with his past, beginning the detective work of unearthing the tragic story of his parents and of his forgotten childhood. In his preface to the novel, James Wood has observed that although Austerlitz is involved in a journey of detection, 'the book really represents the deliberate frustration of detection, the perpetuation of an enigma' (xi). This is not entirely accurate, however. Austerlitz *does* recover significant portions of his past through the memories of others, and, by the novel's end, he even discovers the vital photograph of his mother. His tragedy is that he cannot recognize his mother, in the same way that he

---

[7] I echo here Benjamin's reflection that 'looking at someone carries the implicit expectation that our look will be returned by the object of our gaze. … To perceive the aura of an object we look at means to invest it with the ability to look at us in return' (*Illuminations* 188). On the auratic aspect of Sebald's photographs, see also George Kouvaros.

cannot recollect himself as a boy dressed in the page outfit because that aspect of his past no longer belongs to his memory, but to the archive. And yet, despite this tragic dimension, there is much that we do learn about his past: the time he spent with his adoptive parents in Wales; his university years and travels; the memories shared with his long-suffering companion, Marie. Wood continues: 'at the end of the book, as at the beginning, [Austerlitz] threatens to become simply part of the rubble of history, a thing, a depository of facts and dates, not a human being' (xxvii). This is hardly a fair assessment, as one struggles to find many more authentically depicted characters, in recent fiction, than Jacques Austerlitz. How much memory, moreover, can be legitimately expected of a five-year-old child (the age at which Austerlitz left Prague on a *Kindertransport*)? Contra Wood, I would suggest that the story of Austerlitz's struggle with the Janus memory–forgetting is among the most philosophically subtle accounts of an individual's difficulties in remembering and of the narrational expression of these difficulties.

The question that *Austerlitz* asks, and that this chapter seeks to answer is: How does one – indeed *can* one – remember oneself via the archive? In *W.G. Sebald: Image, Archive and Modernity*, J. J. Long contends that Austerlitz must be read as an 'archival subject', and, as a response to my question, this contention is problematic.

> The protagonist spends his academic career amassing compendious architectural knowledge as a form of compensation for his own lost memories of his past. The archive here thus replaces 'authentic' memory as a kind of 'prosthesis of the inside' (Derrida). And yet the putatively authentic memory that Austerlitz seeks to retrieve also emerges as external to the self, for its retrieval depends on the archives he discovers in Theresienstadt and Prague. The archive is both a symptom of Austerlitz's lack of memory and, at the moment of discovery that constitutes the provisional *telos* of the narrative, the resource of the cure. There is thus no escape: Austerlitz seems to represent an extreme example of a subject *constituted entirely by the archive*. At the same time, however, the archive remains always incomplete … which is why it leaves the end of this particular text open and the subjectivity of Austerlitz in a permanent state of incompletion.
>
> (my emphasis 20)

Long's reading takes its departure from Austerlitz's own claim, when he admits to the narrator: 'I had constantly been preoccupied by that accumulation of knowledge which I had pursued for decades, and which served as a substitute or compensatory memory' (198). Yet we know that this amassed knowledge of history does not serve him at all well as 'compensatory memory', as he later discovers when he experiences what he calls 'the disintegration of the personality' (174). For something to become disintegrated, however, it first needed to be integrated: there needed to be a personality in place, before Austerlitz begins his descent into the realm of oblivion that his story seeks to understand. Long is correct in suggesting that, at the end of the novel, Austerlitz's subjectivity is left – like *any* subjectivity – 'in a permanent state of incompletion'. But the use of the verb 'constituted', in the phrase 'a subject constituted entirely by the archive', needs to be interrogated more closely. To 'constitute', according to the *OED*, can mean:

1. To frame, form, make (by combination of elements) … (Very frequent in reference to the bodily or mental constitution.)
2. To appoint to the office, function, or dignity of; to make, to create.

Austerlitz is 'constituted' by the archive in sense 1, but only in so far as his identity draws on the archival fund about his origins. But there is an even more significant sense in which *he* is the one who is *doing* the 'constituting' of the archive, in sense 2: both by appointing himself to this 'function' and by taking responsibility for the sense that he creates out of the archive's seriality. We might thus invert Long's phrase to read: 'Austerlitz is a subject entirely *constituting* the archive as narrated sequence.'

The imprecision in Long's argument, I think, lies in a presupposition, via a reading of Derrida, that a subject *can* be 'constituted entirely by the archive', which is not quite the point that Derrida is making. In *Archive Fever*, Derrida meditates on the contemporary obsession with the archive and defines the 'fever' as follows:

> It is never to rest, interminably, from searching for the archive right where it slips away. It is to run after the archive, even if there's too much of it … It is to have a compulsive, repetitive, and nostalgic desire for the archive, an irrepressible desire to return to the origin, a homesickness, a nostalgia for the return to the most archaic place of absolute commencement.
>
> (91)

Derrida's encapsulation of this very modern obsession is actually quite prescient in capturing Austerlitz's passion for the story of his origins. Austerlitz, we might say, suffers from archival fever to an inordinate degree. However, Derrida emphasizes that the archive can never *replace* personal memory: 'the archive, if this word or this figure can be stabilised so as to take on a signification, will never be either memory or anamnesis as spontaneous, alive and internal experience'

(11). In Chapter 3, I introduced Aristotle's distinction between *mneme* – an image – and *anamnesis* – an individual's quest for the memory image. The archive introduces us to memory's third instantiation: *hypomnesis* or external memory. Although the archive can never replace *anamnesis*, it nonetheless finds 'lodging space' within the psyche, as Derrida argues:

> Taking into account the multiplicity of regions in the psychic apparatus, this model [of the archive] also integrates the necessity, inside the *psyche* itself, of a certain outside, of certain borders between insides and outsides. And with this *domestic inside*, that is to say also with the hypothesis of an *internal* substrate, surface, or space without which there is neither consignation, registration, impression nor suppression, censorship, repression, it prepares the idea of a psychic archive distinct from spontaneous memory, of a *hypomnesis* distinct from *mneme* and *anamnesis*: the institution, in sum, of a *prosthesis of the inside*.
>
> (19)

And the following is Long's reading of *Austerlitz* via Derrida's argument:

> Austerlitz's archival researches repeatedly lead to the same insight: the buried memories that Austerlitz hopes to retrieve fail to materialise. In pursuing himself and his mother through a series of representations – the photographs of the page, the Theresienstadt film, the theatre archive – Austerlitz continues what he has always done, which is to compensate for his lack of memory by substituting the archive for interiority. He is in the most literal sense an archival subject.
>
> (162)

The problem here is Long's final claim that Austerlitz is, most literally, 'an archival subject'. Long goes further, suggesting that 'Austerlitz is devoid of stable and authentic subjective interiority. His subjectivity is produced largely by the archive' (171). Now we might pretend, for a moment, that we are not reading a work of criticism and are being told of a real person that they are 'devoid of stable and authentic subjective interiority'. Of whom could such a claim be true? The only conceivable situation where we can say this is of someone who is in a state of psychosis: one whose psychic life is compromised and made unstable – yet with the possibility of recovery, the restoration of interiority. Despite his periods of mental breakdown and amnesia, Austerlitz certainly retains his subjective interiority, precisely by making *subsequent narrative sense* of these temporary periods of psychic collapse.

But if we cannot speak of the archive legitimately replacing memory, then how are we to interpret Derrida's radical claim that the archive is a 'prosthesis of the inside'? Derrida explains: 'Freud made possible the idea of an archive properly speaking, of a hypomnesic or technical archive, of the substrate or the subjectile (material or virtual) which, in what is already a psychic spacing, *cannot be reduced to memory*: neither to memory as conscious reserve, nor to memory as rememoration, as act of recalling' (my emphasis, Archive Fever 92). Derrida could not be clearer: the archive may inhere 'in' our psyche, but it may only find psychic space *alongside* personal memory, never in its place. The archive cannot replace personal memory, *anamnesis*, for the simple reason that it cannot become fully integrated into one's interiority.[8] This is because the archive, precisely as it is the archive and consequently exists apart from my subjectivity, independently of me, lacks the vital element of all happy memory: recognition. Hence, Ricoeur speaks of the efforts of recollection being crowned with the 'miracle' of recognition: 'I speak of it as a minor miracle. It is indeed at the moment of recognition that the present image is held to be faithful to the initial affection, to the shock of the event' (*Memory* 416). Re-cognize: know again memory's forgotten possession.

Derrida's internal 'spacing' reserved for the archive is hence better thought of as capacity for a kind of psychic storage space, not unlike the Austerlitz-Tolbiac depot in Paris, where the belongings of a destroyed epoch were stored during the Second World War: 'In the years from 1942 onwards everything our civilisation has produced, whether for the embellishment of life or merely for everyday use, from Louis XVI chest of drawers, Meissen porcelain, Persian rugs and whole libraries, down to the last salt-cellar and paper mill, was stacked there in the Austerlitz-Tolbiac storage depot' (402). But a human interiority is not a storage depot. Rather, these facts rescued from the storage dumps of history that make up the ever-deepening fund of the archive are facts which one can know, but not own. And herein lies the inviolable integrity of personal memory: the things I remember belong to me (even when I rely on technology to recall them). The archive, on the other hand, always occupies the space of interindividual territory; it is the site not so much *of* collective memory, but *for* the activity of commemoration (the tense structure of the archive is futural). I may use the archive to 'cross over' into another's subjectivity or even imagine that subjectivity as though it were my own. But I could never claim it as my own – such is the inviolability of the archive – as belonging to the undisclosed interiority of myself, without doing violence to the integrity of personal memory (as well as to the archive).

[8] For Derrida, one's most personal recollections are also reliant on archival traces, being supported/supplemented by the technology of writing; but admitting this is not the same as claiming that Austerlitz's 'is in the most literal sense an archival subject', in Long's sense.

In *The Generation of Postmemory*, Marianne Hirsch suggests that memory, for those generations fortunate enough not to have witnessed atrocities (her work is largely concerned with representations of the Holocaust), 'can be transferred to those who were not actually there to live an event' (3). She calls this intergenerational transferral 'postmemory':

> 'Postmemory' describes the relationship that the 'generation after' bears to the personal, collective, and cultural trauma of those who came before – to experiences they 'remember' only by means of the stories, images, and behaviours among which they grew up. But these experiences were transmitted to them so deeply and affectively as to *seem* to constitute memories in their own right. Postmemory's connection to the past is thus actually mediated not by recall but by imaginative investment, projection, and creation.
>
> (5)

Hirsch highlights the fact that the memories of witnesses to trauma may only *seem* to become memories 'in their own right' for future generations that allow themselves to be affected by the memories of others.[9] Austerlitz's narration discloses the extent to which many of one's memories are reliant on these kinds of 'postmemorial' encounters with others. In Chapter 3's discussion of reminiscence in Nabokov's *Ada*, we saw how personal memory is often depicted alongside or on behalf of another, and this is what happens during Austerlitz's conversation with his aunt, Vera. Vera's reminiscence of Austerlitz's mother appears to rekindle some small spark of recollection in him, but he is never quite sure whether he is remembering or imagining these moments:

> trying to think my way back through the decades, to remember what it had been like, carried in Agata's arms – as Vera had told me, said Austerlitz – I craned my neck, unable to take my eyes off the vault reaching such a vast height above us. But neither Agata nor Vera nor I myself emerged from the past. Sometimes it seemed as if the veil would part; I thought, for one fleeting instant, that I could feel the touch of Agata's shoulder or see the picture on the front of the Charlie Chaplin comic which Vera had brought me for the journey, but as soon as I tried to hold one of these fragments fast, or get it into better focus, as it were, it disappeared into the emptiness revolving over my head.
>
> (307–308)

'Sometimes it seemed as if' is indeed the most one can say whenever one is reliant on the memories of others about one's own forgotten experiences. 'Postmemory'

---

[9] For a critical response to Hirsch's own reading of Sebald's novel, see Kathy Behrendt.

is archival to the extent that it is external to oneself: even when one is deeply affected by the memories of loved ones, one is only able to *recount* their memories (as Austerlitz, with his prodigious memory for historical narratives, does so well), whereas one re-*encounters* one's own. A personal memory image carries the authority of a witness, what Ricoeur calls its 'minor miracle' of recognition. If this authority is denied personal memory (despite its fallibility), then it loses its essence: *anamnesis* becomes replaced by *hypomnesis* – the self gets erased by the archive.

Although the archive cannot replace memory, it can become incorporated, through narration, into a story about one's life. This is precisely the function narrative form performs for individual consciousness: it permits history, understood as the memories of others, and one's own memories to cohere. The archive is always interpreted, worked upon and finally mediated by narration in order to signify meaningfully. Benjamin's reflections on what he memorably described as modernity's 'disintegration of the aura in the experience of shock' (*Illuminations* 194) may be seen as addressing precisely this relation between archive and personal memory. Writing of modernity's impact on consciousness, Benjamin observes: 'The greater the share of the shock factor in particular impressions, the more constantly consciousness has to be alert as a screen against stimuli; the more efficiently it does so, the less do these impressions enter experience (*Erfahrung*), tending to remain in the sphere of a certain hour in one's life (*Erlebnis*)' (*Illuminations* 163).[10] Benjamin turned to art as a means to redress the 'increasing atrophy of experience', and, significantly, he considered Proust's novel to be exemplary in this regard. If involuntary memory might be regarded as the chance resurrection of a past moment (*Erlebnis*), and voluntary memory as 'experience in the strict sense of the word', then Proust's narrative 'kept producing the amalgamation of these two elements of memory over and over again' (Benjamin 159). Extrapolating from Benjamin's ideas a little, we may say that the photographs in Sebald's prose function precisely as instances of *Erlebnis*, narratively unmediated experiences of reality – invasions of the real into the space of the text. In fact, Benjamin defines *Erlebnis* as 'the quintessence of a passing moment' (185) and one struggles to find a more apt definition of a photograph. *Erfahrung*, on the other hand, designates one's experience as the product of recollection; it represents an *integrated* experience of time made

---

[10] Benjamin is here writing of Baudelaire, arguing that Baudelaire's poetry places 'the shock experience', *Erlebnis*, at its very centre, and that in doing so it is striving after the very modern goal of making moments of crisis be 'given the weight of an experience' (*Illuminations* 194).

possible by narration. The function of the photographs in Sebald's texts is that they demonstrate that the archival real cannot become part of one's memory but can only be *made part of the narration about* one's memory. In *Austerlitz*, the archival real is articulated to personal memory through the mediation of narrative form, and the photographs serve as reminders of its surplus. This is what the archive *looks* like, the quintessence of passing moments, and there is always too much of it ever to be encompassed by a single subjectivity.

The photographs also attest, perhaps, to Sebald's denunciation of a kind of collective hubris (itself the product of technological advancements in so-called memory technologies), a hubris that would claim to remember all, when we would want to claim as our own the memories of others. Ricoeur's question is also the question posed by Sebald's fiction: 'Could a memory lacking forgetting be the ultimate phantasm, the ultimate figure of this total reflection that we have been combatting in all of the ranges of the hermeneutics of the human condition?' (*Memory* 413). Sebald, of course, would be the first to urge the need, perhaps even the duty, to *preserve* forgotten memories, yet preservation is not the same thing as recollection. Photography, to repeat my claim, serves to remind us of all the things that we fail to remember. Despite these reminders of what has been, unless we can recognize ourselves and our own memories in the archive's pictures, we can only learn about that which we never ourselves remembered. The archive thus stands as a silent witness to history, never becoming memory but only *seeming* to remember on our behalf, whenever we turn to its records and photographs.

Ekphrasis and the photograph

During the aforementioned interview, this is the second reason Sebald gives for including photographs in his fiction:

> The other function that I see is possibly that of arresting time. Fiction is an art form that moves in time, that is inclined towards the end, that works on a negative gradient, and it is very, very difficult in that particular form in the narrative to arrest the passage of time. And as we all know, this is what we like so much about certain forms of visual art – you stand in a museum and you look at one of those wonderful pictures. … You are taken out of time, and that is in a sense a form of redemption, if you can release yourself from the passage of time. And the photographs can also do this – they act like barriers or weirs which stem the flow.
>
> (Schwartz 41–42)

In Chapter 1, I argued that Proustian narratives are constructed out of the productive tension between description and narration. All narratives modulate between descriptive delay and narrational progress, as Ricoeur here indicates: 'narrative gives itself to be understood and seen. Dissociation of the two interwoven effects is facilitated when the picture and the sequence, the descriptive stasis and the properly narrative advance ... are separated' (*Memory* 262). Proustian narratives entail an implication of these two fundamental effects, 'picture' and 'sequence', to a far greater degree, precisely because of their indulgence in ekphrasis. Pictorial description seeks to subvert the law of narrative progress: to *slow* the flow of the story and rivet the reader's attention to *this* picture or scene being ekphrastically evoked. In this sense, the photographs' function of 'arresting time' mirrors the function of ekphrastic passages, which are pervasive in Sebald's writing. Sebald's sentences, like Proust's, are known for their length and their slow, ruminative rhythm; reading them, it is as if we were experiencing time in a different way, as we look forward to what each sentence will reveal, but, having become mesmerized, are happy to endure the delay of its resolution. Our mind's eye is engaged in patiently visualizing what the text is depicting:

> Thinking back now, I see again a low block of flats like a fortress standing on the corner of the street; a garish green kiosk with its wares openly laid out, though there was never anyone behind the counter; a cast-iron fence round a patch of grass on which you might think no one had ever trodden; and the brick wall on the right, about fifty yards long and as tall as a man.
>
> (167)

If the novel is not fresh in one's mind, one may be forgiven (as with the example of the missing photograph with which I began this chapter) for thinking that this passage is accompanied by its own grainy picture in the text (it is not). However, even if the photograph were present, we would still feel that it did not quite capture how we visualized the ekphrastic scene in our minds. Archival pictures, particularly photographs (memories external to the self), *exceed* language's descriptive means.[11] We might even say that Sebald's decision to include photographs in his fiction is another novelistic expression of ekphrastic anxiety that plagues every 'visual writer' of memory: language lacks the certificate of presence (Barthes) of photography. The irony of inserting photographs into

---

[11] See also Silke Horstkotte, who argues that Sebald's ekphrasis 'emerges as an attempt at verbal dominance over the visual that constantly falls short of the ephemeral nature of vision and of the polyvalent reference of the image' (119).

narrative is that, while certifying past presence, they remain divorced from the hypotactic signification that narrative bestows on the recounted past; a photograph, as Marshal McLuhan has aptly defined it, is '[a] statement without syntax' (219).

In Sebald, I have argued, photography represents the paratactic record of the archive as opposed to the hypotactic ordering of events that makes up a narrative. Before examining the fluctuation between parataxis and hypotaxis that informs narratives which confront the archive, I would like to examine further Sebald's remark that photographs 'act like barriers or weirs which stem the flow'. This book's contention that Proustian narratives are structured by a dialectic unification of description and narration finds an illuminating resonance in Laura Mulvey's understanding of cinema as a dialectic of stillness and movement. In *Death 24x a Second*, Mulvey argues that since advancements in video technologies – such as the VHS tape and digital film – the spectator's experience of film has changed radically because it now becomes possible to 'freeze frame' a film's progression. Mulvey's insight is that the ability to delay cinema discloses cinema's essence, its previously 'hidden secret': by freezing the individual frame the spectator sees that cinema is really a succession of still moments, and what we see when the film is playing is, in fact, the fictionalization of the photographic real. The still frame dispels the imaginative vision: 'To delay a fiction in full flow allows the changed mechanism of spectatorship to come into play and with it shifts of consciousness between temporalities. By halting the image ... the spectator can dissolve the fiction so that the time of registration can come to the fore' (Mulvey 184). The 'time of registration' refers to the moment of inscription of reflected light onto celluloid or digital film stock – so that what we behold on the paused screen is the very trace of the real. The jarring halt in the cinematic image throws us into that *past* moment when it was still 'one' with the real. Mulvey argues:

> When the presence of the past, the time of registration, rises to the surface, it seems to cancel the narrative flow. In almost any halt to a film, a sense of the image as document makes itself felt as the fascination of time fossilized overwhelms the fascination of narrative progression. But then, once the film begins to flow again and the action takes over, the temporal register shifts again and its fictional present reasserts itself.
>
> (187)

Significantly, Mulvey concludes her book by referring to Sebald's novel, specifically to Austerlitz's discovery of the video of the Theresienstadt Jewish ghetto. When Austerlitz manages to obtain a copy of this rare film, made by the

Nazis authorities to impress officials from the Red Cross with their 'humane' treatments of the ghetto's prisoners, he makes a slow-motion copy of the footage, which, he says, created 'a different sort of film altogether, which I have since watched over and over again' (345). He then freeze-frames a scene depicting a blurred woman with dark hair wearing a necklace, whom he mistakes for his mother, Agata. Austerlitz's manipulation of the film stock in order to discover its 'time of the index', the real concealed by the fiction of narrative flow, may thus be viewed as an illustration of Sebald's own prose-poetics of word and picture. Like Austerlitz freeze-framing the Theresienstadt footage, Sebald is seeking to slow the flow of his own fictions for reality's fragments to emerge before the reader's eye, not only in photographs, but (more riskily) as ekphrases. It is as if 'with a moment of delay, fiction disappears again under the reality of the index that sustains it', as Mulvey puts it (188). Of course, the difference between film and verbal narrative is that the latter does *not* consist of indexical images, and neither can it bring the narrative fiction to a *complete* halt. Therefore, if Sebald's novel is encouraging its readers to draw this kind of parallel between film and prose, it is only to emphasize how much more metaphorical – in the sense of being in an 'as if' relation to reality's index – verbal narratives are.

On parataxis and hypotaxis

Besides utilizing photographs, how could narrative represent the fathomless archive? A striking illustration in the novel of how this can be achieved is the nine-page-long sentence that records Austerlitz's obsessive reading about the Theresienstadt Jewish ghetto. Austerlitz, with the help of Vera's memories, has been searching for his mother, Agata, when he discovers that Agata was deported to the ghetto in the Czech city Terezin, better known by its German name, Theresienstadt. He then reads H. G. Adler's encyclopaedic study of the ghetto – the first book of its kind – and, once begun, seems unable to stop recounting the book's brutal contents. Here is a representative excerpt:

> [S]ome sixty thousand people were crammed together in an area little more than a square kilometre in size – industrialists and manufacturers, doctors and lawyers, rabbis and university professors, singers and composers, bank managers, business men, shorthand typists, housewives, farmers, labourers and millionaires, people from Prague and the rest of the Protectorate, from Slovakia, from Denmark and Holland, from Vienna and Munich, Cologne and Berlin, from the Palatinate, from Lower Franconia and Westphalia – each of whom had

to make do with about two square meters of space in which to exist and all of them, in so far as they were in any condition to do so or until they were loaded into trucks and sent east, obliged to work entirely without renumeration in one of the primitive factories … assigned to the bandage-weaving workshop, to the handbag and satchel assembly line, the production of horn buttons and other haberdashery items …

(331–333)

Reading this exhausting sentence, we are taken out of narrative time and, as it were, confront seriality: a paratactic sequence of information, enumeration rather than narration. On a grammatical level, the sentence is not quite paratactic, since each clause is hypotactically linked to its successor – to re-invoke Rancière's idea of the 'sentence-image': Sebald's sentence seeks to image parataxis itself, and yet it inescapably performs a syntactical role. Narrative emplotment is dictatorial and operates even here: the sentence has a beginning and an end, and what it contains and the order in which it presents this information already emit traces of plot. There is a discernible narrative impulse that *guides* the order of the items in this long sentence of suffering; it narrativizes the individual items making up this list, and thus consigns them to meaningfulness, endowing them with a *particular* meaning (the denouncement of inhumanity, expressed by the incessant, almost machinic rhythm of the clauses, culminating in death). Nevertheless, this is as close as narration can get to representing seriality without subordination and escaping the mastery of hypotaxis that governs its capacity for generating meaning out of miscellany. A purely paratactic sequence would be a randomly compiled list of information or, at best, a chronicling of dates and their accompanying events, as we find both in medieval and bureaucratic records.[12]

Clive Scott argues that Sebald's photographs stand for this kind of enumeration, a record of those objects

> without syntactic intricacy, impediments to hypotaxis, which is the record of a mental activity, of processes of plotting, and of the extraction and projection of meaning, by relational arrangement. Enumeration pushes aside the ratiocinative mind, and human agency more generally; and in the place of syntax of teleology and controlled temporalities and interpretative processing, enumeration, the sequence of photos, installs a paratactic montage of indefinite limits, a problematic temporality, a spirit of contingency, which poses searching questions about continuity, function, epistemology.
>
> ('W.G. Sebald' 126)

---

[12] Although, as Hayden White has persuasively argued, even a medieval chronicle is a narrative *in utero*; see *Content of Form* 1–26.

The fact that this kind of enumeration 'pushes aside human agency' only underscores the impossibility of the archive ever replacing interiority. The archive never enters the individual psyche other than as enumeration, parataxis; it then becomes a 'prosthesis of the inside', in Derrida's phrase: an adjunct of records stored in memory's depot. The archive genuinely *signifies* only when incorporated into the re-inscribable narrative of our lives and memories. Sebald's incorporation of the archive into Austerlitz's story is thereby better conceived as an invasion rather than a boon: it is meant to inculcate humility. This claim risks sounding didactic, yet it is undeniable that Sebald's narratives are pervaded by a sense of guilt in the face of unremembered history, in the confrontation of human ignorance with so much forgotten past. The photographs, in this sense, do not furnish us with knowledge or historical evidence; instead, as Scott suggests, 'Sebald's photos do not fill holes, they create them' (130).

The implication of Sebald's representation of the archive as parataxis is that in the context of a memory narrative a life story cannot be reduced to a paratactic list of the individual events of which it is composed – not unlike a symphony, which cannot be reduced to a list of its measures. To compose a story out of memory's fund, with the aid of the archive, it is first necessary to imagine the possibility of life taking on narrative form: to construe existence as plot. Prior to examining the role of the imagination in this kind of hypotactic ordering of experience, it will be useful to invoke Barthes's distinction between photographic and verbal modes of representation. Barthes affirms the fictionalizing impulse inherent in language as follows:

> It is the misfortune (but also perhaps the voluptuous pleasure) of language not to be able to authenticate itself. The *noeme* of language is perhaps this impotence, or, to put it positively: language is, by nature, fictional; the attempt to render language unfictional requires an enormous apparatus of measurements: we convoke logic, or lacking that, sworn oath; but the Photograph is indifferent to all intermediaries: it does not invent; it is authentication itself.
>
> (*Camera Lucida* 87)

The Sebaldian poetics of photograph and text emphasize, by their contrast, the frustratingly (for the documentarian) fictionalizing nature of narrative, what Barthes calls language's *noeme*. This does not suggest that even those narratives that purport to be nonfictional – for example autobiography, memoir, confession, the letter – are by their very nature fictitious. Rather, the fictionalizing impulse of narrative forces us to rethink the nature of our relation to the past: the verbally rendered past is read *as though* it is again present; the dead are remembered and described *as though* they are again with us; I narrate my life *as though*

I again became my past self. We are thus returned, via these meditations on the gulf separating the archival real from the fictionalizing (rather than fictitious) narrative, to metaphor. In the same way that Austerlitz remembers himself as if he was again that five-year-old boy, sitting in the waiting room of Liverpool Street Station with his adoptive parents, we cannot think the past without recourse to the detour of metaphorical understanding. We cannot, moreover, ever see the story-whole of our past, in the same way that we can gaze on certificates of its presence in photographs. The *story* about one's past lacks its photographic index.

Hayden White has thought through this metaphorical (he prefers the term 'tropological') structure of narrative discourse, which is to 'consider the specific *story* as an *image* of the events *about which* the story is told, while the generic story-type serves as *a conceptual model* to which the events are to be likened in order to permit their encodation as elements of a recognizable structure' (*Tropics of Discourse* 110). White asks the theorist to examine more critically the 'objective' picture of history that all too easily suggests itself to the theoretical imagination:

> [I]t is wrong to think of history as a model similar to a scale model of an airplane or ship, a map, or a photograph. For we can check the adequacy of this latter kind of model by going and looking at the original and, by applying the necessary rules of translation, seeing in what respect the model actually succeeded in reproducing aspects of the original. But historical structures and processes are not like these originals; we cannot go and look at them in order to see if the historian has adequately reproduced them in his narrative.
>
> (88)

White's distinction suggests that history, unlike such models, never reproduces the past – this is photography's privilege – but inherently produces it in mediated form. History constructs the past in representing it.[13] And it is precisely on the narrative construction that is history that we find metaphor's fingerprints. In the following key passage, White elaborates on history's metaphorical relation to reality:

> It is this mediative function that permits us to speak of a historical narrative as an extended metaphor. As a symbolic structure, the historical narrative does not *reproduce* the events it describes; it tells us in what direction to think about the events and charges our thought about the events with different emotional

---

[13] Ricoeur has observed that by focusing solely on form White neglects to give due emphasis to the importance of witness, 'the documentary moment', in historical writing (*Memory* 254).

valences. The historical narrative does not *image* the things it indicates; it *calls to mind* images of the things it indicates, in the same way that a metaphor does. … Properly understood, histories ought never to be read as unambiguous signs of the events they report, but rather as symbolic structures, extended metaphors, that 'liken' the events reported in them to some form with which we have already become familiar in our literary culture.

(91)

White speaks here of historical narratives in much the same way that I speak about Proustian narratives: the latter similarly 'call to mind' images of what they describe, without *actually* imaging (in the sense of reproducing) these events. In Sebald, the photographs' purpose, I have suggested, is *to contrast* the way in which we create meaning via linguistic mediation to the way in which the actual appears to us. Sebald's photographs do not tell a story; instead, they represent actuality before it is made to tell a story: they show the reader the silence of the real in the absence of imaginative mediation. Doubtless, the photographs were carefully selected by the author, but their cumulative effect is to suggest the nakedness of the paratactic historical record, *before* it becomes emplotted as narrative.

In an interview with Arthur Lubow, Sebald provides the following defence for the co-habitation of the fictional and the non-fictional in his prose: 'You adulterate the truth as you try to write it. There isn't that pretence that you try to arrive at the literal truth. And the only consolation when you confess to this flaw is that you are seeking to arrive at the highest truth' (Schwartz 164). Sebald is here addressing the question of whether his texts ought to be received primarily as fiction, or whether they are to be considered as history, and he is suggesting that the distinction is not really necessary for him because he is after the 'highest truth'. Sebald's by now well-established cross-pollination of fiction and non-fiction conveys an understanding of the fictionalizing impulse informing narrative discourse. Sebald, I think, would have been quite sympathetic to White's statement that '[t]he older distinction between fiction and history, in which fiction is conceived as the representation of the imaginable and history as the representation of the actual, must give place to the recognition that we can only know the *actual* by contrasting it with or likening it to the *imaginable*' (*Tropics of Discourse* 98). Hence, the Sebaldian blurred photograph is aimed at depicting how we first get to know the actual, while the narration enacts our sense-making of the actual *in terms of* the imaginable. Sebald's poetics of prose-and-photograph asks us to reflect on how the understanding of memory mirrors the understanding of history, in that both quest for the recapture of the 'actual' in the knowledge that they may only arrive at its approximation. And this is also the basis of ekphrastic desire.

In *Austerlitz*, Sebald is not so much deconstructing historiography as he is illustrating the kinship between history and memory constructions as narratives.[14] Consider, for instance, how the narrator first describes his wonder at Austerlitz's ability to do just this, trans-forming events into history: 'From the first I was astonished by the way Austerlitz put his ideas together as he talked, forming perfectly balanced sentences out of whatever occurred to him … bringing remembered events back to life' (14). Austerlitz's narration echoes the narrator's own in its hypotactic arrangement of the past into a history/story. Hypotaxis, writes White, enables us

> [to] experience time as future, past and present rather than as a series of instants in which every one has the same weight or significance as every other … This experience of historicality … can be represented symbolically in narrative discourse because such discourse is a product of the same kind of hypotactical figuration of events (as beginnings, middles, and ends) as that met with in the actions of historical agents who hypotactically figurate their lives as meaningful stories.
>
> (*Content of Form* 179)

Austerlitz is clearly a 'historical agent', in White's sense, and calling him an 'archival subject' subverts his identity by denying him this kind of imaginative figuration of his life as a story about memory and forgetting. Austerlitz's identity, contra Long, does not find expression *in* the archive; in his role as narrating self, he is not the young boy in the photograph whom he fails to remember. Instead, his identity partakes of the narrating consciousness who is recounting to us the story of his life. Identity becomes meaningful once it is emplotted – this is what Ricoeur means when he argues that 'the characters in a narrative are emplotted along with the events that, taken together, make up the story told' (*Memory* 262). Austerlitz's identity *is* his story that makes up the novel.

The shape (or plot) of Austerlitz's life is mediated in two senses. Firstly, his memories and the memories of others that he incorporates into his story (rather than his memory) are mediated by being transposed into narrative sequence. Secondly, the account of his life is framed within the nameless narrator's own story of contending with history. The narrator and Austerlitz are narrator-cousins, in

---

[14] See also Lynn Wolff: 'While thematising the problems of representation, both literary and historical, Sebald ultimately demonstrates the power of the literary discourse to form human experiences, emotions, and events into a story or "history"' (330).

that they both seek for origins; their life stories comprise a peripatetic journey through the ruins of European history in the face of forgetting. This novel thus charts a dual quest: we follow two footpaths into the past via narrative form.

Ricoeur gives the following helpful definition of narrative's configurative act: 'A story must be more than just an enumeration of events in serial order; it must organise them into an intelligible whole, of a sort such that we can always ask what is the "thought" of this story' (*Time and Narrative 1*, 65). Ricoeur defines here the essence of hypotaxis: the imposition of meaning onto contingent seriality – the always partial victory of personal narrative over the ensnaring loom of the archive. My claim in this chapter has been that *Austerlitz* belongs to an evolving novelistic genre I have been calling the Proustian narrative, and, in Ricoeur's sense, this is how we might state the 'thought' informing this genre:[15] these are nostalgic narratives ironically recounted, seeking to celebrate the past to the same extent that they mourn its irrevocable loss. Sebald's novel expands this genre's framework to encompass the mass of the archive in its singular attempt to illustrate the archive's contentious relation to personal memory.

A reader has the potential to gain interpretative insight into the formal innovation of a literary work, whenever he or she recognizes where this work might fit in the literary 'landscape'. As Ricoeur indicates:

> The received paradigms structure readers' expectations and aid them in recognizing the formal rule, the genre, or the type exemplified by the narrated story. They furnish guidelines for the encounter between a text and its readers. In short, they govern the story's capacity to be followed. On the other hand, it is the act of reading that accompanies the narrator's configuration and actualises its capacity to be followed. To follow a story is to actualise it by reading it. ... The act of reading is ... the final indicator of the refiguring of the world of action under the sign of the plot.
>
> (76–77)

If Proustian narration predisposes readers to conceive memory's articulation as an amalgam of imagetext, and thereby foregrounds the cycle of ekphrastic hope/ ekphrastic fear that pervades this kind of writing, then Sebald's innovation is to enact the clash of words and pictures (rather than mnemonic images conjured by ekphrasis), thus bringing to the fore the writing of unremembered history.

---

[15] See Mikhail Bakhtin's telling statement about genre's historical development: 'A genre lives in the present, but always *remembers* its past, its beginning. Genre is a representative of creative memory in the process of development' (*Problems of Dostoevsky's Poetics* 106). See also Bakhtin, *Speech Genres* 5 and P. M. Medvedev 134.

Sebald's photographs depict what memory alone cannot – the very trace of the past – and, by doing this, the novel reminds us not to forget forgetting. The real that we fail to remember coexists with the real figured in verbal representations of our memories. Knowing this is tantamount both to admitting the finitude of memory and to acknowledging memory's reliance on the resources of the archive, never to displace memory itself, but to become incorporated into the *story* about one's life that, while it reneges 'total reflection', does not give up its quest for a deeper knowledge of self and history.

*

In conclusion, I want to invoke Benjamin's great apology for the novel:

> The novel is significant … not because it presents someone else's fate to us, perhaps didactically, but because this stranger's fate by virtue of the flame which consumes it yields us the warmth which we never draw from our own fate. What draws the reader to the novel is the hope of warming his shivering life with a death he reads about.
>
> (*Illuminations* 101)

The reason we cannot draw this kind of comfort from our own fate is because life is lived in the ongoing moment of precarious temporality. The novel about memory, however, offers hope in the sense that through it we can learn to draw warmth from our own lives, if we allow the past that very human bestowal of a story. Had Austerlitz been a real person and not a character in a novel, one imagines that he would have drawn much warmth from Sebald's novelistic rendering of his history.[16] 'The reader willingly suspends his disbelief, his incredulity, and he accepts playing along as if – as if the things recounted did happen,' Ricoeur observes (*Memory* 261). All fiction demands this kind of Coleridgean suspension of disbelief, yet Sebald's novel requires perhaps an even greater wager on the truthfulness of its depiction. For we must surely recognize our own experience of remembering in that of the fictional narrator; in the absence of such recognition, we accuse the narrative of the more culpable charge of being fictitious, counterfeit, rather than being merely fictional.

---

[16] In Michael Wood's clever observation, certain novels 'show us not the fictional lives of real people but the real lives of people who came extraordinarily close to existing' (*Literature and Knowledge* 180). This refreshing characterization of fiction's capacity for an uncanny verisimilitude is very fitting to Sebald's narrators.

In his final book, *The Practical Past*, White begins fittingly (in the context of this chapter) by referring to *Austerlitz* and how the novel reflects on his book's title. The 'practical past', White argues, is 'a past which, unlike that of the historians, has been lived by all of us more or less individually and more or less collectively' (14). While the professionally sanctioned 'historical past' deals with politics, religion and other matters of public life that have been preserved in official documents, the novel has long been able to imaginatively represent the quotidian past as it must have been lived. Unlike officially documented historical events, White writes, 'It is quite otherwise with a topic like love or work or suffering and the kinds of relationships among them which are (or were) real enough but which are accessible as objects of *practical* study only by way of imaginative hypothesization' (xv). The value of Sebald's novel, in this sense, is that its mimesis of memory's difficult relationship to official history may be seen precisely as a depiction of the 'practical past' encountering 'the historical past' – or as a more affective comprehension of the latter by means of the former. In other words, by immersing us in the 'practical' matter, the matter of memory of Jacques Austerlitz's life, by reconstructing what it must have been like to live a life overshadowed by atrocities, Sebald is doing what the novel has always been able to do so effectively: vicariously immerse us in its prose pictures of past experience. And this is why this novel, for White, is '[t]he kind of presentation of the "mood" or atmosphere of post-Holocaust Europe … [that] is nonetheless "historical" for being an imaginative rather than an exclusively evidentiary construction' (xv). Reading Sebald is not unlike, but not quite the same thing as, reading a historical text.

> In opening a history book, the reader expects, under the guidance of a mass of archives, to reenter a world of events that actually occurred. What is more, in crossing the threshold of what is written, he stays on guard, casts a critical eye, and demands if not a true discourse comparable to that of a physics text, at least a plausible one, one that is admissible, probable, and in any case honest and truthful. Having been taught to look out for falsehoods, he does not want to have to deal with a liar.
>
> (Ricoeur, *Memory* 261)

Sebald passed away before the publication of *Memory, History, Forgetting*, so he could not have read these words. Reading this passage today, though, it is as if Sebald sought to create a work that is 'admissible, probable, and in any case honest and truthful' – without quite being a work of history.

5

Retrospect, prospect and the fiction of the face in Ben Lerner's *10:04*

In both *Leaving the Atocha Station* and *10:04*, Ben Lerner's narrators draw sustenance from the lived experience of their author, and this conceit of fiction shadowing autobiography also informs Proust's *Search*. As Barthes has observed:

> The Proustian oeuvre brings on stage (or into writing) an 'I' (the Narrator); but this 'I', one may say, is not quite a self (subject and object of traditional autobiography) … the person this 'I' brings on stage is a writing self whose links with the self of civil life are uncertain, displaced. … The result of this dialectic is that it is vain to wonder if the book's Narrator is Proust (in the civil meaning of the patronymic): it is simply *another* Proust, often unknown to himself.
>
> (*Rustle of Language* 282)

Barthes speaks of Proust's narrator as creating, within the novel, his own 'writing self', so that, in reading about Marcel's struggle to become a writer, we are witnessing a kind of refracted spectacle of Proust's own preparation in writing his great novel. In this fictional staging, Marcel performs a self-othering operation, whereby the narrating-I writes the narrated-I as a story character on a verbal 'stage' that opens up memory's future. That 'stage' is, of course, narrative form, a form which always adopts the lineaments of a specific literary genre.

In Lerner's second novel, *10:04*, what distinguishes the narrator, Ben, from Marcel is a heightened self-consciousness in writing about the past. Early in the novel, after tutoring his student Roberto, Ben decides not to walk home as he usually does, but, as if 'drawn there by a subtle force' (14), re-enters the school building. This is not the school Ben attended as a boy, but the space still triggers a Proustian moment of recollection. 'Do you know what I mean,' Ben muses, 'if I say that when I reached the second floor … I was in Randolph Elementary School and seven, the wall hangings now letters addressed to Christa McAuliffe in exaggerated cursive, wishing her luck on the *Challenger* mission, which was only a couple of months in the future?' (14–15). To a reader familiar with the conventions of Proustian narration, the answer to this question is affirmative: I *do* know what you mean, one is nudged into replying. We read on:

> I pass through Mrs Greiner's door and find my desk, the chair no longer small for me, Pluto among the planets in the Styrofoam mobile suspended from the ceiling. My parents are at the Menninger Clinic; my older brother is in a classroom directly above mine ... my aorta may or may not be proportional; the radiator sputters in the corner because November in the past is often cold. The classroom isn't empty, but its presences are flickering: Daniel appears at the desk beside mine, Daniel whose arms are always a patchwork of Peanuts Band-Aids and minor hematomas, who will go to the emergency room this spring for inhaling a jelly bean – on my dare – dangerously deep into his nose. ... It is sad work to build a diorama of the future with a boy you know will hang himself for whatever complex of reasons in his parents' basement at nineteen, but that work has been assigned, Mrs. Greiner standing over us to check our progress, the synthetic coconut odour of her lotion intermingling with the smell of rubber cement. I'll make Daniel's effigy and he'll make mine, but we'll co-construct the spacecraft, letting it dangle like a modifier from a string, perpetually disintegrating.
>
> (15)

This passage does not at all sound like ordinary retrospection; there are too many temporal leaps, suggesting that these recollected images have been carefully arranged in light of the narrator's present concerns and thematic aims. What initially signposts itself as a moment captured by mnemonic ekphrasis quickly turns into a commingling of temporalities. This is not a descriptive re-presentation of a single moment but a recounting of the past that contains a reflexive subtext of how this representation relates to the narrator's past, present and future. (In Proust, this kind of palimpsestic overlaying of narrational perspectives tends to happen over many pages; in Lerner's novel, it often gets condensed within the space of a single paragraph.[1]) We see how the prospect of future danger for the present 'I' – the enlarged aorta – insinuates itself into the represented world of the narrator's childhood. Similarly, the remembered seven-year-old Ben is building a 'diorama of the future' with his schoolmate Daniel, knowing that Daniel will one day hang himself. Lerner has said in an interview that his interest as a writer lies in expressing 'how each of us is constantly striving

---

[1] Joshua Landy (138–140) suggests that certain descriptions in Proust are similarly multidimensional, in terms of focalization. While I agree with Landy's suggestion, in Lerner's novel the shifts in narrational perspective are much more condensed than in Proust.

to reorganize mere chronology into some meaningful pattern, to narrate our pasts in a way that makes a future thinkable' (Leyshon 2016). No doubt this is why the narrator is unsatisfied with simply describing what he remembers; description is here all too brief, given insufficient textual space as each clause is dislocated by jump-cuts in time. Rather than a painting, this narrated memory-sequence is suggestive of cinematic montage, a metaphor that helps us grasp identity's temporal fluidity as the self ranges across time in quest of itself.[2]

This kind of temporal mutability is constitutive of narrative identity, which ceaselessly articulates pastness to futurity. Proustian narratives articulate retrospection to prospection, so that the identity of a character *in medias res* is being pulled, so to speak, both backwards into the past and forwards into the future, not unlike the way the present moment is said to consist of retentions and protentions in Husserlian phenomenology. Invoking Husserl, Stiegler argues that the 'technology' of writing affects how present experience is remembered and, subsequently, elaborated (narrated):

> The preservation of memory, of the memorable (the retention of this memorable element creates it as such) is always already its elaboration: it is never a question of a simple story of 'what happened', since what happened only happened in not having completely happened ... selection of what merits retention occurs in what should have been, and therefore also in anticipating, positively and negatively, what will soon will have been able to happen (retention is always already protention).
>
> (*Technics and Time 2*, 115)

We can see in Lerner's novel an expression of precisely this kind of anticipatory memory in action. Description in Lerner, as the example above illustrates, acts as a textual site where the retrospect of memory meets the prospect of temporal becoming. Thinking about 'what will have been able to happen' is formally expressed by narrative as such, so it is not unique to Lerner's novel, but my contention is that Proustian narratives, and Lerner's in particular, provide the clearest insight into this temporality at work.[3] This insight is perhaps most clearly expressed when Ben, while waiting for his cardiogram results, thinks to himself: 'So clearly could I picture the cardiologist walking in to inform me that

---

[2] For cinema's impact on memory, see Stiegler, *Technics and Time 3*, 35–79. For an account of cinema as metaphor for how consciousness apprehends reality in today's moving-image-saturated culture, see Victor Burgin 67–73 and *passim*.

[3] For an analysis of how Lerner's novel thinks futurity, particularly of the ways in which it differs in its use of prolepsis from Proust's *Search*, see my essay, '"an actual present alive with multiple futures"'.

the speed of dilation required immediate intervention that it was as though it had already happened; predicting it felt like recalling a traumatic event' (206). Memory, in Currie's apt phrasing, 'has a form that lends itself to anticipation as much as to recollection' ('Trace of Future' 203), and it acquires this form, we rediscover in Lerner as we also discerned it in Proust, when it is contained within the time-enclosing mould called narrative – memory's needed prosthesis.[4] Memory is about retrospection, narration is about prospection, and when memories become narrative the two terms articulate themselves to each other in a hermeneutic circle of life-imitating fiction. Ekphrasis is that narrative device where the retrospect of memory (consummated in a distinct image) is poised on the threshold of narrational prospect (for every visual description is read 'under the shadow' of what is still to come). Ekphrasis is often figured as if 'a picture' as description slows down – but never to the point of ultimate stasis – a narrative's progress. If the experience of reading narrative, as Currie has argued (*About Time* 99), is about making *present* events already *in the past*, then ekphrasis is the device that *maximizes* such presentification. Visual description seeks to delay the story's unfolding, so that while reading it we might momentarily *not* see the depicted moment of past presence under the shadow of its future explanation.

In this chapter, I want to consider the function that digital image reproductions perform in Lerner's writing. Unlike Sebald, I suggest, Lerner does not seek to emphasize the disjunction between the unmediated archival real that photography captures and the storytelling that processes the archive via narration. Instead, Lerner's insertion of actual pictures into his prose restages the novel's desire to re-present the absent, but with an added dimension: our *shared look* at pictures across time and space that is the troubling privilege of handheld screens. First, though, let us examine a text where yet another auto-fictional narrator makes several revealing remarks about ekphrastic hopes and ekphrastic fears.

---

[4] See Stiegler's reflection on the temporal complexity of 'prosthesis': 'By pros-thesis we understand (1) set in front of, or spatialization; (2) set in advance, already there (past) and anticipation (foresight), that is, temporalization' (*Technics and Time 1*, 152). Like Heidegger before him, Stiegler speaks of a prosthesis not only as what comes before us (in that we are born into a world already technical and prosthetic), but also as what is always *ahead of us*, what allows us to think futurity. Indeed, futurity is invoked by the word's etymology: 'Pros-thesis can be literally translated as pro-position. A prosthesis is what is proposed, placed in front, in advance; technics is what is placed before us' (Stiegler 235). From this perspective, if a narrative genre can be thought of as a prosthesis needed by memory, then it always already anticipates memory, being as though 'set in front of' it, preceding it as its possibility by proposing itself for its meaningful articulation. A genre incorporating mnemonic ekphrasis may be seen as a technics that guides memory's visual representation as its possibility – one that anticipates, but without being able to predict, its own future mutations.

Ekphrases of missing paintings

In Lerner's short story 'The Polish Rider', the narrator helps his Polish friend, Sonya, find her lost paintings that she left behind in an Uber taxi. The story chronicles their difficulties to locate the ghostly taxi driver, difficulties created by Uber's Kafkaesque privacy policy. As in much of Lerner's writing, the story functions, in part, as a critique of some of the absurdities and contradictions that constitute contemporary life: in this case, our frustrating negotiations with digital bureaucracy. Reflecting on their search for paintings which they may never see again, the narrator discusses the challenges that the visual arts pose to writers. Can a writer, he wonders, with his words alone really depict a painting that has been lost? This question leads him to think about writers who have had lost or inexistent paintings as their subjects. He thinks of stories by Henry James ('The Madonna of the Future') and Balzac ('The Unknown Masterpiece') and reflects,

> [T]hese stories are really opportunities for the authors to assert the superiority of their own art, of literature, over painting. James's or Balzac's words can describe paintings the crazy artists can't actually paint, or intuit canvasses that were as yet unpainted, unpaintable. And isn't it really true of all ekphrastic literature, fiction and poetry, that even when it claims to be describing or praising a work of visual art it is in fact asserting its own superiority?
>
> ('Polish Rider')

What is interesting about these particular examples is that neither of them gives us a detailed description of the fictional paintings. For instance, all we are told about the artist Frenhofer's destroyed masterpiece, in Balzac's story, is that it showed 'in one corner of the canvas, the tip of a bare foot emerging from this chaos of colours, shapes and vague shadings, a kind of incoherent mist' (40). Only Frenhofer claims to see the beautiful woman whom he has painted – the other two painters are left bewildered by his canvas and remain blind to the woman's painted image. Therefore, if ekphrastic description is asserting 'its own superiority' in this story, then it is doing so very hesitantly.

The narrator's description of his friend's lost paintings is itself only a little more detailed. Before the paintings go missing, he mentions that every canvas in Sonya's planned exhibition depicted, *à la* Warhol, the same picture: Régis Bossu's much-reproduced photograph, taken in 1979, of the kiss shared by Erich Honecker and Leonid Brezhnev. More accurately, Sonya's paintings were variations on Russian artist Dmitri Vrubel's painting of this photograph – graffitied on the East side of the Berlin Wall in 1990. What is interesting, for my purposes, about the narrator's description of these paintings is its reliance on pictorial allusions: 'The canvases were, as always with Sonia's work, meticulously composed, but each was composed in a different historical style. One canvas depicted the kiss abstracted into Cubist shapes and volumes, another was Caravaggesque in its chiaroscuro ... another involved a mixture of verisimilitude and blur that recalled Gerhard Richter, and so on' ('Polish Rider'). We can here observe how, to help us 'see' these paintings, the narrator is relying on shared cultural knowledge; we might need to look beyond the page and look up, say, 'a blurred Richter painting', to visualize these fictional artworks more accurately. These visual clues, in Brosch's apt phrase, 'facilitate imagination via abbreviation', where, due to ready availability, 'the mere mention of an iconic image ensures shared visualization' ('Ekphrasis in Digital Age' 229).

But is it true to say that ekphrastic literature is 'asserting its own superiority' whenever it invokes visual media? The narrator vacillates between confidence and doubt in language's capacity to conjure the visual. Here, we hear fear: 'I'd always been jealous of painters and sculptors and other visual artists, basically jealous of any artist who worked with something other than words ... jealous because of my unsophisticated but unshakeable sense that a work of visual art is more real, more actual, than writing'; whereas here we discern hope: 'I felt literature's lack of actuality relative to the plastic arts as a power, not a weakness, and that was new to me' ('Polish Rider'). As we read the story, however, it becomes ever more evident that the narrator is much more hopeful in writing's powers than he is afraid of its limits. After their failed attempts to locate the lost paintings, he tells Sonya that they could make a kind of documentary that recreated their frustrated search, creating a new form of art out of missing works of art. When she tells him that they did not document or record anything during their search, he responds confidently: 'I am a writer ... Ekphrastic literature' ('Polish Rider').

Lerner's story illustrates that ekphrastic fear and ekphrastic hope are mutually implicating; they are, in fact, inseparable in any act of writing memory. Ekphrastic hope is the belief in writing's capacity to restore presence of the absent – to resurrect the images of the past on the page. Without this foundational hope, memory would cease to be written. And yet ekphrastic hope is perpetually haunted by its other: ekphrastic fear, the cognisance that language can never tangibly picture the absent. The visual immediacy of the past is lost to time, and ekphrastic fear is what so often compels writers of memory to call to their aid visual media, as though to lend greater semantic weight to memory's description. Like Lerner's narrator, as critics we go astray whenever we attempt to exorcise either hope or fear, for then we either deny language its powers to represent the absent or we grant language too much power and blind ourselves to language's blind spot. Ekphrastic hope and ekphrastic fear are the sight/blindness from which visual writing issues, and they may be said to constitute one another like the helix pattern of red and white stripes on a traditional barber's pole. The red stripe on the pole (in this figure) corresponds to hope, the passion for colourful vision, while the white stripe corresponds to fear of the blank page: the paralysis of writing. If one imagines this pole turning, then the stripes seem to converge on one another, the one leading to the other but without ever blending. Lerner's short story illustrates that it is only when we interpretatively oscillate between these extremes that we begin to appreciate the productive tension between image (whether pictorial or mnemonic) and text and see why imagetext becomes the most fitting way to describe what the ekphrastic text is doing to us.

On faces outside and inside prose

A memorable face appears in the pages of *10:04* that captures ekphrasis' spiralling drama: the satellite photograph showing the 'face' on the surface of Mars. It appears in Part Two of the novel, in the reproduced story titled 'The Golden Vanity'.[5] Ben (himself a fictioned Ben Lerner) says that the narrator of this inserted story should be seen as his *own* fictional avatar – a thirtyish poet living in contemporary New York City, who writes about himself in the third person (54–56).[6]

The narrator describes an evening out with his girlfriend, Hannah, and gives the following account of his difficulty in remembering her face:

> Would you know what he meant if the author said he never really saw her face, that faces were fictions he increasingly could not read, a reductive way of bundling features in the memory, even if that memory was then projected into the present, onto the area between the forehead and chin? He could, of course, enumerate features: gray-blue eyes, what they call a full mouth, thick eyebrows that she was probably careful to have threaded, a small scar high on the left cheek, and so on. And sometimes these features did briefly integrate into a higher order unity, as letters integrate into words, words into a sentence. But like

---

[5] 'The Golden Vanity' was first published in *The New Yorker* on 18 June 2012.
[6] For a reading of *10:04* as auto-fiction, see Alison Gibbons. Gibbons provides an overview of established accounts of auto-fiction (in Genette, Philippe Lejeune and Serge Doubrovsky), suggesting that Lerner's novel enacts an ontological blurring of fiction and autobiographical reference through its singular use of pronouns; see especially 85–94.

words dissolving into sentences, sentences into paragraphs and plots, combining these elements into a face required forgetting them, letting them dematerialize into an effect, and that somehow never happened for long with Hannah, whom he was now beside.[7]

(68)

The difficulty of accurately visualizing a person's face is here used as a metaphor for the way in which the scenes of a narrative become 'dematerialized' into the effect of the overall story. In other words, the difficulty of picturing a person's face is a mirror image of the difficulty of 'seeing' the whole of a story; to comprehend a story in its overall shape requires forgetting, or temporarily *not* seeing, the individual scenes (as it were, the precise facial features) that make it up. But this is not the whole story about remembering and describing faces:

> He watched her tuck strands of black hair behind her ear, noted its pointed helix, only now perceiving her nose ring, silver but appearing rose gold in that light … they were side by side in the booth, leaning against each other a little more with each drink, and he was saying these things about faces to her, how important it is for a writer to be 'bad with faces,' and she had asked if he had ever seen the satellite image of that rock formation on Mars … She took out her phone and Googled it, and he used the excuse of looking together at the little glowing screen to press more closely against her.

(68–69)

As Hannah explains to the narrator, the 'face' in the Googled satellite photograph is a manifestation of the psychological phenomenon called pareidolia, the seeing of 'faces in the moon, animals in clouds' (69). Pareidolia, in sum, is the perception of facial contours or other meaningful shapes in random stimuli in the external world (see Figure 4).[8]

Lerner gives the following reasons for choosing to include this illustration in the novel:

> The author's refusal of the 'fiction' of the face could also be read as a refusal of the traditional claim of prose to be able to flesh out a character. When, instead of 'seeing' Hannah's face, we see a photograph of random stimuli that our brains misinterpret as a face, *the optical realism of prose is being undercut*. And this anticipates how Hannah's presence will flicker in and out of the story. To a

---

[7] Marcel has similar difficulties in visualizing Albertine's face after first meeting her; see *Within a Budding Grove* 589 and 608–610.
[8] Cf. Olney's telling comment: 'man explores the universe continually for laws and forms not of his own making, but what, in the end, he always finds is his own face: a sort of ubiquitous, inescapable man-in-the-moon which, if he will, he can recognize as his own mirror-image' (*Metaphors of Self* 4).

Figure 4 Face on Mars (Photo by © CORBIS). Courtesy Corbis Getty Images.

certain extent, what the reader sees in that image is an image of reading – how fiction itself depends on our combining, often unconsciously, stimuli into some significant but ultimately unstable pattern.

(my emphasis, Leyshon 2016)

The metaphor is on target as a reflection on the imprecision (but also the expressive capacity) of language: unlike the pareidolic picture reproduced in the novel, no one reader will see the same 'face' depicted by its prose. It should be said, though, that this metaphor only goes so far, as the 'faces' that we read about in a verbal description are the intended *focus* of that description, whereas pareidolia is about seeing things that are not really there. And note, too, that Lerner tries to upset 'the optical realism of prose' by substituting one *fiction* for another: 'the fiction of the face' that we find in novels is replaced with the visual fiction seen in pareidolia.[9]

---

[9] In *A Death in the Family*, volume one of Karl Ove Knausgård's auto-fictional novel *My Struggle*, the narrator recollects experiencing pareidolia while watching the news one evening as a boy. The TV footage shows the choppy waters off the north coast of Norway, where a fishing boat mysteriously sank the previous night: 'I stare at the surface of the sea without listening to what the reporter

What is most interesting about pareidolia is that it immediately evokes a visual phenomenon. One can only understand what pareidolia is by *seeing* it; the phenomenon is made alive by a virtual 'picture' of what it is, and this is also the continually deferred hope of ekphrasis. Ekphrasis relies on words to make a fiction of seeing happen, whereas pareidolia evokes fictions within the visual field. But the essential difficulty of writing visually is precisely that the kind of 'optical realism' that Lerner wants to do without has never been realizable; it is an impossibility towards which writing imperfectly strives. Peter Boxall suggests that the impossibility of 'optical realism' may even be at the heart of realism itself, and it surely accounts for why realism has endured as an artistic goal: 'the history of realism itself is the history of an ongoing struggle between word and world, in which the capacity of the word to represent has always been fundamentally shaped by the resistance of the world to its mimetic power' (*Value of Novel* 61). A refusal of the 'traditional claim of prose to be able to flesh out a character' is almost a refusal of novel writing itself, which promises to make present, to 'flesh out' that which is absent (whether the 'absent' happens to be the imaginary, the past or the imaginary past). In this sense, the novel's voice might be defined with Boxall as a voice which brings fictional bodies and faces into being and which it also makes disappear: to narrate is thus 'to perform an act of engendering, of progeneration, which is also and at the same time the overseeing of a general extinction' (71–72). From this perspective, Hannah's face, like the face and body of any fictional character, will, in Lerner's own words, 'flicker in and out of the story', not because of the author's refusal 'to flesh out a character', but because this kind of 'flicker' between presence and absence, vision and blindness is at the very heart of narrative mimesis.[10]

This brings us to the final reason Lerner gives, in the same interview, for including digital reproductions in his writing:

> When the image of the face on Mars is reproduced within the story, this becomes a different kind of looking, a moment in which Hannah and the author and the reader *are all looking together, are all seeing the same image simultaneously.*

---

says, *and suddenly the outline of a face emerges*. I don't know how long it stays there, a few seconds perhaps, but long enough for it to have a huge impact on me. The moment the face disappears I get up to find someone I can tell' (8). What is so poignant about this moment is Karl Ove's loneliness: the only person in whom he can confide this experience is his father, who does not share his wonder and tells him not to give it another thought (9–10). Knausgård italicizes the moment the boy sees the face appear on the surface of the sea, typographically evoking the phenomenon's *ineffable* surprise. See also Lerner's review of the novel, 'Each Cornflake', where Lerner reflects on Knausgård's exhaustive narration of the past.

[10] See also Boxall, *Value of Novel* 72–92.

That echoes the notion of correspondence that recurs throughout the piece, moments of co-presence between the living and the dead, the fictional and the real, 'the author' and the author and the reader. There's a line that appears twice in the story: 'From their respective present tenses, they all watched the same turbulent point'.

(my emphasis Leyshon 2016)

Aware of the way in which, when reading narratives, we make present events already belonging to the past, Lerner seeks to produce a sense of presence within his readers by making them contemplate digital pictures. He thus gestures towards a new kind of mimesis: a collective gazing at screens signalling a new instantiation of intermediality, fostered by online media culture. By including a picture Googled by a character, Lerner's novel mirrors the act of looking at a glowing screen that has become part of daily life; the reader, the characters and the author 'are all looking together', as he puts it. This intermedial invocation speaks the need for a closer contact to be established between two moments of presence (narrator's and reader's), two moments in time impossible to reconcile, yet necessary to attempt.

In a sense, Lerner's fiction begins at this uncertain juncture. *Leaving the Atocha Station* opens with the narrator, Adam Gordon, describing his morning's ritual during the first few days of his research fellowship in Madrid. After breakfast, he would make his way to Room 58 of the Prado to contemplate Roger van der Weyden's *Descent from the Cross*. He provides us with a brief but evocative ekphrasis of the painting: 'Mary is forever falling to the ground in a faint; the blues of her robes are unsurpassed in Flemish painting. Her posture is almost an exact echo of Jesus's; Nicodemus and a helper hold his apparently weightless body in the air. C. 1435; 220 × 262 cm. Oil on oak panelling' (8). We join Adam's looking, as his eye first scans over van der Weyden's canvas and then reads the painting's date, dimensions and technique. But what is remarkable about the novel's opening is not this ekphrasis, but the following description of what happens to Adam, when, one day, he finds that someone else has taken his habitual place in front of the painting. 'He was standing exactly where I normally stood,' Adam says, 'and for a moment I was startled, as if beholding myself beholding the painting' (8). The sense of dizzying self-externalization passed, he gets annoyed at this importunate man not moving on, when, unexpectedly, the man bursts into tears. Is he crying because of grief, Adam wonders, 'Or was he having a *profound experience of art*?' (8). The man's emotional reaction prompts Adam to reflect that, unable to respond to art in this fashion himself, he has always been interested 'in the disconnect between my experience of actual artworks and the claims made on their behalf' (9). He then follows the man around the Prado, watching this art connoisseur/broken-hearted soul have several more fits of crying in front of masterpieces.

Another possibility now occurs to Adam: What if this man is only pretending? What if he is a performance artist who intends to reveal the contradictions of the museum guards' functions – the guards who follow the weeping man around the gallery, fearful that he might be 'a potential lunatic loose among the treasures of their culture' (10), yet equally fearful to interfere should his response be genuine? The novel's opening section – a section concerned with seeing and misrecognition – concludes with Adam 'following this man, this great artist, out of the museum and into the preternaturally bright day' (10). A detail of the *Descent from the Cross* appears on the following page, with the caption: '*I thought of the great artist for a while*' (11). The detail shows the tear-streaked face of Nicodemus's 'helper', the man in the golden robe who is supporting Christ's legs. The helper's face is identified with the face of the crying man, who may be a performance artist playing at crying, and whom Adam first contemplated as if beholding his own self rapt before a canvas towards which he can only feel disconnected. Nothing conveys more powerfully both the disconnect Adam feels while looking at art and the real/fake crying of the man than this visual illustration, taken from van der Weyden's canvas. But let us note that, in every sense of the word, we are drawing this impression *from a fiction*: another face, and yet another fiction of the face.

Words may say more than a picture, but a picture, as this scene illustrates, is often what makes this saying possible – the picture *illuminates* the saying. Ekphrasis, perhaps even more obviously in the digital age, enacts the imaged presence of the text's outside within the text, delineating their osmotic permeation.[11] No narrative is hermetically sealed off from its 'outside', as the world diffuses within it during the reading encounter. The following chapter attempts to capture the osmosis of picture into text as well as the text's voicing of the picture's permeation, as it occurs in yet another iteration of Proustian concerns.

---

[11] The *OED* defines the figurative sense of osmosis as the 'gradual, usu. unconscious assimilation or absorption of ideas, knowledge, etc.' ('osmosis'). In this sense, the pictures that 'osmose' into the text via ekphrasis often do so unconsciously, establishing a connection with another medium that might not be immediately apparent.

6

Commemoration via intermedial lamination in Ali Smith's *How to Be Both*

One writer's essay about another is often self-reflective. In 'Loosed in Translation', Ali Smith gives a piercing description of Sebald's voice when she writes, 'He works with the opening of the eyes, and the opening of the I, the open first person' (75). Sebald achieves these ocular and narratorial openings by including reproductions of archival photographs in his prose, and this collocation of picture and text enables his fiction to explore the rift between the paratactical real that the photograph stages and the hypotactical mediation of the real that narration encodes. Sebald is most interested, Smith suggests, in depicting narrated memory's movement across 'liminalities, in the space between lost and found, ruin and construction, imprisonment and liberation, blindness and seeing … shifts between states which seem as irreconcilable as fact and fiction' (77). *How to Be Both* might in its own way be described as a movement between these elements, but what this novel shares most with Sebald and Proust, I suggest, is a distinctive *rhythm*; as Smith writes of Sebald's writing: 'It's an art of storytelling in which reported speech becomes a kind of enfolding, a state of inclusion as intimate as breath pattern' (75). Smith's novel is punctuated by its own 'breath pattern', which correlates stylistically with Sebald's parataxis-cum-hypotaxis elaboration of memory's entanglement with the archive, and Proust's lengthy, patient sentences that unveil, clause by clause, a renewed perception of the past.

How to Be Both has a binary form. One story, set in contemporary London, is about a teenage girl called George, whose mother dies from cancer. George commemorates her mother's memory by recollecting their conversations about art, notably the frescoes by Francesco del Cossa. The other story is about this little-known Renaissance artist – referred to in the novel as Francescho. Francescho gets brought back to life in the National Gallery, inexplicably ghosting George and, in the process, recollecting her own past in flashbacks, conjuring a vivid portrait of artistic awakening in fifteenth-century Italy. 'It is a well-known fact',

Liliane Louvel suggests, 'that many writers construct their worlds from a seminal picture which, by triggering off a reverie, structures the work by representing its aura, a sort of creative horizon' (*Poetics of Iconotext* 17). This adage about writerly inspiration certainly applies to this novel, one that is, in many ways, about the 'aura' emanating from pictures. Smith's novel attests to the *pull* of neighbouring media upon memory's writing – media that cause narration to warp and adapt to their passage across the text. In previous chapters, we have already considered these kinds of cross-media resonances in Proust, Nabokov, Sebald and Lerner. The present chapter seeks to unravel the still more complex network of intermedial passages in *How to Be Both*, and it begins by examining these passages' importance in commemorating the departed.

There is an intimate connection between intermediality and commemoration at the heart of Proust's *Search*. A mnemonic ekphrasis in Proust is an elegy (mourning those lost to Time) turned paean (resurrecting their memory in writing). The departed in Proust are often described by recourse to visual media, either in metaphor or via a textual sampling of a medium because of its close ties to those whom one mourns. In the *Search*, this is particularly felt in Marcel's recollection of his grandmother. During Marcel's first stay at Balbec, Robert de Saint-Loup one day offers to take the grandmother's photograph. The young Marcel, noticing that 'she had put on her nicest dress for the purpose and was hesitating between various hats' (*Within a Budding Grove* 423), becomes annoyed with her for what he mistakenly takes to be an uncharacteristic display of childishness and vanity. (The grandmothers' photograph, as we will shortly see, will carry its burden of remorse and pain for him.) During the final days of his grandmother's illness, Marcel unforgettably describes her anguished face as though a sculptor had carved suffering's insignia on its surface: 'her face, worn, diminished, terrifyingly expressive, seemed like the rude, flushed, purplish, desperate face of some wild guardian of a tomb in a primitive, almost prehistoric sculpture' (*Guermantes Way* 372). When she dies, the sculptural image recurs, but this time in a different emotional hue; her death, Marcel says, seemed to unburden her face from signs of suffering: 'A smile seemed to be hovering on my grandmother's lips. On that funeral couch, death, like a sculptor of the Middle Ages, had laid her down in the form of a young girl' (397). In both instances, sculpture functions as an intermedial support that allows Marcel to articulate both the suffering he saw 'carved' upon his beloved grandmother's face and the release from it bestowed by death.

But it is by considering the second mention of the grandmother's photograph that we can fully appreciate the link between intermediality and commemoration in the novel. Upon returning to the room in the Grand Hotel at Balbec, where, years ago, young Marcel had stayed with his grandmother and where she had her photograph taken by Saint-Loup, the older Marcel bends down to unbutton his boots. Suddenly, he is again that young self and his grandmother is right there with him, unbuttoning his boots to get him ready for bed (*Sodom and Gomorrah* 179–180). Exhilarated by this resurgence of memories, he is also pained by them: it is only now, when he can again feel her presence (near to him whom he once was) that he truly understands – she is gone forever. And it is at this moment that her photograph, which he has with him, reminds him of having caused her pain with his callousness. His regret at having muttered 'wounding words' (183) to his grandmother will only be compounded, once he learns from Françoise about his grandmother's real intentions for having the photograph taken. (Jacques Austerlitz, let us recall, likewise relies upon the memories of his aunt, Vera, to shed light upon photographs of the departed.) Françoise, having come to Marcel's hotel room to inform him that Albertine is waiting for him downstairs, notices the photograph in his hand and proceeds, unasked, to tell him its backstory (203). Marcel learns that his grandmother had already felt very ill at Balbec and, fearing that she did not have long, wanted to leave behind a happy memory for him and his mother. She had asked Françoise to request Saint-Loup to take her picture and to instruct him never to reveal her secret to Marcel. The photograph now causes Marcel even greater anguish, yet he refuses to part with it as it preserves the one lasting connection with his beloved grandmother's memory.[1]

A few days after Françoise's disclosure, he studies the photograph and admits that his grandmother's ruse worked: she looks elegant in it, even '"carefree" beneath the hat which partly hid her face' (207). However, peering closer and examining her expression, concealed by the carefully placed hat (and here we can observe a palimpsest of perspectives occurring, as the older Marcel's gaze overlays the narrated-self's perspective), he retrospectively reads into it her future:

> And yet, her cheeks having without her knowing it an expression of their own, leaden, haggard ... my grandmother had an air of being under sentence of death, an air involuntarily sombre, unconsciously tragic, which escaped me

---

[1] See also Kaja Silverman, *The Miracle of Analogy* 115–135, where Silverman discusses the challenges that photography poses for Marcel's memory, particularly when he writes about the deaths of his grandmother and Albertine. For a suggestive comparison of the grandmother's photograph in Proust to Barthes's reflections on photography and the death of his mother in *Camera Lucida*, see Bal, *Mottled Screen* 195–200.

but prevented Mamma from ever looking at that photograph, that photograph which seemed to her a photograph not so much of her mother as of her mother's disease.

(207)

Marcel also describes how Mamma, who comes to Balbec to mourn, commemorates her mother by reading her favourite books – the *Memoirs* of Mme de Beausergent and the *Letters* of Mme de Sévigné. Grandmother loved to quote the latter in her correspondence, a predilection which Mamma often criticized. Marcel then says the following poignant line: 'When, in reading the *Letters*, [Mamma] came upon the words "my daughter", she seemed to be listening to her mother's voice' (197).

How to Be Both is a novel that thinks through this kind of layered remembrance by similarly staging the ways in which two people commemorate their departed with the help of visual media. There is a striking evocation of a painting in the novel that enlightens the intimacy between intermediality and recollection. Towards the end of her story, Francescho remembers a painting that she'd painted as an apprentice when she still practised her craft in a study built for her by her father. The painting showed Marsyas the musician, having lost the proverbial contest, being flayed alive by Apollo, the god of music. Francescho shifts into the present tense to describe this image-spectre, as though she were again before a canvas that no longer exists:

> It's a story I've puzzled over almost all my years : right now though I've found the way to tell it : the god stands to one side, the unused knife slack in his hand : he has an air near disappointment : but the inner body of the musician is twisting up out of the skin in a kind of ecstasy like the skin's a thick flow of fabric coming rich in one piece off the shoulder and peeling away at the same time from the wrists and ankles in little pieces like a blown upward snow of confetti : the body appears through the skin's unpeeling like the bride undressing after the wedding : but bright red, crystal red : best of all the musician catches the skin over the very arm it's coming off and folding itself, neat.

(360)

This image is spectral in two senses: first, it haunts Francescho's memory because the painting was stolen. The day prior to the painting's disappearance, Cosmo – modelled on Cosimo Tura, one of del Cossa's contemporaries – unexpectedly visits the studio and spends a long time gazing at it. He criticizes Francescho for depicting Marsyas exulting in his loss and thus offending the classical model that requires the proud musician to be in agony before the god. Despite his criticisms of her approach, however, Cosmo is enraptured. The reader observes him studying the painting, as the text gives further details of this fictional work of art being seen by scrutinizing eyes. We see a vivid depiction of a character gazing at a picture that does not exist:

> He's as close to the surface of the painting as he can get, so close it's as if his eyelashes might be brushing the twigs and leaves of the crown on Apollo : he puts himself equally close to the place where the skin of the musician's face and neck, all that's left still attached to the body, meets the red of the underflesh.
>
> (362)

The ekphrasis of the flaying of Marsyas is among the most vivid descriptive passages in the novel. Smith's verbal conjuration makes it seem as if we, too, can see both Marsyas's flesh sliding off his body with the ease of a silk garment and Cosmo with his nose and eyelashes right up against (the verbal ghost of) this painting's surface, gazing upon Apollo's leafy crown and the place where the skin of Marsyas's face and neck barely clings on to his gloriously revealed flesh.

But what does one *see* when *hearing* the voicing of this painting that does not exist in any art gallery? Phenomenologically, one sees what is given one to see, and this 'given' is determined by one's imaginative response to this fictional painting, a response bolstered by familiarity with extant representations of this mythological scene, as well as an indeterminate plethora of potential images kindled by phrases like 'unused knife', 'an air of disappointment', 'a thick flow of fabric', 'a blown upward snow of confetti', 'the skin's unpeeling', 'bright red, crystal red'. This response, though, cannot be entirely contingent (ideally it is fortuitous) as the loose context of 'Renaissance art' focuses the stream of associations, so that one sees this virtual painting according to the rough conception one has of the visual grammar of this type of representation. The 'pictorial model' – the flaying of Marsyas – calls out both to the reader's memory and imagination, in that one *recollects* previous sightings of kindred paintings to the same extent that one *imagines* the images being vocalized.

This brings us to the second reason that the image voiced by ekphrasis is spectral: it is that which haunts the text with the promise of its arrival, but an arrival which can only be imagined, virtual, approximate. The image of Francescho's lost painting, so present and yet so absent, so visible and yet so invisible, is exactly the kind of image that haunts the ekphrastic voicing of memory with the possibility of its realization. The spectrality of memory images in writing is responsible for the rich ambiguity in the distinction between seeing/hearing, image/text and the order of their emergence (even in the act of writing itself).

What is most characteristic about ekphrastic narratives is that their 'speaking' of memory is often laminated with pictorial allusion. I want to suggest that it is precisely this intermedial convocation, spoken by ekphrasis, that fosters the sense of our *participation* in the protagonist-narrator's seeing through the *agency* of a visual referent or allusion. In this way, we see alongside Francescho, as she gazes upon the photographic collage of George's late mother, which George has put up on her bedroom wall:

> I now sense this girl has had a death or a vanishment perhaps of the dark-haired woman in the pictures on the south wall above her bed … in which the woman is both young and older, sometimes with a small infant who resembles this girl, and sometimes with another small infant who then matures to become the brother, and sometimes with strangers : in this instance the pictures mean a death : cause pictures can be both life and death at once and cross the border between the two.
>
> (344)

If a photograph of a person 'can be both life and death at once' (as we saw in Chapter 4, this phrase finds much resonance in Sebald's fiction), then this descriptive passage can be both sight/image and hearing/text; we see a text-cum-image collage of family photographs emerging before our mind's eye, even if we cannot precisely picture it in the way a photograph can. Francescho observes George like a fly on the wall, invisible to the subject of observation, in the same way that we observe George sitting on her bed in grief, and Francescho observing George. This layered looking by means of voicing may be aptly described with a note Louvel makes regarding intermedial allusion: 'It is … a movement in the mind of the reader, who recognizes the still veiled and imprecise image rising from between the lines of the quivering text, but also a change of rhythm, since the pace of the text and that of reading are affected, modified' (*Pictorial Third* 174). The image of George's late mother is more 'veiled and imprecise' to the reader than the elaborate image of Marsyas disrobing his own skin; nonetheless, both are instantiations of *enargeia*: the event of seeing inwardly what is no longer there. 'Once the girl held one picture of this woman so close to a source of light', Francescho continues, 'to see it more fully, as if to illuminate things in its dark, that I thought surely the picture would burn' (344). This mimesis of myopic looking represents the attempt to see more clearly an image one is verbally presented, as one tries to imagine both what George's mother looked like and George's looking at her mother's photograph. And we see (the senses of) all this looking in the novel only by hearing a voice tell us about it.

The vortex

Let us consider the following scene: over breakfast, a novelist is paging through *Frieze*. Having taken a mouthful of coffee, she nearly chokes when she sees a full-page reproduction of a singular painting

> of a man in clothes that were nothing but dirty white torn rags. At the same time, it looked like the richest, most gorgeous thing anyone could ever find himself or herself wearing. His tunic was frayed at the wrists and at the same time sort of kilted, ribboned, elegant, billowing richly round the tops of his thighs, which were showing through the piecemeal tied-together threadbareness of legwear ripped open at the knees too so the knees came through.
>
> He was black, or maybe Arab, or maybe very southern Italian. His wrists and arms were veined and strong. He was obviously a worker of some sort, at leisure but ready for anything, whatever'd come next, friend, foe, love, work, with one hand on his hip and the other holding out one of the ends of a length of thick rope he'd tied round his waist for a belt, at its end a delicate little fray of strands, as if to say, look – I'm tied to nothing – nobody's slave – but if you need me to do something for you, here, just take hold of this. The other end of the rope-belt hung down between his legs almost cockily long, and the whole man, a piece of strength, beauty, fierceness and waiting alertness, was standing as if floating in a field of deep bright blue.
>
> (Smith, 'He Looked Like the Finest Man')

Smith is describing a detail from the *Allegory of March*, a fresco painted *c.* 1476 by Francesco del Cossa in the halls of the Palazzo Schifanoia in Ferrara. Readers familiar with Smith's fiction will readily recognize the peculiarities of her voice, such as the unpunctuated set of adjectives describing the rags as 'dirty white torn', a flow of qualifiers lending this description greater visual immediacy; her clever use of adverbs in 'He was black, or maybe Arab, or maybe very southern Italian', making the writing sound less weighty and more disarming in its colloquialism; and, perhaps most characteristic of all, Smith's knack for encapsulating a scene, character or picture with lexical economy by using nouns to great effect, in 'the whole man, a piece of strength, beauty, fierceness and waiting alertness'. 'Every image [whether pictorial or mnemonic]', Jean-Luc Nancy suggests, 'is a "portrait", not in that it would reproduce the traits of a person, but in that it pulls and *draws* (this is the semantic and etymological sense of the word), in that it *extracts* something, an intimacy, a force' (*Ground of Image* 4). We might say that the painting of the man in rags 'extracts' Smith's intimacy, guiding her voice to speak in a certain way about it. This picture draws out of her a 'something' that is characteristic of her manner of writing, so that she might say of the man holding out one end of the rope, 'look – I'm tied to nothing – nobody's slave'. This picture, in other words, compels its own ventriloquizing by the descriptive voice, realizing itself in prose as an image. Of course, it could only 'realize' itself through a writer's agency, as we hear in Smith's characteristic vocal rhythm the affective impact of this picture, but the picture needed to be there for this address (both to itself and to the writer) to take place. I think this is the import of Nancy's contention that, when confronted by a verbal rendering of the visual, 'the object and the subject are given together and give themselves to one another, or even in one another' (84). It almost seems as if the usual subject-to-object correlation, characteristic of the Age of the World Picture, gets reversed here: instead of the sovereign writer-subject acting on her object (del Cossa's fresco), she instead becomes as if acted upon by this object. This move of 'as if' is precisely the open space where ekphrasis (and, arguably, mimesis itself) takes place.

In the novel, both George and Francescho will also memorably describe the man in rags 'as if floating in a field of deep bright blue'. I have added Smith's own voice to the two fictional voices which we will hear over the course of this chapter to emphasize how her idiosyncratic writing *speaks* the ekphrasis of the man in rags in a distinct way. But what is it that makes this kind of descriptive writing *distinct*? To answer this question, I want to invoke a striking image used by Giorgio Agamben. In *The Fire and the Tale*, Agamben deploys a metaphor that perfectly captures ekphrastic deceleration amid narration's flow: the vortex that forms in swirling water. Agamben thinks of the vortex as a metaphor for the idea of 'the origin' in historical writing,[2] but it works equally well as a suggestive image of what happens whenever we encounter visual description in narrative. The strange thing about a vortex is that, despite consisting of water's substance, it operates by its own movement principle:

> [I]t is a shape that is separated from the flow of water of which it was and somehow still is part; an autonomous region closed onto itself that follows its own laws. *It is strictly connected*, however, with the whole in which it is immersed, made of the same matter that is continuously exchanged with the liquid mass that surrounds it. It is an independent being, yet there is no drop that separately belongs to it, and its identity is absolutely immaterial.
>
> (my emphasis, Agamben 58)

---

[2] As Agamben (*Fire and Tale* 58–60) sees it, the origin is not to be found entirely 'in' the past. Paradoxically, it arises (like a vortex in moving water) only in the present's unfolding, suggesting that historical becoming is contemporaneous with its own origin and yet cannot be fully conflated with it.

Description, like the vortex in flowing water, consists of 'the same matter' (the matter of language) as the rest of the text, and yet it seems to operate according to its own law: it creates a pause in narration's flow – a pause with variable temporal depth – using artful language to distinguish itself from more prosaic narration and effecting a change in rhythm.

The following ekphrasis from Smith's novel will perhaps convey the aptness of Agamben's figure. Francescho, having been resurrected as a ghost in the National Art Gallery, begins to remember her childhood, in fits and starts, when she suddenly recalls the following scene. She is sitting out in the yard with her mother nearby, soapily stomping clothes in a half-barrel of laundry:

> Sunlight hitting the yellowing leaves, I was a child, small, on a stone slab warm from the sun, almost too small to walk I think and something was twisting itself down through the air and landed in the middle of the pool of horse piss, the foam and the bubbles nearly all off it but the smell of it still fine in the dip in the stone ... The thing that fell caused a circle to happen, a ring to appear in the piss : the ring widened and widened until it got to the edges and vanished.
>
> (202–203)

The spiralling thing that Francescho watches (and that we watch beside her) fall into the pungent image of 'horse piss' is a sycamore seed. She goes on to describe it as 'a small black ball like the head of an infidel : it had a single, a hard and feathery-looking thing stuck straight out of it' (203). That space on either side of the colon is intended, we discover, to signal a pause for breath. Before Francescho left her father's house to pursue her artistic vocation, her father told her that she inherited this idiosyncratic punctuation sign from her late mother, who taught her to write (337). What we are thus seeing in this passage is not only the memory described, but also the trace (akin to early musical notation) of the *voice* doing the describing, whose breath we read as the two dots with a space on either end ' : ' – inhale, exhale. This is the way her mother wrote, and each time this sign appears in Francescho's narration, her mother's memory is preserved.

The spiral and the vortex are both visual concepts – they signify images – and perhaps that is why this prose picturing of a sycamore seed, spinning on its own axis, is so effective in conveying the difference between descriptive and diegetic voices. Visual description distinguishes itself here by means of a kind of discursive delineation: the opening phrase, 'Sunlight hitting the yellowing leaves', frames the passage as a visual scene, and the details that follow about the movement of the falling 'something' into the puddle of urine; the puddle's foam and bubbles; the ringed ripples caused by the seed's landing; their gradual disappearance at the pool's edge – all these details add to the scene's immediacy. (This scene is also compelling my own paraphrase to follow its rhythms, producing an ordered paratactic sequence which is ekphrasis' distinctive trait.) Louvel suggests that the function of a framing device in discourse is 'to present and [its] role … is deictic' (*Pictorial Third* 115). Ekphrasis is deictic in the sense that it *points* the reader's imagination at these objects, present-ing them for contemplation. This is not to suggest, however, that it is always possible to trace a *precise* demarcation of this kind of discursive framing. As Nancy puts it, there is a threshold at play in verbal description (and also in the difference between an image and what it represents), 'whose division [*partage*] is at that moment traced by something that makes us cross it without eliminating it (the distinction)' (*Ground of Image* 5). This threshold might be imaged as a scuffed line in the sand – blurred yet preserving its deictical force. For instance, Francesho is again out in the yard, when her mother starts to draw figures on the ground:

> Another time : hot, and the cicadas : my mother was drawing a line in the ground with a stick.
>
> I saw what it was before it became it : it's the neck of a duck!
>
> Then she moved to a new piece of ground and drew a line and then another then joined them to 2 other lines and a curve : it's the place where a leg of a horse meets its body!
>
> She finished the horse, started again, drew a line, then another, made a scuff in the dust and drew lines in the scuff : it's a house! It's our house!
>
> (211)

This is not the kind of lengthy ekphrasis that we have come to expect of Proustian narratives; nonetheless, the passage invites us to picture the tracing of these lines in the sand, to visualize these movements of a drawing hand. This is a descriptive sequence filled with movement, compelling the reader to 'see' the figures being drawn in the sand *through* Francescho's budding-artist's gaze – a gaze that foresees each line's destination before it arrives there. In other words, there is something operating over and above description itself – *a voice is guiding us to see*, blurring the threshold separating two distinct functions of narrative, picturing and sequencing, characteristic of the Proustian model.

Similarly, another voice guides our mind's eye to see towards the end of George's story. After her friend Helena has left London, George decides to cycle the 'DNA Cycle Path', running for two miles from Addenbrooke's Hospital in

Cambridge.³ She cycles the length of the path and then takes a photograph of the DNA sculpture that marks the end of the trail. She compares the picture on her mobile phone with the artwork itself and reflects:

> It resembled a joyful bedspring or a bespoke ladder. It was like a kind of shout, if a shout to the sky could be said to look like something. It looked like the opposite of history, though they were always going on at school about how DNA history had been made here in this city.
>
> What if history, instead, *was* that shout, that upward spring, that staircase-ladder thing, and everybody was just used to calling something quite different the word history?
>
> (172)

The unusual metaphors here, 'a joyful bedspring or a bespoke ladder' (both happy instances of *ostranenie*), add to the vividness of a recognizable visual icon, but it is the DNA sculpture's comparison to 'a kind of shout' that is most suggestive. What it suggests is that history (etymologically, according to the *OED*, 'history' encompasses both learning through narration and pictorial description) might be construed as 'that upward spring' whose spiralling movement over time connotes a 'shout'. Voice and vision commingle in this figure, as history becomes a shout that can, paradoxically, only be given expression visually.

'A third thing'

In *Image Science*, a typically exciting venture into the semiosphere of images, Mitchell thinks of the pictorial image as expressive of a futural, anticipatory orientation. 'My sense', he posits, 'is that something [is] in the painting waiting to be described in a new way, waiting for language to catch up with a compelling picture. In that sense, the image (as always) goes before the word, foreshadowing the future if only we knew how to read it' (88). The 2015 Penguin UK paperback of *How to Be Both* literalizes this sense of a painting preceding its own articulation. The insides of the covers show the two key figures that appear in both parts of the novel: the front cover's overleaf shows the man in torn shirt with the fraying rope tied around his waist, while the back overleaf shows an androgynous figure dressed like a courtier, holding a golden hoop in one hand and a golden arrow in the other (see Figure 5).

---

³ Created in 2005, the cycle path celebrates the 10,000th mile of the national cycle network in Britain, as well as the discovery by researchers of the Sanger Institute of the BRCA2 protein, responsible for breast cancer ('DNA Cycle').

Figure 5 Triumph of Minerva, Sign of Aries and Borso d'Este, who administers justice and goes hunting, scenes from *Month of March*, c. 1470, by Francesco del Cossa (c. 1435–1477), fresco, east wall of Hall of the Months, Palazzo Schifanoia (Palace of Joy), Ferrara, Emilia-Romagna. Detail. Italy, fifteenth century. Courtesy DeAgostini Getty Images.

The man in the frayed shirt appears in the fresco that Smith beheld in *Frieze* magazine, the fresco that almost made her choke on her morning coffee, compelled her to visit the Palazzo Schifanoia, and inspired her to write *How to Be Both*. In the novel, George's mother likewise sees it in a magazine and is compelled to travel to Italy to see it in the flesh. As readers of the novel, when we first see this cover illustration, we anticipate both what it might have to say in response to the text we are about to read and what the text will have told us of it. In *Poetics of the Iconotext*, Louvel identifies several picture–text instantiations, ranging from pictorial allusion, inter-semiotic translation, narratives featuring both text and pictures, and so on (55–57). One of these instantiations she calls (invoking Genette's concept of the paratext) 'parapictoriality', which occurs when a picture 'appears at the "threshold" of the text', relates to the text's content and thereby 'fulfils a mnemonic and didactic function' (Louvel 68–69). From this perspective, the verbal translation of the picture of the man in the torn shirt reactivates a reader's remembrance, and the reason that this is significant is that it allows this novel to enact the collocation-becoming-imbrication, the weird intersemiotic blend that is the phenomenological product of ekphrasis.

'The pictorial contribution', Louvel argues, 'an oblique flash of glazing light projected onto the text, activates the pictorial third that is actualized once an image-in-text, an in-between phenomenon, rises in the reader's mind; it is a dynamic, oscillating between an imagistic reading and a read image' (*Pictorial Third* 188). Smith, coincidentally, has herself alluded to a 'third' something that emerges whenever words encounter pictures. In an interview, she was asked whether she ever uses the collage technique when planning her novels. Smith responded by saying that she does, in fact, often produce collage-like arrangements on the wall of her study, putting varied objects and pictures beside each other. As she tells the interviewer, collages 'do what narrative does when two things come together in it, *they make a third*, they cocktail together to produce their own new thing' (my emphasis, Elkins). Suggestively, Mitchell too speaks of a 'third thing' that emerges when texts seek to picture; as he puts it, 'Let's say, then, that the normal relation of text and image is complementary or supplementary, and that together they make up *a third thing*, or open a space where that third thing appears' (my emphasis, *Image Science* 43).

How to Be Both is full of dense textual sites where this intermedial 'cocktail', this strange 'third thing', appears before us. It is most apparent at those moments when an actual picture is being described – invoked in retrospect. When that happens, as it so often does in Smith's novel, we find ourselves travelling along, in Louvel's apt phrasing,

> The passage between the two media [that] is read in-between as the reader is never totally inside the one, nor completely outside the other. This instability of the text/image ... fascinates the writer and the reader, since it constantly places them inside the transposition, the transaction, the negotiation, and imposes a kind of writing or a dynamic, active reading where the image provides an impetus throughout the text, throughout the language that allows it to rise.
>
> (*Pictorial Third* 187)

We find ourselves placed inside this kind of unstable intermedial 'transposition' while reading a passage such as the following one. In George's story, Carol takes her family to Ferrara to see the del Cossa frescoes in the Palazzo Schifanoia. She asks George several pointed questions about how one looks at art and what this looking entails. 'And which comes first? her unbearable mother is saying. What we see or how we see?' (104). George – understandably enough – shakes her head. However, Carol then draws her attention to certain details in the *Allegory of March* fresco (see Figure 5), pointing out something about its composition that is not immediately apparent. Suppose that the artist was a woman, she tells George. Certain details in the painting could support a thesis on this subject, as Carol points to the opening in the shirt over the man's breastbone:

> the vaginal shape here on that beautiful worker in rags in the blue section, the most virile and powerful figure in the whole room ... And how the open shape at his chest complements the way the painter makes the rope round his waist a piece of simultaneously dangling and erect phallic symbolism –
>
> (her mother did an art history degree once) (110)

Carol is making this painting imbibe a specific sense, a sense which George's parenthetical interruption tries to undermine. She then refers to the 'effeminate boy' who appears opposite the man in the fresco and asks both George and reader to notice 'how this figure holds both an arrow and a hoop, male and female symbols one in each hand. On this alone I could make a reasonably witty argument for its originator being female, if I had to' (111). Carol knows that this is very unlikely to have been the case and the historical artist was likely male, but this is hardly the point. The point is rather how George subsequently reflects upon this *memory* of her mother saying these things about this *fresco*, one which they both looked at not long before Carol's death. 'I saw the same room', George thinks to herself, 'the exact same room as she did, we were both standing in the very same place, and I didn't see *any* of it' (111). George's not seeing of what Carol sees in the fresco-detail might echo the reader's own failure to do so or it might not; in either case, having heard this fresco 'speak' through Carol's *enargeiac* voicing, it becomes difficult to *un*-see these details – the opening in the shirt above the man's breastbone having a 'vaginal shape', or the dangling and erect ropes representing the respective phallic postures. The 'erect' part of the rope, the end held out by the man, is most likely a 'pointing' gesture, a compositional prompt to the viewer's eye to 'look over there'. Indeed, this kind of deictic hint is about all that a picture can denote, as if verbally. For the rest, a voice is necessary *to let a picture speak through it* (note that if the italicized clause is dropped from this sentence, and all sense-making thereby entrusted to the voice, then the picture's own meaning-producing agency gets silenced).[4]

---

[4] Lewis calls an artwork's claim on our attention its 'beholding': 'When I behold something, I am also its object: I am *held* by it. ... The object that I behold is co-actor with me in a visual happening' (141). Drawing on Michael Fried, she argues that 'the visual dynamics of *How to Be Both* consistently unsettle comfortable distinctions between viewing subjects and viewed objects' (142). I share Lewis's contention that Smith's novel thereby expresses a 'shifting epistemology of vision' (136), constantly challenging the reader's gaze by staging so many acts of looking. By Lewis's count, the word 'look' appears no fewer than 400 times in the novel.

Carol's description of the fresco is conveyed by the cadences of her voice, which we hear in George's narrativization of her recollection. And, despite George's mocking of her mother's interpretation of this fresco, she will herself interpret another del Cossa painting in similar fashion. Later in the novel, when George and Helena decide to present a school project on the life of del Cossa, Helena finds a painting of 'a handsome man with brown eyes holding a ring' (142). As they look over this painting on Helena's iPad, they notice that the rocks in the background, to the left of the sitter's head, are 'shaped a bit like a penis' (142), while the rockface on the opposing side has a cave set in it.[5] Here, we are presented with the painting's symbolism as seen through George's eyes: 'If you notice, it changes everything about the picture, like a witty remark someone has been brave enough to make out loud. ... It isn't lying about anything or feigning anything. ... It can just be rocks and landscape if that's what you want it to be – but there's always more to see, if you look' (142). George is describing this painting as if it had a capacity for speech and could make 'witty remarks' and even be 'lying' or 'feigning' things. Nancy offers a helpful account of this kind of address made by pictures to those who behold them: 'An image always says, simultaneously, "I am this, a flower," and "I am an imaged flower, or a flower-image." I am not, it says, the image *of* this or that, as if I were its substitute or copy, but I *image* this or that, I present its absence, that is, its sense' (*Ground of Image* 70). Nancy endows the pictorial image with voice and lets it speak, precisely in order to trace the sense of both what it means 'to image' (where 'imaging' is intransitive) and what it means to be 'an image of' something (where a picture is in a transitive relation to the subject of representation). The voice is relied upon to illuminate that which does not speak but only images, as Nancy emphasizes. His point, of course, is that pictures do not only image, just as words do not just speak.

This is precisely the double sense in which the del Cossa painting of a man holding out a ring speaks to George and Helena: it is imaging (speaking) sexual symbolism, but it also images (shows) a young man extending his hand beyond the picture frame, with the rock formations, mountains and sky in the background. That is, it is imaging the one as superimposed upon the other, which is how the visual makes narrative sense. In this way, the painting's function in narrative becomes very close to that of metaphor: the moment a metaphor's constituent parts are literalized and separated, it loses sense. It only gains sense when these

---

[5] For readers wishing to make a visual pilgrimage, the painting is titled *Portrait of a Man with a Ring*, c. 1472–1477.

parts are working together to produce 'a third thing': the semantically 'higher' sense conveyed by the metaphorical comparison.

What is seen in ekphrastic evocation is not only the visual scene (actual or remembered) that is its point of departure and destination, but equally the voice that expresses it, as voice and seeing are caught up in each other and as our attention oscillates between them. According to Nancy, the mask of Bacchus was often used in antiquity as a scarecrow and hung in the vines of a vineyard. The mask was called *Oscillum*, the diminutive form of *os*, 'which signifies the mouth and, by metonymy, the face' (Nancy, *Ground of Image* 73). The mask of Bacchus turned whenever the wind blew, producing a movement of oscillation, 'swing[ing] between mouth and face, between speech and vision, between the emission of sense and the reception of form' (Nancy 73). Hence, the infinitive 'to oscillate' derives from the word for mouth and, through the figure of the *Oscillum*, also connotes the face, the look – sight. Ekphrasis, from this perspective, is that shifting space within the text where this rhythmic turning, this process of intersensory exchange between 'mouth' and 'eye', happens. As Nancy suggests: 'What one paints, the other depicts. But precisely that, their common cause and their common thing [*chose*], oscillates distinctly between the two in a paper-thin space: recto the text, verso the image, or vice (image)-versa (text)' (78). The 'common thing' shared by text and image is their combined sense, and the remainder of this chapter will argue that this sense emerges most concretely out of the *enargeiac* voicing of a narrative's scenes.

Narrational modulation

The George half of the novel, due to the focalization assumed throughout, is told in the vernacular of adolescence.[6] The narrated world is seen through George's eyes, as we hear her voice in passages like this one: 'This will be the first year her mother hasn't been alive since the year her mother was born. That is so obvious that it is stupid even to think it and yet so terrible that you can't not think it. Both at once' (4). Like Marcel, George has a discerning eye, and this is particularly evident towards the end of her story, when she and Helena research

---

[6] There is one exception in the novel where a third-person voice narrates over George's point of view. When George first goes to the National Gallery to look for one of del Cossa's paintings, she enquires after 'St Vincent of Ferrara', and the authorial narrator corrects her: 'Actually, George had been wrong about that. It's not Ferrara. It's a painting of a saint called Ferrer and nothing to do with the place George has been to in Italy' (151).

the life of del Cossa for a school project. Del Cossa's paintings moved both George and her mother, Carol, when they visited Ferrara a year before Carol's death. George discovers that there is a painting by del Cossa at the National Gallery, and she visits the gallery several times to look at *Saint Vincent Ferrer*. Upon first glance, the painting seems to be intended to inculcate obeisance to the Church, the 'severe-faced monk' with sternly lifted finger not making much of an impression (154). But George looks past first impressions and notices that the figure of Jesus resembles a 'well-worn human being or a tramp who's been dressed up as Jesus' and that the androgynous angels surrounding him appear to be holding 'torture implements like the people in an S&M session online but really unlike an S&M session in their calmness' (155). Likening objects held by angels in a Renaissance painting to sadomasochistic 'torture implements' is, needless to say, a startling comparison, one that lends greater immediacy to George's description. Of course, the reader looking at this painting will not necessarily see the angels' implements *as* 'S&M session' devices, but George's disjunctive comparison incites a curiosity to see it through her eyes. In this way, this instance of ekphrastic *ostranenie* lends credence to Nancy's claim that '*mimesis* encompasses *methexis*, a participation or a contagion through which the image seizes us' (*Ground of the Image* 9). *Methexis*, as conceived by the rhetoricians, denotes participation or 'sharing' by an audience in a theatrical performance, and, as Nancy contends, it is present in all mimetic practices ('The Image' 74–77). The painting's description, in other words, is an invitation to the reader to participate (*methexis*) in George's *way of seeing it*; George's surprising ekphrasis is contagious, precisely because of its bathos.

Although there are many moments of compelling description in George's narrative, it is in Francescho's ekphrastic perorations that we can most clearly see the merger of the seeing eye and the speaking voice. Francescho's story opens with a typographically rendered spiral (another vortex), as the text mirrors the passage of her ghostly re-birth, over five centuries after her death, into the world of George's present:

> Ho this is a mighty twisting thing fast as a
>   fish being pulled by its mouth on a hook
>   if a fish could be fished through a
>   6 foot thick wall made of bricks …
>   home again home again
>   jiggety down through the up
>   like a seed off a tree with a wing. (189–190)

The final image, 'like a seed off a tree with a wing', anticipates the spiral movement of the falling sycamore seed, to appear later in the story. Then, at narrative's end, Francescho's voice spins back to silence, with the text of the voice once again becoming a spiral:

> ... the seed still unbroken
> the star still unburnt
> the curve of the eyebone
> of the not yet born
> hello all the new bones
> hello all the old
> hello all the everything
> to be
> made and
> unmade
> both. (372)

George's wish for history to have an 'upward spring' is thus realized in Francescho's story – insofar as this novelization of a historical painter's life can be considered 'history'. What lends Francescho's story greater immediacy than George's, though, is our hearing of a visually impelled phrasing made by her voice, with the visual acting precisely as the narration's 'impeller'. The OED suggestively defines 'impeller' not only as someone or something that impels but also 'a part of a machine or apparatus designed to impart motion to a fluid by rotation, esp. in a restricted space'. Hence, the pictorial image propels ekphrasis, causing it to send out semantic ripples even as our eye is drawn to this textual vortex. Francescho's narration allows us to see, in other words, how the narrating voice acquires a certain *modulation* peculiar to ekphrastic word painting. One reason for this is that Francescho is an artist, and her perspective is naturally more coloured by the experience and knowledge of her profession. Her rhetorical adeptness at describing visual perception equips her with the evocative language needed to make verbal seeing happen, a seeing produced by what ancient rhetorical manuals referred to as *enargeia* (see Chapter 1).

Two modulations of the narrative voice can be heard in *How to Be Both*, what I will be referring to as the 'narrational keys' of diegetic and *enargeiac* voicing. There are two passages in the novel that illustrate this modulation. The first passage comes from George's story: Helena has come over for a visit and surprises George by handing her an A4 envelope.

> George opens it. Inside there's a photograph on thick paper. It's summer in the picture. Two women (both young, both between girl and woman) are walking

along a road together past some shops in a very sunny-looking place. Is it now or is it in the past? One of them is yellow-haired and one of them is darker. The yellow-haired one, the smaller of the two, is looking at something off camera. … She's wearing a gold and orange top. The dark-haired taller girl is wearing a short blue dress with a stripe round the edging of it. … The yellow-haired one looks preoccupied, intent. The dark one looks as if something that's been said has struck her and she's about to say a yes.

(81–82)

We are given here to hear George's voicing of an iconic photograph showing Sylvie Vartan and Françoise Hardy walking along a sunny street. As we read on, we learn that the 'yellow-haired one' (Vartan) represents George, who is said to look a little like her, and the 'dark one' represents Helena. George and Helena are likewise 'between girl and woman', and, upon rereading the novel, we realize that Hardy being 'about to say a yes' is suggestive of George's desire for Helena to say 'a yes' to their relationship. George, in the focalized voicing of this photograph, is inadvertently describing her own desires, but this only emerges into light once we have read the novel.

The publisher's fortuitous decision to use Jean-Marie Périer's photograph of Vartan and Hardy as a cover illustration (of the Penguin 2015 edition) actually supports the conventions of ekphrastic representation in antiquity; as Webb indicates, what lends an ekphrasis its affective power is the *familiarity* of the material being re-presented to the audience (*Ekphrasis, Imagination* 122). Hence, by re-presenting the cover photograph via George's description before our inner gaze, the Penguin edition of the novel gives the reader (one is tempted to say 'the viewer') a sense not only of George's physical appearance (the comparison with Vartan) but, more importantly, the emotional accents with which she imbues this photograph. As Louvel puts it, the 'writer's appropriation and restitution of an iconographic representation is a means for the reader to revel in the contemplation of a lost object that is thus retrieved … a way of sharing knowledge with the reader by fostering a sense of complicity' (*Poetics of Iconotext* 104). This sense of complicity is made possible because, with the aid of the cover illustration, the reader is invited to look alongside George at *this* picture and to see it through her eyes – in the same way that we were earlier invited to look at the del Cossa painting in the National Gallery. Affective ekphrasis has 'the power to make us feel "as if" we can perceive [the absent things] and share the associated emotions', Webb writes (*Ekphrasis, Imagination* 168), and this is precisely the sense in which we contemplate 'a lost object that is thus retrieved'. The cover photograph of Vartan and Hardy, temporarily lost to the reading eye in its encounters with the novel's imaging of various scenes, suddenly presences itself again, but this time as ekphrasis, and its emotional impact is felt through a vicarious complicity (*methexis*) with the protagonist's point of view.

Enargeia, the sense of immediacy and presence produced by ekphrasis, is central to the project of fiction. However, what ekphrasis makes present is not only a scene, person, object or moment described but also the *voice* producing the description. I have suggested that the *enargeiac* key is distinct from the diegetic within the tonality of narrative voice, and the second ekphrasis of the Vartan-Hardy photograph, in the Francescho half of the novel, further illuminates their distinction. Francescho, from the moment that she is brought back to life in the National Gallery, follows George wherever she goes. Once in George's bedroom, she observes George grieving:

> Back in that room, the room with the bed in it, back comes the sadness : she sits behind the veil of it for many whole minutes then she shakes herself to her feet and takes off her dusty shirt, shakes the dust and stuff off it out of the window she shoulders the shirt back on … and sits on the bed again.
>
> (287)

This is narration in the diegetic key: the passage gives us an indication of space ('the room with the bed in it') and action ('shakes', 'takes', 'shoulders', 'sits'), but it is neither vivid nor does it draw our eye to particular features in George's room. The following paragraph, however, is quite different:

> The south wall, along which the narrow bed runs, has a picture of two beautiful girls seen walking along like friends do : one has gold hair, one has dark but the dark of her hair is sunlit to lightness – both the heads of the girls are : they are walking along a street with awnings : it's a warm place : their clothes are mosaic gold and azzurrite : the girls are in conversational commerce and look as if between sentences : the goldener one is preoccupied : the darker-headed girl turns her head towards her in a most natural gesture in open air and so she can see the other better : her looking has about it politeness, humility, respect, a kind of gentle intent.
>
> (287)

This is narration sounding in the *enargeiac* key. Notice the repetition of Francescho's signature breath sign, ' : ', which appears more frequently as her narration *slows* in pace, creating a beat particular to an eye taking its time to look and giving the reader time to appreciate the evocative power of this re-description of a scene already seen, already interpreted (that is, if your own copy of the novel happens to coincide with mine in the order of its two parts).[7] Francescho's descriptive language is also more precise than George's, as it features words like 'mosaic gold' and 'azzurrite' for the respective colours of Vartan and Hardy's clothes, and the concluding series of nouns adds precision to George's reading of Hardy's open demeanour. *Enargeiac* voicing, as these two ekphrases of a single photograph show, is not only the voicing of seeing again but of seeing *anew*.

Enargeiac voice operates according to its own rhythm, and this rhythm belongs to the character from whose point of view we see the unfolding events. Louvel contends that '[t]he gaze through which the describing subject emerges is rhythm' (*Poetics of Iconotext* 175), and the reason that the visual sense is so intimately involved with the sense of hearing, implied by the word 'rhythm', lies in the intermedial 'transposition' into which our comprehension is immersed, especially when actual pictures are the objects of the narrator's gaze. We can now examine another example in the novel where this kind of descriptive rhythm distinctly announces itself. Francescho recollects having nearly completed the frescoes in the Palazzo Schifanoia, when the Duke's overseer, Mr de Prisciano or 'the Falcon', pays the courtyard one of his visits of inspection. Scrutinizing the frescoes, he tells her that he is unhappy with the way she has painted one of the deacons, who appears 'in the shape of an infidel', and one of the Grace's skins is 'far too dark' (310–311). She, in turn, defends her artistic choices. This scene consists largely of dialogue (the diegetic key of narration) between Francescho and the Falcon, who is eventually persuaded to allow some of her unorthodox representations to dwell for ages to come upon the walls of the Palazzo. A modulation is introduced into the narrative voice, however, when Francescho describes her approach to painting the scene with the Three Graces:

> I had given the Graces fashionable hairstyles : I had given them fleeting bodily resemblances, Ginerva and Agnola both facing, Isotta with her back to us : I had painted them holding apples and painted some Vs in 2 spindly trees to catch and repeat the shape of the place on the facing Graces where all human life and much pleasure originates : I had placed 2 birds in each spindly tree : everything rhythmic : even the apples and breasts were resemblances. (311–312)

This is a precise visual description of the surviving fresco in the Palazzo, titled the *Allegory of April* (see Figure 6). Ginerva, Agnola and Isotta are all women who work in the 'house of pleasure' which Francescho would frequent in the

---

[7] Regarding Smith's decision for the novel's two parts (both labelled 'One') to be printed in random order for each copy, see Alex Clark.

company of her friend, Barto. She surprised these women both by her gender (concealing herself as a man in order to pass in the world as an artist) and, even more, by her request to draw their likenesses. The women like these drawings so much that they eventually begin to pay her for them. Francescho's descriptive rendering of the Three Graces thus refers the reader back to an earlier scene in the novel and thereby infuses a real fresco with a particular story. Francescho invests this *enargeiac* depiction of the Three Graces with her own personality through the rhythm of her narrating voice, and, not unlike the Falcon who cannot take his eye off the 'infidel in his white work rags', this reader finds it difficult to look away from this *textually rendered* painting. This ekphrastic image is so distinct and vivid not simply because it has an extant referent but precisely through the agency of the voice that speaks it in *this* particular way. (That said, its verbal unfolding does acquire an added weight, once one has seen the painting that it invokes, and that impels it.)

Louvel refers to this kind of pictorial quotation as 'a call to the reader from inside the text', and it is entirely up to the reader to respond to it (*Pictorial Third* 194). Having made my own response and looked up the del Cossa painting, I want to dwell a while longer on the implications of this gesture. In what precise sense is Louvel correct, as I suggest she is, when she argues that the significance of an actual picture is that it 'subtly enlightens the text, supplementing and complementing it, bringing in meaning and energy that would not have been possible otherwise' (191)?

To look up (search for) a picture that the text is voicing is also to look up to it (respect its sovereignty). In del Cossa's *Allegory of April*, the V-shaped branches mirroring the lines delineating the groins of the forward-facing Graces, the Three Graces' echoing postures, the similarity between the breasts and the apples – all these visual details are fastidiously reproduced in Francescho's description. The correspondences of these painted objects, as Francescho tells us, make 'everything rhythmic' compositionally, and, mutatis mutandis, their *enargeiac* emulation also acquires its rhythm, signposted by Francescho's breath sign signalling the measured pace in which her sentences are spoken, as she reads the fresco's details to the reader's ear and eye.

There is, however, a deeper sense in which Louvel is correct, when she says that a picture 'enlightens' the text. This concerns memory and the reason why pictorial allusion illuminates our understanding of the ekphrastic hope involved in the writing of memory's own pictures. Louvel defines a pictorial citation as follows: 'it is the trace of a mnemonic presence, the imprint of a passage, an already crossed territory, put in memory and signalling the presence of a

Figure 6 Idyllic love, detail from Triumph of Venus, scene from *Month of April*, c. 1470, by Francesco del Cossa (c. 1435–1477), fresco, east wall, Hall of the Months, Palazzo Schifanoia (Palace of Joy), Ferrara, Emilia-Romagna. Italy, fifteenth century. Courtesy DeAgostini Getty Images.

figured absence' (*Pictorial Third* 174). A key 'mnemonic presence' conjured in Smith's novel is the picture of the man in the torn shirt, whose verbal image we repeatedly encounter in the novel. This image represents a 'figured absence' as this nameless worker's story has not been told, and only his fresco-ghost keeps a vestige of his existence. But all painted figures lack memory and voice within the silence of the historical record. They only *image* intransitively, leaving their allegorical or symbolic deciphering to verbal interpretation. In Smith's novel, as we've seen, paintings' invocations act as signs informing memory's verbal evocation; the *OED* defines the verb 'to inform' as to give shape but also to imbue with a feeling or a quality, to permeate, inspire, animate. Francescho's telling us that she modelled the Three Graces on Ginerva, Agnola and Isotta lends their representation her own affect, and it is one which the reader may come to share, knowing their backstory and being in a position to see three unremarkable (at first glance) female figures imbued with the *memories* of this character. The actual fresco figures, which the reader is able to look up, thus function as reminders, even *indices* of the ekphrastic hope that sounds within the rhythmic beat of memory's *enargeiac* evocation. In other words, the text gestures at these figures, and allows itself to be animated by them from within, imbued with the feelings they give and hoping that the reader will see them and feel their affect too – even in the tangible picture's absence within the text.

The picture of the man in the frayed shirt similarly indexes its presence in Francescho's story, and the descriptive language brings his image before the reader's gaze. Francescho encountered this man, she tells us, one day while walking along the road and passing by a field:

> Further on down the road someone springs out from a copse of trees : he's one of the working men. ... I pass quite close to him : his white clothes are ragged, but less from poverty, I see as I come closer, than from what seems the strength of his own body, as if it can't help but break through : his sleeves are frayed by the strength of his hands and forearms : his knees have made holes in the cloth, being so strong : the line of dark hairs above his groin sits visible : his eyes are reddened by work.
>
> (283)

In the same way that the man appears before (in front of) Francescho as she walks along the road, he appears before (in sight of) the reader as the lines of prose sound his image. The man tells Francescho that he needs a belt, something to tie his flapping shirt. She remembers that she has a rope in her haversack, a rope that she had bought at a market in Florence and which was used for hanging and quartering and said to bring good luck. 'I walk back towards him', she narrates, 'as he comes towards me : I hold out the rope to him : he looks at it, takes it, weighs it in his hand, then smiles at me as if to pay me with the smile' (285). Francescho and the man have sex in the copse of trees: 'We stood up after and I was covered in grass and earth, so was he : he dusted me down : he picked one grass piece off my shoulder and smiled a goodbye, put the piece of grass between his teeth, slung my rope over his shoulder and walked back openly to the fields and the work he'd left' (285). We can hear in this scene a modulation of the narrative voice between *enargeiac* depiction, producing a prose picture of the man's physicality, of his strength that seems to tear his own clothing, his eyes 'reddened by work', and the subsequent diegetic narration that is almost as vivid. This episode can be read as narration that transposes ekphrastic description (the man's appearance) into diegetic recounting (the scene with the rope), oscillating effortlessly between them: the sense of immediacy produced here is the result of description and narration working together, producing an image-cum-text blend of stillness and motion.

*

In *Artful*, an essayistic novel based on Smith's series of lectures first given at Oxford University, the narrator's late partner was a lecturer on art history. The narrative consists, in part, of the narrator's reflections on her/his partner's lecture notes, a lecture which she/he did not manage to complete. The lecture ends on a hopeful but incomplete word:

> Here's to the place where reality and imagination meet, whose exchange, whose dialogue, allows us not just to imagine an unreal different world but also a real different world – to match reality with possibili
>
> (237)

The missing syllable is easily filled in by the reader's eye.[8] In ekphrastic narratives, the place 'where reality and imagination meet' to enact a 'dialogue' is the shifty sight/site within the text that pictures the past. Reality (the narrator's past) meets imagination (ekphrastic images) and, vice-versa, the *enargeiac* text (another kind of reality) permits the reader to imagine this past. *Enargeiac* conjurations of a character's past are also the drawing forth of 'a real different world' out of the vortex of ekphrasis, instead of merely being the creation of 'an unreal different world'. This is because the phenomenological experience of this conjuration makes a reader complicit in it, witnessing a process of remembering unfold and

---

[8] Syllables and words often disappear in Smith's fiction. For instance, in *Hotel World* the opening section, narrated by the ghost of a young woman who fell to her death, has several missing words: 'I will miss the, the. What's the word? Lost, I've, the word. The word for. You know. I don't mean a house. I don't mean a room. I mean the way of the . Dead to the . Out of this . Word' (30). See also Mark Currie, 'Ali Smith and the Philosophy of Grammar', where Currie argues that *Hotel World* graphically encodes philosophical problems about time by presenting us with 'a world in which time is made visible by the form of writing' (60).

being *reminded* of how one recalls one's own past. One bears witness to another's memory-picturing by participating in co-producing the images that the text is voicing, with the help of memory (what one has seen) and imagination (what one has not seen).

The missing syllable in 'possibili' is a textual acting out of what possibility is: a promise of fulfilment that, by definition, carries no guarantee (the writer of the lecture dies while writing this hopeful word). But it also extends an invitation to complete it. To read ekphrastic memory writing is to experience how the reality of the past is matched by its mediated possibili(ty) – where what the text is inviting or trusting us to see is the missing, spectral part that it has not managed to make into a picture. Recall Mitchell's almost tactile distinction between 'picture' and 'image', which he here restates: 'The picture is a material object, a thing you can burn or break or tear. An image is what appears in a picture, and what survives its destruction – in memory, in narrative, in copies and traces of other media' (*Image Science* 16). A memory image, in other words, is inherently spectral, a phantom that always speaks of lost time. Of course, verbally imaging a past is infinitely more uncertain – and thus all the more hopeful – than filling in a syllable that we rightfully expect should be there. But the sense of expectation created by both is comparable in its anticipatory gesture, if not in the assurance of hitting the mark. 'Possibili' anticipates its own completion as 'possibility', so that it can become fully present on the page, while the ekphrastic text performs the opposite gesture, as it seeks to efface itself in order to let the reader glimpse the image centrifugally arising out of its vortex. Ekphrasis seeks to be a calligram whose words give way to the shape they create, the scene that both impels the words and that is drawn under by the maelstrom of phrases which compose it, covering it over with verbal sense, even as the flow of narrative dissolves the calligram's borders.

7

Writing forgetting in Lydia Davis's *The End of the Story*

Of all the writers considered in this book, Lydia Davis shares perhaps the closest connection with Proust. Davis has translated *Du côté de chez Swann* (*Swann's Way*) and, more recently, *Lettres à sa voisine* (*Letters to the Lady Upstairs*).[1] She has also written several essays wherein she ponders Proust's style and its impact upon her as a writer. Unlike Proust, though, Davis is celebrated for her short stories, some of which can be anywhere from a sentence to several pages long. She is among the best practitioners of flash fiction, and, to date, has written one novel, *The End of the Story*. This novel is about a writer's difficulties in narrating a past romance with a younger man, and it both echoes Proust's *Search* and departs from it in significant ways.

Before turning to it, however, it will be helpful to consider Davis's own comments about Proust's style. In 'Loaf or Hot-Water Bottle: Closely Translating Proust', Davis discusses how her translation of *Du côté de chez Swann* differs from previous efforts, in particular the revised C. K. Scott Moncrieff and James Grieve versions.[2] I would like to focus on Davis's self-conscious attempt, in the opening paragraphs of the essay, to write a Proustian sentence. The sentence gives a summary of Davis's work as a translator, and it plots the essay's story about her translation of Proust:

> After having worked as a translator from the French quite consistently for thirty years or so, pausing only briefly to work on my own stories, and stopping for an

---

[1] Discovered only a few years ago, these are letters Proust wrote to his neighbour, one Mme Marie Williams, who lived above his Paris apartment at 102 Boulevard Haussmann. A chance remark Proust makes in one of the letters is particularly revealing. Early in their correspondence, Proust had complimented Mme Williams on her imagination in describing her past (her letters to Proust have not survived). In a later letter, he writes: 'I have so often dreamed of them [the sights described in the earlier letter]; and you, with your pictorial and sunlit words, have brought colour and light into my closed room' (22). Few phrases could be more fitting to describe the experience of reading Proust.

[2] See also Michael Wood's essay, 'Translations', where Wood assesses translations of Proust from the original Scott Moncrieff to the latest English versions undertaken for Penguin and edited by Christopher Prendergast.

extended time once only, as far as I can remember, to finish a novel, continuing to enjoy translating most of the time, working on a range of books of all degrees of excellence and non-excellence, of interest and of no interest, since this was how I earned most of my money and was therefore not in a position to choose, most of the time, what I wanted to translate, books ranging from a sentimental biography of Marie Curie to histories of China and art catalogues, and including several innovative novels by Pierre Jean Jouve, a volume of travel essays by Michel Butor, several books of fiction and literary philosophy by Maurice Blanchot, I was thinking, one day, though not for the first time, that sooner or later I would like to give less attention to translation and more to my own fiction, when, in the early afternoon, the phone rang.

('Loaf or Hot-Water Bottle' 52)

Readers of Davis's fiction will readily notice the difference between this lengthy, multi-clausal sentence and a typical Davis sentence, which is a model of concision. Nonetheless, even this 'Proustian' sentence is marked by Davis's style. Phrases such as 'books of all degrees of excellence and non-excellence, of interest and of no interest', and 'I was thinking, one day, though not for the first time' are carefully weighed, the commas acting as fulcrums upon which the preceding and following clauses are balanced. Rhythmic precision is Davis's outstanding stylistic mark and her prose, as it were, always comes with its own time signature. A representative example is the opening passage of the short story, 'To Reiterate':

> Michel Butor says that to travel is to write, because to travel is to read. This can be developed further: To write is to travel, to write is to read, to read is to write, and to read is to travel. But George Steiner says that to translate is also to read, and to translate is to write, as to write is to translate and to read is to translate. So that we may say: To translate is to travel and to travel is to translate. To translate a travel writing, for example, is to read a travel writing, to write a travel writing, to read a writing, to write a writing, and to travel.

(*Collected Stories* 215)

The adventure of this story, we might say, is discovered within its manner of telling: the sense of semiotic travel it imparts via its play with definitions. It is a story about language leading us to surprising destinations, and it is this aspect of Davis's style that reveals her philosophical concerns about language and how it does what it does.[3] This is not to suggest that Davis cares *only* for rhythm at

---

[3] See Christopher J. Knight, 'Interview with Lydia Davis', where Davis remarks: 'I guess that my higher value is on some sort of philosophical investigation' (534).

the expense of representation or, indeed, depiction. Some of her stories conjure intensely vivid prose pictures, such as the disturbing *tableau mort*, 'The Great-Grandmothers', a story about a rather odd family gathering. In it, the eponymous great-grandmothers are 'put out on the sun porch' (288) and then forgotten by the rest of the family. Eventually, the glass door is opened and everybody makes their way out onto the sunlit porch:

> [I]t was too late: their gnarled hands had grown into the wood of their cane handles, their lips had cleaved together into one membrane, their eyeballs had hardened and were immovably focused out on the chestnut grove where the children were flashing to and fro. Only old Agnes had a little life left in her, we could hear her breath sucking through her mouth, we could see her heart laboring beneath her silk dress, but even as we went to her she shuddered and was still.
>
> (288)

Davis is clearly able to do both things: in stories such as 'To Reiterate', to draw attention to words, phrases and their cadenced arrangement for a particular, often surprising sense, and in stories like the 'The Great-Grandmothers', to conjure vivid images that the aptly chosen words bring forth.

In *Essays One*, her first collection of critical and autobiographical writing, Davis makes several remarks that will be helpful both to a reading of her novel and to a surer grasp of its relation to Proust. One essay in particular is crucial in this respect. In 'Fragmentary or Unfinished', Davis considers writers who have practised the art of the literary fragment – Jourbet, Mallarmé, Barthes and others. Her conclusion is that fragmentary writing's frisson is that it promotes interruption (both of subject matter and reading process), and thereby 'keeps returning the reader not only to the real world but also to a consciousness of his or her own mind at work' (*Essays* 222). In other words, the literary fragment is self-conscious writing par excellence because it acts as a mirror for the reader's mind to take note of its own sense-making, enabling it to witness the process of meaning unfolding. The literary fragment is the place where language is most ostentatious, and, in Davis's assessment, 'It can be seen as a response to the philosophical problem of seeing the written thing replace the subject of the writing' (225). What Davis is suggesting here is that the fragment – and, clearly, her own writing – is valuable for the way it discloses the written as a construction, a vehicle that carries meaning, and which drives right over the illusion of the text 'as invisible purveyor of meaning' (222). The fragment, because it does not pretend to be a complete 'picture' of something, is 'less of an illusion, therefore paradoxically more realistic' (Davis 213).

There is a contradiction, one implicit in all writing concerned with seeing, lurking within these claims: for if the fragment is a way to respond to the problem of 'seeing the written thing replace the subject of the writing', then it responds to this problem by posing it in a new way. The fragment captures a small part of its subject, but, as Davis concludes: 'We have written about it, written it, and allowed it to live on at the same time, allowed it to live on in our ellipses, in our silences' (225). In other words, we see the subject of the fragment *through the gaps* in representation that it necessitates, and yet, because of these gaps, we cannot help but take notice of the fragment itself.

In *The End of the Story*, the subject, I want to suggest in this chapter, is forgetting, and Davis's fragmentary novel allows us to glimpse forgetting's elliptical agency. Incorporating its own process of composition, this novel is fragmentary without ceasing to be a story with discernible plot. The narrator continually shifts between recalling scenes from the past and returning back to her present moment of writing the novel, while also relating the difficulties she has (and has had) writing it. The plot concerns her quest for the young man, both in her own elusive memories and in her struggle to write about her past self's time with him. It is true, as Jonathan Evans has pointed out, that 'Davis subverts the teleological goal of Proust's novel in her own writing', but not for the reason that Evans gives, namely that she is 'writing a narrative that has no goal to reach other than its own telling' (175). I want to suggest that Davis's novel subverts the teleology in Proust for a different reason: whereas Marcel's goal is to rise above Lethe's waters upon anamnestic waves arisen by the tremors of involuntary memory, the goal of Davis's narrative lies in its attempt *to write forgetting* – an attempt that encompasses the effort of composition.

This chapter attempts to shed light on the darkness always implicit in the ekphrastic writing of memory's images, a darkness to which Davis's novel is especially attuned. A consideration of *The End of the Story* alongside Proust's *Search*, however, also needs to take stock of Samuel Beckett, whose work is a key intertextual presence in Davis's writing. The chapter will thus close with a coda that triangulates Proust, Beckett and Davis, suggesting the ways that, when placing Proust and Davis's writing over the foil of Beckett's, 'our eye', in Nancy's wonderful phrase, 'begins to hear' ('The Image' 86).

'As I was then and as I am now'

I have suggested that *The End of the Story* both shares certain features with Proust's *Search* and departs from it in significant ways. What it shares most with Proust's novelistic model is its questioning approach to identity. Perhaps the most poignant observation about Proustian identity comes from Beckett's classic essay, *Proust* (1931). 'We are not merely more weary because of yesterday', Beckett writes, 'we are other, no longer what we were before the calamity of yesterday' (3). Paraphrasing Marcel, he continues, 'The aspirations of yesterday were valid for yesterday's ego, not for to-day's ... The subject has died – and perhaps many times – on the way' (3).[4] *The End of the Story* is likewise peppered with passages where the narrator reflects upon the difference between herself as present narrator and her past self as 'another' character, whose story she is presently fashioning. Indeed, the narrator (who is nameless in the novel, as is the young man who haunts its pages) at one point observes:

> At times the novel seems to be a test of myself, both as I was then and as I am now. In the beginning, the woman was not like me, because if she had been, I could not have seen the story clearly. After a while, when I was more used to telling the story, I was able to make the woman more like me.
>
> (52)

In Proust, Marcel mourns the death(s) of his old self as he narratively navigates his past; in Davis's novel, however, this self-othering operates even at the level of the narrator's present – that is, in her writing the *process* of writing the story. Unlike Marcel, Davis's narrator is a lot less certain of how to go about telling the story in the way it needs to be told. The novel thus consists of two narratives: one story is about the narrator's memory-quest for the young man with whom she had a brief romance, and another story is the narrator's telling of this story and the myriad difficulties she faces not only in writing it but also in remembering things accurately. The hardest thing about writing, she says, is doubt, specifically doubt about the order in which to place the story's events. There is something almost Beckettian in her voicing of the struggle to write and remember: 'I still find myself forgetting things I had intended to do, and doing things I had not planned to do. I find myself doing things sooner than I had planned to do them: Oh, I say to myself, so I'm already at *this* stage' (85). As the novel is taking her several years to complete, the narrator manages to capture the uncanniness of self-narration, an uncanniness emerging out of forgetting's darkening:

> At times I have the feeling someone else is working on this with me. I read a passage I haven't looked at in weeks and I don't recognize much of it, or only dimly, and I say to myself, Well, that's not bad, it's a reasonable solution to *that*

---

[4] Marcel often admits that his greatest horror has always been the thought of a future where his present (already past) self will die, taking with it the joys that he holds (or once held) so dear: 'it would be in a real sense the death of the self, a death followed, it is true, by resurrection, but in a different self, to the love of which the elements of the old self that are condemned to die cannot bring themselves to aspire' (*Within a Budding Grove* 288).

problem. But I can't quite believe I was the one who found the solution. ... I have the curious feeling that my decision of several months ago was made by someone else. Now there has been a consensus and I am suddenly more confident: if she had the same plan, it must be a good one.

(67)

This kind of uncertainty is caused, I have suggested, by her compulsion to tell what happened as accurately as she can, making her all the more aware of the way in which narrative (an envisioned story-shape) will often mould memory in its own image.

Proust's novel is, of course, not blind to this 'moulding' aspect of self-narration. Marcel is aware of story's demands for order and coherence, demands which memory hardly obeys; as he puts it, 'our memory does not as a rule present things to us in their chronological sequence but as it were by a reflection in which the order of the parts is reversed' (*Within a Budding Grove* 176). But in Davis's narrative this awareness operates at a much greater intensity. As Evans argues, the conclusion of the *Search* gives Proust's novel 'a unity and a teleology' (the artistic maturation of its narrator) but in Davis's case, 'It is as if the narrator of *The End of the Story* would like to arrive at the epiphanic conclusion that Proust's narrator does, but at the same time cannot' (186). Indeed, the ending that she does arrive at is perhaps the very antithesis of epiphany.

W. C. Dowling offers the following description, using Aristotle's terms, of a customary understanding of narrative endings:

> [T]he reader is always conscious of viewing events through the eyes of a narrator who, knowing the story as a whole, is already viewing the outcome as an order of moral or ethical significance. *Telos* thus becomes a movement toward that moment of *anagnorisis* or recognition when those following the story will have revealed to them what the narrator has known from the outset.

(49)

This is certainly true of the *Search*, where the massive eruption of writing that makes up the novel is crowned by the final metaphor of Time ekphrastically captured upon a vast 'canvas' of the past. *The End of the Story*, however, proceeds quite differently. The novel *opens* with its ending: the narrator describes how, several years earlier, while touring with a friend in the desert near the West Coast of the United States, she decided to visit the young man's apartment. After a long time spent walking around an unnamed city, she tracks it down but discovers he no longer lives there and, exhausted, decides to rest inside a nearby bookshop. The bookseller, seeing that she is tired, offers her a cup of tea. The tea (and here we start to notice the novel's uncertain relationship with Proust's text) is very bitter and parches her tongue. The novel's conclusion then revisits this scene, as the narrator tells us:

> I have not moved the cup of bitter tea from the beginning, so it may make sense to say the end of the story is the cup of bitter tea brought to me in the bookstore as I sat in a chair too tired to move after searching so long for his last address. Yet I still feel it is the end, and I think I know why now.
>
> (235)

The moment of anagnorisis, such as it is, is now disclosed: the reason that this scene seems like the right ending, she says, is that this was the last time that she searched for the young man, and a stranger's offering her a cup of tea seemed to be 'a ceremonial act, as though the offer of a cup of tea became a ceremonial act as soon as there was a reason for ceremony, even if the tea was cheap and bitter' (236). Why is this significant? Not least because Proust's novel *begins* with a cake dunked in a cup of tea that opens Marcel's eyes to memories hidden in forgetting's depths, whereas Davis's novel begins with a cup of tea that also ends the story, and, far from heralding painterly visions of memories to come, the black of bitter tea portends the oblivion with which the narrator will have had to contend.

By way of the conjunction 'or'

There are other, discreet ways in which Davis's text engages critically with Proust. After her final break-up with the young man, the narrator describes her difficulty falling asleep, and states, as if in wry homage: 'I could not go to bed early' (167). Unlike Marcel, she is not privy to memory's secrets disclosed by involuntary prompts. Towards the end of the novel, while driving home from a party where she had hoped to see the young man, she stops at a traffic light in the early hours of the quiet morning, and 'music came suddenly from somewhere very loud in the stillness and then stopped just as suddenly, and I felt two or three things coming together to reveal something to me. Then there was no revelation, after all, only a blank space' (215).[5] Indeed, reading this novel one has

---

[5] There is one moment in the *Search* where Marcel encounters a similar 'blank space' within him, instead of the revelation gifted by involuntary memory. This occurs during his stay in Balbec, while riding in Mme de Villeparisis's carriage with his grandmother: the carriage passes by a driveway with three trees and Marcel is convinced that the trees are about to reveal something important about his past: 'I looked at the three trees; I could see them plainly, but my mind felt that they were concealing something which it could not grasp' (*Within a Budding Grove* 343). Then: 'In their simple and passionate gesticulation I could discern the helpless anguish of a beloved person who has lost the power of speech, and feels that he will never be able to say to us what he wishes to say and we can never guess' (345).

the sense that the narrator is uncommonly attuned to the presence of these kinds of 'blank spaces' in her memory.

This is not to suggest that there are no prose pictures to be found in *The End of the Story* – only that they are few and far between. Davis's novel is unique in this respect: it is a novel written by a writer who has an intimate connection with Proust, and, as Christopher J. Knight puts it, a writer for whom 'memory is central' ('Lydia Davis's Investigation' 210). The reason it is unique – certainly in terms of this book's argument – is that unlike Proust, Nabokov and the other writers whose ekphrastic picturing we have already sighted, Davis's novel is far more sceptical of writing's ability to make present, in her own phrase, the elusive 'landscape of memory' (*Essays* 478). Davis, in fact, mentions Nabokov's autobiography in her essay 'Remembering the Van Wagenens'. This essay, characteristically enough, consists of fragments thematically tied, of which the following paragraph about Nabokov is an example: '*Speak, Memory*, by Nabokov, in which the raw matter of his memory was developed and refined by the efflorescence of his language into more than it ever was in itself. He did not remember as much as he said. *The memories grew in his language*' (my emphasis 487). In Davis's essay about the past, however, memories are seldom permitted this kind of flourishing growth. Rather than depicting the eponymous neighbours, the essay is preoccupied with meditations upon her *failure* to remember them. Examining a carton of old family papers, Davis reflects that it can be said to contain 'a thick pile of thin sheets of memory – since each piece of paper … or almost each one, yields a bit of memory or large piece of memory' (486). Upon examining her own memory, however, she admits: 'where there should be a memory there is often a blank' (482).

Davis is wary of mnemonic description, particularly of imaginary memories growing in language, as she claims (erroneously or not) happens in Nabokov's autobiography. Orhan Pamuk's distinction between the 'verbal' and the 'visual' novelist is worth revisiting at this point. Pamuk, we recall, thinks of some writers' work as 'addressing our verbal imagination', while others 'speak more powerfully to our visual imagination'. Where, upon these axes of 'verbal' and 'visual', do we place Davis's writing? To answer this question, we can turn to Davis's own view on the matter. In 'Fragmentary or Unfinished', she describes reading two types of literary texts, depending on her mood:

> I read *Anna Karenina* in somewhat the same way I read Stephen King's *Firestarter* in the sense that I lose sight of the text as artifact, the text becomes invisible, and I also lose sight of myself – my thinking mind, my discriminating mind. I lose

my self as I lose myself in certain kinds of movies: the illusion is complete, the fiction has more reality than I do …

The other way I read is the way I read when I read a work in which the text itself remains visible and present to me, an object of interest by its language and/or form; and in these cases I remain present to myself as well (i.e., conscious of my own thoughts).

(*Essays* 222–223)

Davis gives two examples from Flaubert's oeuvre: *Madame Bovary*, she says, is an example of the first kind of text, while *Bouvard and Pécuchet* represents the other kind. 'I could also imagine', she adds, 'that it is easier to make a movie from a written work in which the text disappears – for me, *Madame Bovary* – than from one in which the text is foregrounded as object of interest' (223). We have seen that when it comes to her own writing, Davis is capable of engaging the reader's mind in both ways. 'To Reiterate', a tightly constructed game with polysemy in verbs like 'read', 'write', 'translate' and 'travel', is a work where the text is very much 'visible and present' to us. 'The Great-Grandmothers', on the other hand, allows us to lose ourselves in its weird, intensely vivid reality.

The End of the Story is concerned with achieving both kinds of effects, but here the 'verbal' novelist within Davis carries the day over the 'visual'. This is already apparent in the novel's opening paragraph. It presents us with a visual scene, but one beset by uncertainty:

The last time I saw him, though I did not know it would be the last, I was sitting on the terrace with a friend and he came through the gate sweating, his face and chest pink, his hair damp, and stopped politely to talk to us. He crouched on the red-painted concrete *or* rested on the edge of a slatted wooden bench.

(my emphasis 3)

There is something very peculiar about the conjunction 'or' when it appears in a visual description. It is a moment of double take – 'or' jumps out before our reading eye as our imagining of this scene is upset by the sense of uncertainty that 'or' propagates. We are compelled to picture *two* eventualities – the young man crouching on the red concrete *or* resting on the edge of a wooden bench – but we cannot visualize them simultaneously, as a single image. As we read on, we discover that 'or' keeps upsetting the narrator's descriptions of her memories of the young man. Recalling the first time she met him at a party, her account is full of uncertainty: 'I'm not sure whether we walked on dirt or asphalt, what we passed, or how he walked next to me, whether awkwardly or gracefully, quickly or slowly, close to me or a few feet away' (16). Soon, this game of either/or becomes almost comical. The narrator and the young man arrive at her house, and this is how she describes their walk along the driveway:

> Now I walked ahead of him, and by the front wall he lifted a stem of thorns that hung down from an overgrown climbing rose so that I could pass without scratching myself. Or maybe he couldn't have done this in the dark, and it was on another day, in the daylight. Or it was that night, but the night was not entirely dark. In fact, it is only *dark in my memory* of that particular night, because I know there were two bright streetlamps nearby: one of them shone into my room.
>
> (my emphasis 18)

One would certainly be surprised to find this kind of profusion of 'or' in Proust's writing. Its effect is not only to add verisimilitude to Davis's (or, rather, the narrator's) narration of memory (after all, we do tend to forget how much we tend to forget when talking about the past). More importantly, 'or' brings the writing itself before our eyes as we scan the page, interrupting the mind's picturing of these scenes and introducing doubt where it is not accustomed to appear.

The young man is allied with 'or' in the narrator's story. Her uncertainty about the accuracy of her recollections is most acute whenever she is trying to verbally evoke his presence. At times, our inner eye does encounter the kinds of ekphrastic images that characterize Proustian narration. For instance, the narrator here verbally frames the view from her study window: 'If I looked up from my work, I saw dark green pine branches waving slowly against the sky, a shrub of rich red roses beyond the trees, rubbery, arching spears of succulents with serrated edges, and the soft powdery dirt scattered with pinecones at the base of the tall cypress that leaned away from my house' (27). When it comes to her descriptions of the young man, however, the most detailed (suggestively) is presented with the aid of a photograph. 'The only photograph I have of him', the narrator says, 'shows him frowning at me from a distance of about fifteen feet. He is on a sailboat belonging to a cousin of mine, he is bending over, his hands are busy, perhaps fastening a rope, and he is looking up sideways at me, frowning. The picture is not very sharp' (64). Elsewhere, we learn that he has reddish-gold hair, freckles, prominent cheekbones and blue eyes, is stocky and athletic, and usually wears either 'white painter's pants, or blue jeans torn at the cuffs', either 'a red plaid lumber jacket, or a light blue flannel shirt' (12–13).

In sum, the novel presents us with few ekphrases of moments past, and, whenever it does so, the conjured sights are often dispelled – *veiled* – by the presence of 'or'. In this way, Davis's text makes palpable the sense of absence that haunts every ekphrasis of memory's sightings. It reminds the reader not only of memory's frailty and imperfect recall, but more importantly of the medium of expression through which memory can be made to speak. The text as 'artifact', to borrow Davis's own term, makes itself present, and, by doing so, it exposes what Peter Boxall has referred to as 'a finely tuned dialectic between presence and absence, between limpid, luminous expression and a kind of darkness that … is part of the expressive mechanism of narrative itself' (*Value of Novel* 61). Over the course of this book, I have argued that the language of fiction about memory is made anxious by visuality: the visual is that possibility towards which literary discourse can only imperfectly aspire, especially when it is claiming to 'outdo' the visual. Ekphrastic writing, as Proust, Nabokov, Sebald, Smith and Lerner practise it, seeks to efface itself, so that the images being conjured before the reader's eye appear all the more 'present', but it is also writing that draws attention to itself, whenever it is heard euphoniously by the ear as well as noticed by the eye. As Derrida aptly remarks: 'reading proceeds in no other way. It listens in watching' (*Memoirs of the Blind* 2). It is precisely at the site (and in sight) of ekphrastic text that hearing and watching appear to become one. In Davis's text, however, we encounter something different: a writing of memory that seeks to forestall this reconciliation.

The blind side of the image

In a chapter titled 'Speaking is not Seeing', from *The Infinite Conversation*, Maurice Blanchot is critical of a visual conception of mimesis, where '[t]he novelist lifts up the rooftops and gives his characters over to a penetrating gaze' (29).[6] What Blanchot is after, and what he was arguably attempting to do in his own fiction, is to give voice to the kind of speech that, in his words, 'frees thought from the optical imperative that in the Western tradition, for thousands of years, has subjugated our approach to things, and induced us to think under

---

[6] Peter Brooks believes visual mimesis to be at the heart of realism in the novel: 'Removing housetops in order to see the private lives played out beneath them: the gesture … suggests how centrally realist literature is attached to the visual, to looking at things, registering their presence in the world through sight' (*Realist Vision* 3).

the guaranty of light or under the threat of its absence' (27).[7] And, crucially, he adds, '[T]here is a speech in which things, not showing themselves, do not hide' (29). A speech, that is, which does not attempt to depict, and yet still unveils things, allowing them to come out from their hiding within absence.

I would argue that Blanchot's description of a kind of speaking (and, by extension, writing) that does not show us things but neither does it hide them is a fitting way to describe the uncertainly ekphrastic description of mnemonic images that Davis's novel stages. This will become clearer if we turn to Blanchot's intricate definition of 'image': 'The image is what veils by revealing; it is the veil that reveals by reveiling in all the ambiguous indecision of the world reveal … it is a folding, a turn of the turning, the "version" that is always in the process of inverting itself and that in itself bears the back and forth of a divergence' (30). Ekphrasis similarly 'veils by revealing', in the sense that it veils the originative image with language and, in so doing, presents it as a figure – an image, for Blanchot, is what 'permits to be figured' (30) – revealing it to the reader's eye in verbal form. Blanchot's characterization of the image as 'a folding, a turn of the turning' might also be read as evocative of the spiral of ekphrastic hope and ekphrastic fear that, I have argued, operates in even the most self-assured of memory's descriptions. 'Revealing implies', Blanchot continues, 'that something shows that did not show itself' (29). The something that 'shows' itself whenever we interrogate ekphrastic description, I want to suggest, is the impossible possibility of visuality in prose discourse, and Davis's text makes this aporetic nature of visual writing palpably felt.

In this respect, the novel's representation of the young man may be seen to pose the question of the very possibility of verbal picturing. But the aporetic nature of this representation – with the conjunction 'or' repeatedly staging ekphrastic aporia – also sheds its own dark illumination. It illuminates, that is, the blind side of every image: the 'dark' side against which an image is staged, of which it forms a part, and from which the image can never sever itself. Perhaps this is why the narrator associates the young man alternately with darkness and with light. She relates how, before she learnt the young man's name, he seemed less substantial to her, and 'came and went through darkness and shadow more than light' (38). Later in the story, attending a poetry reading where they were

---

[7] Davis has translated six of Blanchot's literary and philosophical texts. See Jonathan Evans's essay, 'Translation and Response between Maurice Blanchot and Lydia Davis' for an overview of Davis's translations, as well as a fascinating analysis of how her short text, 'Story', engages critically with Blanchot's 'The Madness of the Day', which Davis has also translated. For Davis's own reflections on Blanchot's canny writing, see *Essays* 367–370 and 380–384.

to meet, she is anxious that he will not come and sees darkness: 'Because I did not know where he was, I located him in all of the large darkness, filling it, as though I had to make him large enough to fill the darkness and the night' (198). Elsewhere, she remembers him as being in the light: 'It was dark outside, where I was, and light inside, in his rooms' (152); 'I could see him sitting in the office that was so fluorescent in the darkness it was like a showcase where he was behind glass, flooded with light' (157). The narrator's struggle to hold 'his image' before her mind's eye, while she writes her memories, is the very theme of this novel, her reason for writing it; yet it is a goal that always recedes, veiling itself from her sight. Reading this novel, it is as though we were witnessing the struggle between light/revealing and dark/concealing that inheres (without, however, always being visible) in every mnemonic description.

Near the end of the story, this is how the narrator assesses her writing about the past:

> The center is missing, the original is gone, all that I try to form around it may not resemble the original very much. I am thinking of some example from the natural world in which the living thing dies and then leaves a husk, sheath, carapace, shell, or fragment of rock casing imprinted with its form that falls away from it and outlasts it.
>
> (176–177)

This is a fascinating metaphor for writing the past, and the reason it fascinates has to do with the density of absence it captures: few objects express absence or, which is almost the same thing, the desire for presence as well as an empty shell. As Nancy puts it, '[t]he absence of the imaged subject is nothing other than an intense presence, receding into itself, gathering itself together in its intensity' (*Ground of the Image* 9). There is a singular image in the novel that captures this intensity of absence: the narrator describes how she would sometimes manage to dream about the young man by thinking of him before falling asleep, conjuring 'his image standing in a well-lit place, against the wall of a room. I had him there, though he looked irritated, but as I began to fall asleep, of his own accord he turned and walked away, out of my sight' (192–193). Startled awake and saddened at having lost his image, she writes: 'Even though he was only an image, he had his own feelings, and he was there under protest, and as soon as I grew too weak to hold him, he walked away out of my sight' (193). In the narrator's summoning of the young man before her mind's eye, his very image protests this summoning, as his absence refuses the presence she seeks to give him. And neither are *we* given much of a description of his image: all we see is an abstract male figure standing irritably against the wall of a well-lit room. As Nancy puts it, 'giving presence means giving to someone who is not there something that one cannot give him ... The image gives a presence that it lacks ... and it gives it to something that, being absent, cannot receive it' (*Ground of the Image* 66). The absent cannot receive the presence the image gives them – yet writing memory cannot help but assign the absent what falls short of presencing them. The way in which Davis's narrator differs from the other fictional memoirists whose stories we have read is in showing how, when writing (and reading) memory, in Blanchot's words, 'what reveals itself does not give itself up to sight, just as it does not take refuge in simple invisibility' (29).

In Davis, we are not presented with lengthy ekphrases of the young man, certainly not the kind of indelible descriptions which we've encountered in Proust, Nabokov, Sebald and Smith. Instead of verbal portraits of the absent, what the novel makes present is the sense of absence the narrator is experiencing. The following passage, for instance, may be read as illuminating the blind side of descriptive language, the darkening that always puts it in danger:

> Waiting for him again that night, when he would not come, created a dark space like a large room, a room that opened into the night from my room and filled it with dark draughts of air. Because I did not know where he was, the city seemed larger, and seemed to come right into my room: he was in some place, and that place, though unknown to me, was present in my mind and was a large dark thing inside me. And that place, that strange room where he was, where I imagined him to be, with another person, became part of him, too, as I imagined him, so that he was changed, he contained the strange room and I contained it, too, because I contained him in that room and that room in him.
>
> (117)

Where exactly, in this image, is the young man? He is in a room somewhere the narrator cannot see, which is also somewhere within her, a dark 'place' that blooms inside her mind and that darkens this description, clause by clause. 'The absent', Nancy suggests, 'are not there, are not "in images". But they are imaged: their absence is woven into our presence. The empty place of the absent is a place that is not empty: that is the image' (*Ground of the Image* 68). The absence of the young man, that is, is presented as a darkness, a 'place' that is inside the narrator herself and one that only her *writing* presences.

In the narrator's earlier metaphor, her writing was depicted as an empty shell, a carapace with no living occupant: the absent young man acts the lacuna around which she forms the 'casing' that is her narrative. As this metaphor implies, he is gone (from her present) and all that may be salvaged of him is the ghostly mark that his past presence 'imprints' on the inside of her narrative about him. The reason that the (story) shape she forms around his absent image 'may not resemble the original very much' is because this shape reflects her *own* presence, in writing the story, as much as it indicates his absence. In Benjamin's wonderfully fitting image, every story 'bears the marks of the storyteller much as the earthen vessel bears the marks of the potter's hand' (*Illuminations* 159). It is precisely in this sense that the young man's absence becomes woven into the narrator's presence.

Following forgetting's arrow

'In Proust', Evans suggests, 'memory is more of a possibility for creation than something to be interpreted or a site of multiple possibilities' (180). It would be more precise to say, though, that it is *forgetting* that acts as Marcel's 'possibility for creation'. We have seen that the Proustian conception of memory is Bergsonian, in the sense that the 'cone' of memory has ever-present depths of which we remain unconscious, but which accompany us throughout our lives. It is out of these depths that involuntary prompts retrieve Marcel's forgotten experiences; as he puts it, 'the better part of our memories exists outside us, in a blatter of rain, in the smell of an unaired room or of the first crackling brushwood fire in a cold grate: wherever, in short, we happen upon what our mind, having no use for it, had rejected' (*Within a Budding Grove* 254). Habit is to blame for these rejections because it dulls perception; as Beckett aptly observes, 'Strictly speaking, we can only remember what has been registered by our extreme inattention and stored in that ultimate and inaccessible dungeon of our being to which Habit does not possess the key' (*Proust* 18). This 'ultimate and inaccessible dungeon' is forgetting, what Ricoeur has called the 'reserve' upon which memory draws. Marcel thus qualifies his original claim: 'Outside us? Within us, rather, but hidden from our eyes in an oblivion more or less prolonged. It is thanks to this oblivion alone that we can from time to time recover the person that we were' (254).

Davis seems to share this conception as can be seen in her comment from 'Remembering the Van Wagenens': 'Memories creating three-dimensional space – recent memories shallow space, older memories deeper space, oldest memories deepest space' (*Essays* 489). But she differs from Proust in what her writing gravitates towards in its approach to the 'three-dimensional spaces' of time past. Her novel departs from Proustian narration in one crucial respect: whereas Marcel derives the impetus to write from, in his own words, 'having extracted from myself and brought to light something that was hidden in my inner darkness' (*Within a Budding Grove* 364), Davis's narrator seeks to *represent* her own 'inner darkness'. The novel may be read, in this sense, as a story that progresses from one moment of darkness to another, stitching together these moments of un-remembering, sentence by sentence.

Forgetting, as paradoxical as this may sound, has *agency* in Davis's writing. When dealing with paradoxes, Blanchot is always helpful: 'Forgetting causes *language* to rise up in its entirety by gathering it around the forgotten thing' (my emphasis 194). Forgetting, that is, causes the verbal to congeal over the absent visual, placing language under the spotlight of consciousness. (It is difficult to be a visual writer, when you are writing about forgetting.) In *The End of the Story*, forgetting is sounded in every appearance of 'or' that continually qualifies, unsettles and interrupts the narrator's story. This uncertain conjunction appears so frequently in the novel's pages that it seems to possess a will of its own, producing speculation (as writing) seemingly for the sake of voicing it. Evans – who, like myself, thinks of *The End of the Story* as 'a Proustian novel' (175) – suggests that Davis's 'writing is a way of investigating the past, putting into words a process of remembering it' (177). But we might equally say that this novel voices the process of *failing* to remember the past. For instance, after the narrator has described her visit to the young man's garage, she thus annotates forgetting's operation:

> I did not visit him in his garage again after that, as far as I can remember. I did not help him move, when he moved a month or two later … I can't remember just when the move was. I think I was away, I think I had gone back East. There was a dispute surrounding the move. *Either* he owed rent, *or* the landlord did not like him, *or* a friend came back and claimed the place, *or* that friend *or* a different friend was angry about the books, *either* that they had been left behind in the garage *or* that they had not been left, *or* that the landlord had kept them, *or* that they had been damaged, *or* that some were missing.
>
> (my emphasis 96)

The first few sentences relate common enough expressions of uncertainty in the recollection of particular events. Beginning with the first appearance of 'either', however, the proliferation of either/or verges on the absurd. The narrator appears to be belabouring the point: *all* of these are indeed possibilities. The question is: what narrative purpose does this comical parataxis of the unverifiable serve?

An answer suggests itself if we return to Blanchot's thoughts on forgetting. The first comment Blanchot makes is reminiscent of Proust's own conception: 'Forgetting is the very vigilance of memory, the guardian force thanks to which the hidden of things is preserved' (315). Davis's novel, I have suggested, seeks to *write* this vigilance. However, Blanchot goes on to say: 'what is forgotten is a marker enabling a slow advance: the arrow designating *direction*' (my emphasis 315). In memory's narration, the 'arrow' of forgetting initially points backwards towards the past, guiding the mind to an approximation of what it seeks after, should memory become restored to it. (In Proust, it could also be said to be pointing forwards, in that the narrated Marcel has had to *await* future moments of involuntary revelations of the forgotten – but ever present – past.) In Davis's novel, on the other hand, forgetting's 'arrow', in a circular loop, points back at itself: 'What is forgotten points at once toward the thing forgotten and toward forgetting, the most profound effacement where the site of metamorphosis is found' (Blanchot 315). When the narrator indulges her whims of 'or', we glimpse precisely this: an effacement of memory, where the only thing left to do is let what has been forgotten metamorphose into shadows of what might have been. In Knight's fitting figure, 'For Davis, the past is never a simple thing; rather, it always shadows forth its eidolonic others, those silent footfalls that echo in our memories and are approached via imagination' (210). What could have happened and what may have been misremembered are indeed 'eidolonic', ghosting the narrator's story. But her story does not merely capture these spectral realms of 'or'; it also gives voice to writing's uncertainty, which happens to be its vigilance.

The narrator, when trying to recall the house where she saw the young man at a party, presents us with yet another glimpse of 'the site of metamorphosis' that is forgetting, a site productive of words:

> These memories are sometimes correct, I know, but sometimes confused, a table in the wrong room, though I keep moving it back to where it belongs, a bookcase gone and another in its place, a light shining where it never shone, a sink shifting a foot from where it was, even, in one memory, an entire wall absent in order to make the room twice as large.
>
> (233)

Why might a forgotten room need to be 'twice as large'? Surely because, as Mary Warnock suggests, 'the story is a construct, a work of art; and that is why memory by itself, without imagination is not enough. The peculiar value we attach to discursive memory, the recollection of what things were like, seems to derive from its connection with imagination in the developing story of a life'

(127). This is certainly the case, but Davis's novel also shows us that memory's possibility, the site of its unfolding, is grounded on forgetting; and forgetting itself may only be *heard* as it sounds in narration's rhythm – unseen.

A difficult promise

In the final pages, summing up her effort to tell the story as accurately as possible, the narrator confesses:

> There are some inconsistencies. I say he was open to me, and I say he was closed to me. I say he was silent with me, and that he was talkative. That he was modest, and arrogant. That I knew him well, and that I did not understand him. … Either all these things were true at different times or I remember them differently depending on my mood now.
>
> (234)

There is a see-sawing rhythm about this paragraph, one that characterizes the entire novel: a vacillation between the poles of either/or, both telling the story and questioning its telling. The young man keeps receding from the narrator's grasp, only revealing glimpses of himself as our eyes peer through black marks on the page after him. Yet the text keeps foregrounding itself. After dreaming of the young man, the narrator says, '[S]omewhere in my brain there must be a clear memory of his face that is hidden most of the time and is uncovered once, like a photograph, in the dream' (139). Nowhere in the novel do we find this kind of uncovering – we see only glimpses. Describing her conversations with the young man on the telephone, the narrator says that she could then 'bring him so close to me that his voice was in my ear, his thin voice coming through a wire into my ear like a face inside my head' (182). This is a very fitting metaphor of ekphrastic hope: ekphrasis, too, is a voice that promises to become a sight. But this is a promise that the novel defers, so that we are left listening to the narrator's voice as it follows forgetting's arrow, ever seeking the unremembered, probing its way blindly but not without giving insight.

The insight that it imparts to this book's reading of ekphrastic narratives is the light it sheds on what lies beneath, what foils (like the invisible metal inside a mirror) the visual. *The End of the Story* illuminates what *voices* memory: the text lighting its way. It can be said to stage, to borrow Nancy's phrase, 'a vision operating as a mode of listening' ('The Image' 79). Prose pictures image by being heard; while reading, as Derrida put it, we listen in watching. Let us again listen in watching, then, as the narrator describes the young man's recurring periods of silence: 'His vast silence seemed as heavy as a cloud pressing down on a landscape that shrinks beneath its bulk, every living thing bending to the ground, continuing to wait in the airless presence of that awful cloud' (213). Silence is here being imaged as something that darkens sight. The absence of sound is made palpable as a cloud which oppresses, and this metaphor is representative of what happens to our reading (both hearing and seeing) in the novel as a whole. Nancy argues that a consideration of any type of image 'cannot stop at the visual any more than at the auditory … We should only say: the one rhythms the other' ('The Image' 87). This is because '[t]he image draws me into the rhythm it imprints in (the) sense(s) by cutting and opening sense anew. In its own way, the image then speaks … the image makes its own phrasing reverberate – it brings forth that mode of *ekphrasis* which pushes sound to the surface rather than positing sound upon it' (Nancy 83). Whereas in ekphrastic writing we are accustomed to seeing a prose picture, that, so to speak, has sound posited upon it by the text, the way an image may *speak* to us is only by emphasizing the sound that voices it at the expense of itself. This is precisely what happens in the novel, where ekphrasis – whenever it appears – rebounds (springs back, reverberates) to the rhythm of its own uncertain saying.

'Hear, simply hear'

One writer who is crucial to Davis, and whose presence in *The End of the Story* this chapter has so far not addressed, is Samuel Beckett.[8] Beckett's presence is clearly felt in *The End of the Story*: it can both be heard in the narration's cadences and seen in the narrator's imagery. For instance, the narrator recounts how, after the break-up, she would often read to distract her mind from dwelling on the young man: 'I did not choose books that really distracted me, only books that left part of my mind still free to wander away from what I was reading and search around restlessly for the same old bone to gnaw on' (178). Near the end of the story, she confesses to having thought about abandoning the novel altogether, with an allusion to the much-quoted refrain from *The Unnamable*: 'maybe I will become too exhausted to go on' (196). Returning us to the moment of wry

---

[8] For Davis's own assessment of Beckett's influence on her writing, see *Essays* 6–7. See also Jonathan Evans, *Many Voices of Lydia Davis* 135–138, where Evans discusses Davis's creative pastiche of Beckett's late novella, *Worstward Ho*, in her story 'Southward Bound, Reading *Worstward Ho*'.

homage to Proust, in the following passage the narrator's cadenced narration is Beckettian in its bodily references:

> I could not go to bed early. It was hard to get into bed and stop moving, and hardest of all to turn off the light and lie still. I could have covered my eyes and put earplugs in my ears, but that would not have helped. Sometimes I wanted to plug up my nostrils, too, and my throat, and my vagina.
>
> (167)

The one Beckett text that speaks most directly to *The End of the Story* is *Malone Dies*.[9] Moribund Malone has reached a point where memory and imagination have become indistinct. He is what Proust's Marcel might have become, had he lived on into senility and forgetfulness, exhausting the vast reserves of memory in writing. The older Marcel could be describing Malone in the following anticipation of the inevitable: 'It comes too soon, the moment when there is nothing left to wait for, when the body is fixed in an immobility which holds no fresh surprise in store, when one loses all hope' (*Within a Budding Grove* 561).[10] On the verge of death, Malone lies supine on his bed, in a room presumably his own. He gets tended to by a woman, whom he does not remember. He passes the time he has left by telling stories, wishing to prevent himself from thinking about himself. Occasionally, though, memories slip into his fictions. In the following concluding remarks on Beckett's novel, I want to focus on the ways in which it can be said to haunt Davis's own and reflect on why Beckett's writing is significant to a reading of prose pictures.

Let us consider some striking similarities. Firstly, there are the narrators' writing situations: both are isolated in their rooms (while writing her novel, for Davis's narrator; permanently, for Malone), and both reflect on the difficulties of writing their stories. Davis's narrator, for instance, admits: 'Now, even though I work on it almost every day, I still become confused and forget what I was doing when I left off the day before. I have to write instructions to myself on little cards' (22). Malone is on even more familiar terms with forgetting, constantly reminding the reader both of how much he is forgetting to tell and what he could not be bothered to tell. 'I have a short memory,' he confesses bathetically, 'My little finger glides before my pencil across the page and gives warning, falling over the edge, that the end of the line is near. … At first I did not write, I just said the

---

[9] See also James Baxter 231–236.
[10] See James H. Reid 117–137, where Reid examines how irony and allegory structure both *Malone Dies* and the *Search* (which Reid reads as a key intertext in Beckett's writing). See also Garin Dowd for a fascinating discussion of how the 'image' in Proust was read by both Beckett and Deleuze and how Raúl Ruiz's 1999 adaptation of *Le Temps retrouvé* cinematically evokes Proust's narration.

thing. Then I forgot what I had said. A minimum of memory is indispensable, if one is to live really' (235). Malone's struggle is further compounded by forgetting what he has already written:

> I now add these few lines, before departing from myself again. I do not depart from myself now with the same avidity as a week ago for example. For this must be going on now for over a week ... since I said, I shall soon be quite dead at last, etc. Wrong again. That is not what I said, I could swear to it, that is what I wrote. This last phrase seems familiar, suddenly I seem to have written it somewhere before, or spoken it, word for word.
>
> (*Malone Dies* 237)

His writing is made still more difficult as even the light in his room is uncertain; in this strange illumination, he says, '[A]ll bathes, I will not say in shadow, nor even in half-shadow, but in a kind of leaden light than makes no shadow ... there is really no colour in this place except in so far as this kind of grey incandescence' (250). When Davis's narrator suffers the emotional tremors of the break-up, her room is presented in similarly dull tones: 'Real things in the room looked thin and transparent, part of a flat surface of colours and patterns lining the sides of the room' (148).

There are still louder echoes between the two texts. Both narrators pay attention to *sounds*, rendering what they hear as images sounds give to sight. Here is Davis's narrator:

> At night, the air, soft and fragrant, was clear of most of [the day's] noises, as it was clear of the hot sun and the profuse colors, as the plants, in the dark, were only soft shapes against the walls of buildings ... and through this emptier air I could hear wheels of the train clattering along the track and hoot of its whistle, as pure as its single yellow eye.
>
> (28–29)

One is here startled by the appearance of the concluding image – not unlike an absent-minded traveller crossing the tracks who, forewarned by a loud hoot, sees the 'single yellow eye' of an oncoming train. In Beckett, similarly, Malone describes lying in bed at night and listening to the noises outside his window:

> Then in my bed, in the dark, on stormy nights, I could tell from one another, in the outcry without, the leaves, the boughs, the groaning trunks, even the grasses and the house that sheltered me. Each tree had its own cry, just as no two whispered alike, when the air was still. ... There was nothing, not even the sand on the paths, that did not utter its cry.
>
> (234)

It is striking how easily one is able to visualize 'the leaves, the boughs, the groaning trunks', the grass and the sand, not least because the word used to conjure them is 'cry'.

My final example concerns the flat, almost two-dimensional description that we often find in both novels. In the aforementioned passage, where Davis's narrator states that she 'could not go to bed early', she goes on to describe her struggle to fall asleep:

> I would lie on my right side, my bony knees pressing together until they were bruised, the right on top of the left and then, when I turned over, the left on top of the right. I would turn on my back, then onto my stomach, first with my head on the pillow and then pushing the pillow aside and lying flat, then turning on my right side again, holding the pillow between my knees and arms, then turning onto my back again.
>
> (168)

In a very Beckettian gesture, the narrator is paratactically notating her movements, as if we were looking down upon her from the top and observing this restless geometry of the body.[11] Malone describes the character Macmann (earlier called Sapo) performing similar bodily permutations. When Macmann is caught in a downpour, he first decides to lie prostrate, reasoning that it is best to protect his back, which he thinks is more vulnerable from the damp ground. Then, when his front gets soaked,

> instead of springing up and hurrying on he turned over on his back, thus offering all his front to the deluge … his hat having remained in the place which his head had just left. For when, lying on your stomach in a wild and practically illimitable part of the country, you turn over on your back, then there is a sideways movement of the whole body, including the head, unless you make a point of avoiding it, and the head comes to rest at x inches approximately from where it was before, x being the width of the shoulders in inches, for the head is right in the middle of the shoulders.
>
> (274)

The strange effect of both descriptions is that, despite or perhaps because they aim to be so geometrically precise, they emphasize their cadenced narration instead of the images they are after. In Beckett's case, the degree of precision

---

[11] The narrator's description brings to mind similarly sketched figures in Beckett's 'Imagination Dead Imagine', where we find two bodies curled up foetally inside a white rotunda, around which the narrating voice guides us; see Beckett, *Texts for Nothing* 87–90.

becomes absurd, as the phrase 'at x inches *approximately*' implies that the shoulders' indeterminate width, 'x', could ever be in doubt and would ever even come into question when talking about a body's turning over. In effect, both passages stage text (narration) more than vision.

What I want to suggest, with the help of these examples, is that in Beckett and Davis the sense of hearing often plays the same if not a greater role than the sense of seeing. As Blanchot observes apropos of Beckett's *How It Is*: 'We find justified in Beckett's case the disappearance of every sign that would merely be a sign for the eye. Here the force of seeing is no longer what is required … Hear, simply hear' (329). Like the speaker's spare narration in that later work, Malone's narration undercuts prose's ability to picture, almost at every turn. Consider, for example, Malone's description of what he sees while looking out his window at night:

> I open my eyes and gaze unblinkingly at the night sky. So a tiny tot I gaped, first at the novelties, then at the antiquities. Between it and me the pane, misted and smeared with the filth of years. I should like to breathe on it, but it is too far away. It is such a night as Kaspar David Friedrich [*sic*] loved, tempestuous and bright. The name that comes back to me, those names. The clouds scud, tattered by the wind, across a limpid ground. If I had the patience to wait I would see the moon. But I have not.
>
> (224–225)

The allusion to Caspar David Friedrich is the kind of allusion to visual art that is de rigueur in Proust; in Beckett's text, however, its function is to give the reader a glimpse of what is missing. There will be no painterly visions here, the text appears to be telling us, misspelling the painter's name in the process. Reading this passage, we listen to a voice ('The name that comes back to me, those names') and only purblindly see prose's picturing (the scant details of the window being 'misted and smeared with filth', and clouds that 'scud, tattered by the wind, across a limpid ground').

In Beckett, Blanchot suggests, 'The term hearing would befit this act of approach better than reading' (329). Writing about *How It Is*, he continues, '[I]mages, in this narrative where there is almost nothing to see … have a fascinating force, as do the rare words corresponding to things that are representable and still capable of evoking them: *the sack the tins the mud the dark*. Strange, this need we have to see and to give to be seen that survives nearly all else' (330). Blanchot, in that important final sentence, points us towards the very heart of the matter of prose pictures, which haunt even those who would wish to escape their attraction. In

Malone Dies – where there are certainly more visual descriptions than in the descriptively meagre *How It Is* – whenever the few ekphrases do appear, they are certainly memorable. Malone, it should be said, would be the first to admit that he wants to be done with prose pictures; the following comments, concerning his opening story about Sapo, are to be read with not a little irony (certainly the first two sentences): 'For I want as little as possible of darkness in his story. A little darkness, in itself, at the time is nothing. You think no more about it and you go on. But I know what darkness is, it accumulates, thickens, then suddenly bursts and drowns everything' (215). This is an uncanny image of darkness, and it is not the only one to appear in the novel.[12] However, whenever our eye encounters the prose pictures that are there, they appear all the more striking. Towards the end of the novel, Malone hears an aeroplane pass noisily above his room, and this reminds him (or so it seems) of a childhood memory:

> It was above a racecourse, my mother held me by the hand. She kept saying, It's a miracle, a miracle. … One day we were walking along the road, a hill of extraordinary steepness, near home I imagine, my memory is full of steep hills, I get them confused. I said, The sky is further away than you think, is it not, mama? It was without malice, I was simply thinking of all the leagues that separated me from it. She replied, to me her son, It is precisely as far away as it appears to be. She was right. But at the time I was aghast. I can still see the spot, opposite Tyler's gate. … You could see the sea, the islands, the headlands, the isthmuses, the coast stretching away to the north and south and crooked moles of the harbour. We were on our way home from the butcher's. My mother? Perhaps it is just another story, told me by someone who found it funny.
> (305–306)

Malone's effort of recollection is not crowned by 'recognition', in Ricoeur's sense, because he can no longer be sure whether he is seeing memory's images, or simply recalling a story he once heard about somebody else. (I prefer to think that Malone is here describing a scene from his own childhood, one of the few left him to recall.)[13]

---

[12] There is a particularly unnerving description of encroaching darkness when Sapo sits by the kitchen window at the Lamberts': daylight filters into the dark kitchen and is immediately absorbed by the darkness within: 'it entered at every moment, renewed from without, entered and died at every moment, devoured by the dark. And at the least abatement of the inflow the room grew darker and darker until nothing in it was visible any more. For the dark had triumphed' (230).

[13] The same image also appears in Beckett's late novella *Company*: 'It is late afternoon and after some hundred paces the sun appears above the crest of the rise. Looking up at the blue sky and then at your mother's face you break the silence asking her if it is not in reality much more distant than it appears. The sky that is. The blue sky' (5).

The sense of seeing offered by Beckett's novel seems to be beyond ekphrastic hopes and ekphrastic fears because it is a 'seeing' not overly concerned with ocular sights. What is vital in Beckett's writing (of memory most of all) is located in its rhythm, what Blanchot wonderfully describes as 'a slightly accentuated movement or cadence marked by returns and at times by refrains. It is a tacit song' (329). However, even writing preoccupied by cadence and its song-like sounding of the limits of ocular representation cannot forgo visual imagery.[14] To invoke Beckett's *Ill Seen, Ill Said*: perhaps an author's wish to move aside from ekphrastic concerns is manifested as a quest to see what can be said when it is seen 'ill', and vice versa.

Davis's writing, and her singular novel most of all, is similarly concerned with saying the limits of seeing, and seeing the limits of saying. The young man's absence haunts the narrator with the possibility of his image becoming present, but this is forestalled – ill seen because ill said. Though, from a different perspective, something else is given us to be seen because it is so *well* said: this is forgetting, and forgetting's agency. By saying forgetting well, Davis's novel, like Beckett's *Malone Dies*, allows us to glimpse the invisible foil behind prose's picturing: the foil of voice that allows us to see both our own awareness reflected back to us by the text and the images that the text is conjuring whenever it becomes a screen where ekphrastic sights appear. For when that happens, there is no longer a mirror with its foil – only a frame through which we look, forgetful of words.

The most fragmentary and cadenced writing still sounds a 'rhythm [that] is always this, that one sensible order interrupts (itself) and resonates from another (or against the other of all the senses)', as Nancy has us observe ('The Image' 87–88). Hearing and seeing, voice and vision are always resonant of each other, and ekphrastic writing is veiled and unveiled within this resonance. Ekphrastic hope is the wish to deafen the voice, so that only the image remains present before the mind's eye; ekphrastic fear, on the other hand, is the knowing that voice may blind vision, that the text may engulf the scene it is conjuring.

This chapter has sought to address ekphrastic fear, the blind spot in visual writing that has haunted this book's argument from the start. But, as I hope to have shown by looking at Davis's writing of forgetting, it is a blind spot that sheds its own illumination.

---

[14] In Beckett's novel *Watt*, there are two striking ekphrases – in the customary modern definition as description of an artwork – of two paintings hanging up in Mr Erskine's room; see 109–111 and 219. I am grateful to Peter Boxall for reminding me of these text-produced pictures, long dormant in memory.

The image trembles … the shiver of that which oscillates and vacillates: it constantly leaves itself, for always already outside itself and always the inside of this outside, there is nothing in which it can be itself, being at the same time a simplicity that renders it more simple than other language, and in language being like the source from which it 'departs' – but because this source is the very force of a 'setting out', the streaming of the outside in (and through) writing.

(Blanchot 325)

The absent young man in Davis's novel – and in her narrator's quest for him as her language gropes after his absence – might be seen as expressive of that which haunts (and also that which produces) the sight of *enargeiac* vision staged at the site, within narrative, of ekphrastic prose. Like the actual sights that ekphrastic prose wants to conjure, the young man is outside the text, beyond its scope, and yet his ghostly image is found within it, as his absence produces the text's gaps and silences.

A prose picture is the textual site where the outside streams into writing, and it is also the sight that allows for this insight, caught up as it is in a ceaseless movement between outside and inside, image and text, as text mimetically plays at being a picture. The absent young man's image, veiled by forgetting, reveiled in writing, caught up in the uncertainty of 'or', expresses language's yearning for ocular vision – and the aporias with which it has to contend. Every writer of memory after Proust has had (and will have had) to face these aporias and singularly write through them. Prose pictures cannot give us ocular vision, but they do unveil to the mind's eye what a singular kind of literature alone conceals.

Conclusion

In László Krasznahorkai's novel *Satantango*, this is the opening sentence that first lets us see in hearing: 'One morning, near the end of October not long before the first drops of the mercilessly long autumn rains began to fall on the cracked and saline soil on the western side of the estate (later the stinking yellow sea of mud would render footpaths impassable and put the town too beyond reach) Futaki woke to hear bells' (3). The novel's descriptive opening pages are then recited at its conclusion, where we realize that the third-person narrator is no omniscient voice, but one of the inhabitants of the impoverished Hungarian village being described. In the final chapter, 'The Circle Closes', we thus find ourselves in the house of the village doctor. He takes up hammer, nails, planks and boards up his door against unwanted visitors. He sits down at his writing desk, facing the window: 'He gazed and thought, then suddenly his eyes brightened and he took out a new notebook' (271). Having abandoned his first attempts at describing what he had been patiently observing in the village over the past several days, he finally sees a way to write the story we are about to complete reading:

> He saw before him, as clear as if by magic, the path prepared for him, the way the fog swam up from either side of it and, in the middle of the narrow path, the luminous face of his future, its lineaments bearing the infernal marks of drowning. He reached for the pencil again and felt he was back on track now: there were enough notebooks, enough *pálinka*, his medication would last till spring at least and, unless the nails rotted in the door, no one would disturb him. Careful not to damage the paper, he started writing: 'One morning near the end of October not long before the first mercilessly long autumn rains began to fall on the cracked and saline soil on the western side of the estate …
>
> (272)

For Béla Tarr's cinematic adaptation, Krasznahorkai and Tarr (they collaborated on the screenplay) made a vital change to the novel's closing scene.[1] In the film

---

[1] Tarr's film is infamous for its length: 7 hours and 19 minutes of glacially paced black-and-white footage, capturing the bleak but mesmerizing world of Krasznahorkai's novel.

version of *Satantango*, the doctor nails up not only his door but boards up all the windows of his house too. Having covered up even the smallest cracks letting in rays of light, the doctor now sits at his desk in utter darkness, takes up his pencil (we hear it scribbling) and begins to write down the sights that we saw in the film's opening scenes.

In the film's final two minutes, we gaze upon nothing but darkness, hearing the doctor's gravelly voice resume his narration, and we realize that he is retelling the story we are about to conclude watching. We hear and (at least for anglophone viewers reliant on subtitles) see language, as hearing displaces seeing. The closing black screen allows us to witness the process of recollected images issuing out of the darkness of forgetting *as language*. In this way, it illustrates the reader's experience of re-visiting the novel's opening pages, word for word. In the novel's final chapter, that is, we reread the text we encountered in its opening pages in just *this manner*, the manner not of a citation but of seeing the writing take place on the page (in the same way that we *hear* it take place in the film), as if witnessing the very *event* of writing and overlooking the memories of what we have read. In realizing that we have already read these words, we are made conscious of *the words themselves* and gaze upon writing, the inky seer.

Derrida: 'Language is spoken, it speaks to itself, which is to say, *from/of blindness*. It always speaks to us *from/of the blindness* that constitutes it' (*Memoirs of the Blind* 4). *Satantango*'s closing scene discloses language's blindness-cum-vision, by letting the viewer see nothing while hearing, and thus prose picturing, everything. When encountering ekphrasis, we *see* with language. To see with language we have to look beyond it by looking through it (it always returns before the gaze; it is already returning). By rereading the opening pages of *Satantango* at novel's end, with the help of the film's closing scene, we can see more clearly what we cannot but forget while being immersed in prose pictures: language's blindness, precisely as we take for granted its blind belief to make seeing happen with words.

This book has explored how recollected images can be made to issue out of black marks on a white page, just like memories of what was *seen* on the cinema screen issue out of the voice that *retells* them, once the screen has gone dark. I have cited the passage from Krasznahorkai's singular text alongside its cinematic adaptation to foreground the paradoxical nature of ekphrastic writing. The ekphrastic text seeks to efface itself and become a kind of pane through which the reader may see the scenes it is describing. This is particularly important for the kinds of novels that can be said to have adapted Proust's model for writing about the past. The narrator's aim in these novels is to stage the mimesis of retrospective sight, turning the reader into a 'spectator' of what once was. And yet we have also seen that the ekphrastic text is *distinct* from narration, as it delays the progress of events and uses artful language to achieve its aims. Mnemonic ekphrasis after Proust thus not only shows us the recollected past but itself becomes memorable in its lexical remarkableness and choice of metaphors (recall Marcel's unforgettable phrase, 'clear as frozen daylight', used to image the translucence of a wine glass). The paradox of ekphrasis, then, is one of vision as opposed to voice, image as opposed to text, and their dialectical exchange-cum-composition (both intersensory and intermedial) produces textual seeing.

The ekphrastic novels of Proust, Nabokov, Sebald and Lerner foreground vision, while those of Smith and Davis emphasize voice. Nabokov's most ekphrastic novel, *Ada*, differs from Proust's *Search* in that it exhibits an imbrication of imagination and memory in memory's description, as the narrator produces ornate ekphrases expressly intended to serve the novel's elaborate plot. Like Proust's novel, it also shows how the delay of description can never freeze time, remaining submissive to the needs of narration yet without ceasing to be vital in serving the needs of memory – whenever a recalled moment is given the time needed to make its *presence* felt. In *Austerlitz*, similarly, the ekphrastic evocations of the people, places and objects that Jacques Austerlitz presents to us act like 'weirs which stem the flow', to use Sebald's own phrase, foregrounding the narrational delay needed for the pensive look to register that which is ever fleeting – a past fast becoming unremembered. What Sebald's novel adds to Proust's model is the prosthesis of the archive, exemplified by the grainy, auratic photographs that elude memory's verbal capture. In Sebald, we discern how the collective record of what once was can never replace anamnesis, personal memory, but only inhere alongside it as paratactic sequence. Unlike Sebald's fiction, which is preoccupied with melancholic retrospect, Lerner's novels feature a prose picturing of the past made unstable by anxious prospect. If memory typically faces the past, then narrated memory faces the future in Lerner's fiction, as past moments ekphrastically rendered become palimpsests of time past, time present and time future to a much more radical degree than in Proust. Both *10:04* and *Leaving the Atocha Station* also feature digital reproductions of paintings, film stills and satellite photographs, with the aim of capturing moments of looking at screens that characterize contemporary life. In this way, Lerner's fiction stages ekphrasis' classical conception not only of making present what is absent but also vicariously sharing, alongside the narrator and characters, the contemplation of moments thus conjured.

In Proust and after, mnemonic ekphrasis often proceeds by way of intermedial comparison and pictorial allusion, and this is perhaps most clearly seen in *How to Be Both*. Smith's novel features two protagonists, the ghost of a fifteenth-century Italian artist and a teenager living in present-day London, through whose eyes we contemplate echoing narratives about commemoration of lost artworks and persons. The novel formally expresses how the departed, as in Proust, are remembered with the aid of visual media, media that have historically lent both verbal description and memory the support they need to become more immediately apprehended. In ekphrasis' classical conception, hearing produces seeing, and *How to Be Both* makes this aspect of ekphrasis felt in the way narrative voice modulates between two 'keys': *enargeiac* showing and diegetic telling. In Smith's novel, that is, we not only see prose pictures, but also more distinctly hear how the voice of narration alters pace and rhythm, once showing takes over from telling. This is especially clear in Francescho's story, as the eccentric punctuation symbol which she inherited from her mother's handwriting, ' : ', signalling an extended pause, proliferates whenever she either describes vivid moments from her past, or contemplates paintings in the past of Renaissance Italy and photographs in the present of contemporary London. *The End of the Story* also gives priority to voice over vision, but for a different reason. Davis's novel intends to write forgetting and show us the side of mnemonic ekphrasis that wants to stay hidden: the darkening of oblivion that always puts memory in danger. Unlike memory images, forgetting can neither be seen nor described – only gestured at. In *The End of the Story*, we discern its active force in the narrator's struggle to remember her past every time we hear (and see) the conjunction *or* that appears whenever the narrator is unsure either about the recalled details she is describing or the order of the events presented in her story. In Smith, we hear two voices *enargeiacally* (vividly) evoking actual pictures, while in Davis we hear the narrator's struggle to evoke an elusive young man, whose image ghosts her narrative with the promise of its imminent appearance.

These novels thus jointly express the three key features of descriptive ekphrasis: first, it is inveterately intermedial because even ekphrases that do not describe artworks are still informed by the 'idea' of visual art, yearning after its immediacy and distinctness for perception; second, it makes present an absent person, place, object or moment being described; and third, it represents said things in a detailed, vivid manner, emulating sight. This book has focused on the ways that an ekphrasis of memory's sights, what I have called mnemonic ekphrasis, continues to be practised by writers whose fiction is either implicitly or explicitly indebted to Proust's generic model. By doing so, it has demonstrated the extent to which verbal signification, especially where memory is concerned, is implicated with the extratextual realms of visual media, not least because philosophical reflection on memory has itself continually drawn on them – from wax tablets, paintings, photographs, all the way to digital pictures glowing on handheld screens – in an effort to make better sense of memory's more polysemic, more elusive images.

In contemporary writing, ekphrastic description is, of course, not confined to evoking the distant past, so in what follows I want to suggest three directions for future research, arranged according to ekphrasis' key features specified above.

Ekphrasis as intermedial passage. Intermediality is a growing field of inquiry, one characterized by its interdisciplinary approach. Intermediality, as its name suggests, is interested in how various media have historically cross-fertilized one another's respective fields; for instance, how a technique derived from painting – such as cubism during the heyday of Modernism – was used by novelists to represent an aspect of contemporary experience that called out for it in prose.[2] An investigation of how ekphrasis has been and continues to be deployed to help realize these kinds of aims promises to bear fruit, not least because many contemporary writers remain interested in exploring the ways in which words respond to the indelible impression made by certain pictures and works of art. Intermediality is also related to the study of objects, thinghood and prostheses, and the novel's ability to capture their originary role in human experience. This is the subject of Peter Boxall's *The Prosthetic Imagination* (2020), and the following observation about prosthetic objects echoes the argument about ekphrastic delay presented in this book: 'There is a tension,' Boxall writes, 'at the heart of the prosthetic as an object, between stasis and movement, between its reproduction of a particular moment of being and its role as a conduit that brings its user or wearer into relation with moving time, with time still to come' (2). This kind of tension captures the temporal drama at the heart of the Proustian narrative, so that we might well call descriptive ekphrasis its key prosthetic 'object', one that both reproduces 'a particular moment' and acts 'as a conduit' establishing a relation, for the narrated subject, between the past thus restored and the 'time still to come'. Additionally, a consideration of the role ekphrasis plays in the novel's mimetic capture of historically changing prostheses (and the ways that such tools have themselves made an impact upon descriptive language) seems to be a worthwhile endeavour in this area.[3]

---

[2] This subject has been explored, for instance, in Cara L. Lewis's *Dynamic Form*, where Lewis considers ekphrasis to be one of the literary devices where intermedial resonance is most powerfully felt in key modernist texts.
[3] A fascinating essay that explores material objects' active role in shaping language is Bruno Latour's 'The Berlin Key or How to Do Words with Things'.

Ekphrasis of the contemporary. Ekphrasis intends to reproduce an 'act of seeing', re-presenting a visual impression in words, suggesting that there is an inherent delay to this kind of writing: it shows us what has *already been seen* (even if what has been seen is purely fictive). This raises the question whether ekphrasis could ever 'show' us the contemporary moment, whether it can make 'present' that which is presently unfolding. In 'What Is the Contemporary?' Agamben has offered a promising approach to this question: To be truly contemporary with one's own time, Agamben argues, one must keep a certain distance from it, not belong to it without reservations. 'The contemporary', in Agamben's typically arresting phrase, 'is the one whose eyes are struck by the beam of darkness that comes from his own time' (*Apparatus* 45).[4] The reason Agamben spotlights 'darkness' in this way is because '[t]hat which impedes access to the present is precisely the mass of what for some reason (its traumatic character, its excessive nearness) we have not managed to live. The attention to this "unlived" is the life of the contemporary' (51). The present's 'unlived' moments are those aspects of life which are 'too close for comfort' and given insufficient scrutiny, and it is the writer's task to illuminate these areas with the light shed by words. If contemporary writers are successful in this task, then their work allows us 'to return to a present where we have never been', and they can only bring this about by being 'contemporaries not only of our century and the "now", but also of its figures in texts and documents of the past', Agamben writes (52; 54). Ekphrasis is that part of a text which is brightest, given the *most* illumination, and which establishes a connection between past and present.[5] But this also means that there will be areas of present experience left in the shadows cast by this illumination. The critic of the contemporary thus needs to examine not only what has been shown in ekphrastic passages but also what has been left in darkness. It is precisely by attending to a text's omissions and blind spots, as well as its illuminations, that criticism can best 'respond to the darkness of the now' (Agamben 53).

Ekphrasis of what has not yet happened. What has not *yet* happened is a theme that pertains both to fiction and non-fiction, whenever narratives seek to either conjure up or impart predictions of possible or, in some cases, inevitable states

---

[4] See also Ben Davies's essay, 'The Darkness Within-the-Light of Contemporary Fiction', which draws on Agamben's essay to explore the role of the contemporary reader in Lerner's *10:04*.

[5] Any list of exemplary recent fiction that has illuminated various aspects of present experience in this manner would surely include Ali Smith's quartet-cycle, beginning with the ekphrastic *Autumn* (2016), and Karl Ove Knausgård's own seasonal quartet, with the first volume, also titled *Autumn* (2017), meticulously describing various objects to a child, including chewing gum, jellyfish, oil tankers, vomit, Flaubert and eyes.

of affairs concerning the future of humanity. Jeff VanderMeer's novel *Borne*, for instance, is an eerie, retrospective tale of post-human survival and adaptation that employs visual description to great effect in its imaginative projection of life in a dystopian future. Recent notable fiction that depicts what has not yet happened in similar fashion includes Cormac McCarthy's still contemporary novel, *The Road*; Margaret Atwood's *The Year of the Flood*; Rita Indiana's *Tentacle*; and Kim Stanley Robinson's *The Ministry for the Future*. Visual description may not be the key formal component in these narratives that it is in Proustian fiction, but it still plays a significant role in bringing before the reader's inner eye the disquieting visions compellingly written on the page. Outside fiction's arena, descriptive ekphrasis is also used effectively in ecocriticism and theory that reflect on climate change and our species' precarious future. For instance, in Roy Scranton's collection of essays, *We're Doomed, Now What?*, we are presented with scenes of devastation caused by Hurricane 'Isaiah', an imagined storm that, many climatologists fear, may one day really hit Galveston Bay in Texas, a coastal area pregnant with oil refineries. Scranton's descriptive narration is recounted in the present tense, thus heightening the *enargeiac* effect of immersing the reader into the depicted scenes (28–29). Before reading about the imaginary calamity, however, we encounter the following prose collage:

> Imagine an oyster. Imagine waves of rain lashing concrete, a crawdad boil, a fallen highway, and a muddy bay. Imagine a complex system of gates and levees, the Johnson Space Center, a broken record spinning on a broken player. Imagine the baroque intricacy of the Valero Houston oil refinery, the Petrobras Pasadena oil refinery, the LyondellBasell oil refinery, the Shell Deer Park oil refinery, the ExxonMobil Baytown oil refinery, a bottle of Ravishing Red nail polish, a glacier falling into the sea. Imagine gray-black clouds piling over the horizon, a chaos spiral hundreds of miles wide. Imagine a hurricane.
>
> (28)

This descriptive list juxtaposes surprising visual details: a composite image gradually emerges before the mind's eye of the places and objects being described, and its paratactic sequencing also emits narrativity, offering us a kind of micro-story about a hurricane's aftermath plotted backwards. Other thinkers whose writing descriptively gestures towards similar events that have not yet happened include Timothy Morton (in both *Hyperobjects* and *Dark Ecology*); Donna Haraway (*Staying with the Trouble*); Bruno Latour (*Facing Gaia*) and Jan Zalasiewicz (*The Earth after Us*). These books all impart a vivid sense of environmental fragility, precisely by *redescribing* (as in Proustian ekphrasis), and thus reinvigorating, our apprehension of the human race's relation to the natural world. They return us 'to a present where we have never been', in Agamben's phrase, and they do so by often placing us into distant moments in time, so that it is as if we were remembering the present as something which has already been lost. Ekphrastic description, with its vivid mimesis both of present instability and future eventuality, thus continues to aid contemporary writing and theory to come to terms with their own time.

There is a particularly affecting evocation of what has not yet happened in *The Earth after Us*, which may well serve as an ending. Zalasiewicz asks the reader to picture a coastal city one hundred years hence, when sea levels are expected to rise between 2 and 5 metres, with the skyscrapers partially underwater:

> The deep skyscraper roots form inverted concrete and steel spires beneath a New Orleans that is slowly sinking into the Gulf of Mexico, as the detritus of half a continent, washed on to the top of the Mississippi delta, presses down on the malleable crust. Around the tops of the concrete piles snake the thick tangle of pipes for water, electricity, gas, sewage, optical cables, of subways, underground car parks, and nuclear fall-out shelters. Once in the burial realm, these abandoned foundations of our human empire can begin their transformation into the Urban Stratum that may, in the yet more distant future, be discovered, analysed, explored, marvelled at.
>
> A millennium on, these foundations may lie in water that is twenty metres deep or more, as the ice caps continue inexorably to melt. ... This will now resemble an archaeological site, akin to that of some ancient Greek or Egyptian city drowned by tectonic subsidence following an earthquake or volcanic eruption.
>
> (180)

In Lerner's *10:04*, we recall the narrator's strange but suggestive sentence: fearing the worst about the state of his heart, he tells us: 'So clearly could I picture the cardiologist walking in to inform me that the speed of dilation required immediate intervention that it was as though it had already happened; predicting it felt like recalling a traumatic event.' In Zalasiewicz's prose picturing of a sobering future, it is as if we, too, were already there, already recalling the 'traumatic event' of climate change.

Even when projecting imagination's light into such distant vistas, with nothing but words to effect the journey, the temporal logic characteristic of Proustian narratives, with their immersive delays and the flow of time wherein such moments find their fulfilment, remains far-seeing.

Works cited

Agamben, Giorgio. *The Fire and the Tale*. Trans. Lorenzo Chiesa. Stanford: Stanford University Press, 2017.
Agamben, Giorgio. *What Is an Apparatus? and Other Essays*. Trans. David Kishik and Stefan Pedatella. Stanford: Stanford University Press, 2009.
Alexandrov, Vladimir. *Nabokov's Otherworld*. Princeton: Princeton University Press, 1991.
Angier, Carole. *Speak, Silence: In Search of W.G. Sebald*. London: Bloomsbury Circus, 2021.
Aristotle. 'De Memoria et Reminiscentia'. Trans. and ed. Richard Sorabji. *Aristotle on Memory*. London: Bristol Classical Press, 2012. 47–61.
Aristotle. *Poetics*. Trans. Malcolm Heath. London: Penguin, 1996.
Attridge, Derek. *The Singularity of Literature*. London: Routledge, 2004.
Auerbach, Erich. *Mimesis: The Representation of Reality in Western Literature*. Trans. Willard R. Trask. Princeton: Princeton University Press, 2013.
Augustine. *Confessions*. Trans. Henry Chadwick. Oxford: Oxford University Press, 1998.
Bakhtin, Mikhail. *Problems of Dostoevsky's Poetics*. Ed. and trans. Caryl Emerson. Minneapolis: University of Minnesota Press, 1999.
Bakhtin, Mikhail. *Speech Genres and Other Late Essays*. Trans. Vern W. McGree. Ed. Caryl Emerson and Michael Holquist. Austin: University of Texas Press, 2010.
Bal, Mieke. *The Mottled Screen: Reading Proust Visually*. Trans. Anna-Louise Milne. Stanford: Stanford University Press, 1997.
Bal, Mieke. *Narratology: Introduction to the Theory of Narrative*. Toronto: University of Toronto Press, 2017.
Baldwin, Thomas. 'Proust's Picture Plane'. Ed. Nathalie Aubert. *Proust and the Visual*. Cardiff: University of Wales Press, 2013. 131–148.
Bales, Richard. 'Proust and the Fine Arts'. Ed. Richard Bales. *The Cambridge Companion to Marcel Proust*. Cambridge: Cambridge University Press, 2010. 183–199.
Balzac, Honoré de. *The Unknown Masterpiece*. Trans. Richard Howard. Introduction by Arthur C. Danto. New York: The New York Review of Books, 2001.
Barthes, Roland. *Camera Lucida*. Trans. Richard Howard. London: Vintage Books, 2000.
Barthes, Roland. *Image, Music, Text*. Trans. Stephen Heath. London: Fontana Press, 1987.
Barthes, Roland. *The Rustle of Language*. Trans. Richard Howard. Berkeley: University of California Press, 1989.

Barthes, Roland. *Signs and Images: Writings on Art, Cinema and Photography*. Trans Chris Turner. Chicago: University of Chicago Press, 2016.

Barthes, Roland. *S/Z*. Trans. Richard Miller. Oxford: Blackwell, 1990.

Bateman, John A. *Text and Image: A Critical Introduction to the Visual/Verbal Divide*. London: Routledge, 2014.

Baudelaire, Charles. *Selected Writings on Art and Literature*. Trans. P. E. Charvet. London: Penguin, 2006.

Baxter, James. *Samuel Beckett's Legacies in American Fiction: Problems in Postmodernism*. London: Palgrave Macmillan, 2021.

Beckett, Samuel. *Company/Ill Seen, Ill Said/Worstward Ho/Stirrings Still*. Ed. Dirk Van Hulle. London: Faber and Faber, 2009.

Beckett, Samuel. *Molloy, Malone Dies, the Unnamable*. Everyman's Library. London: Alfred A. Knopf, 2015.

Beckett, Samuel. *Proust*. New York: Grove Press, 1978.

Beckett, Samuel. *Texts for Nothing and Other Shorter Prose, 1950–1976*. Ed. Mark Nixon. London: Faber and Faber, 2010.

Beckett, Samuel. *Watt*. Ed. C. J. Ackerley. London: Faber and Faber, 2009.

Behrendt, Kathy. 'Hirsch, Sebald and the Uses and Limits of Postmemory'. Ed. Russell Kilbourn and Eleanor Ty. *The Memory Effect: The Remediation of Memory in Literature and Film*. Waterloo, ON: Wilfrid Laurier University Press, 2013. 51–71.

Benjamin, Walter. *Illuminations: Essays and Reflections*. Trans. Harry Zohn. Ed. Hannah Arendt. New York: Schocken Books, 2007.

Benjamin, Walter. *On Photography*. Ed. and trans. Esther Leslie. London: Reaktion Books, 2015.

Benjamin, Walter. *Reflections: Essays, Aphorisms and Autobiographical Writings*. Trans. Edmund Jephcott. Ed. Peter Demetz. New York: Schocken Books, 1995.

Bergson, Henri. *Creative Evolution*. Trans. Arthur Mitchell. The Modern Library. New York: Random House, 1944.

Bergson, Henri. *Key Writings*. Ed. John Mullarky and Keith Ansell Pearson. London: Bloomsbury, 2014.

Bergson, Henri. *Matter and Memory*. Trans. Nancy Margaret Paul and W. Scott Palmer. New York: Zone Books, 2005.

Bergstein, Mary. *In Looking Back One Learns to See: Marcel Proust and Photography*. Amsterdam: Rodopi, 2014.

Berlina, Alexandra. 'Translator's Introduction'. Trans. Alexandra Berlina. *Viktor Shklovsky: A Reader*. London: Bloomsbury, 2017. 1–50.

Beistegui, Miguel de. *Proust as Philosopher: The Art of Metaphor*. Trans. Dorothée Bonnigal Katz, Simon Sparks and Miguel de Beistegui. London: Routledge, 2013.

Bewes, Timothy. 'Introduction: Temporalizing the Present'. *Novel: A Forum on Fiction* 45.2 (2012): 159–164.

Bilmes, Leonid. '"An Actual Present Alive with Multiple Futures": Narrative, Memory and Time in Ben Lerner's *10:04*'. *Textual Practice* 34.7 (2020): 1081–1102.

Bilmes, Leonid. 'Oneself as Character: Emplotment, Memory and Metaphor in Ricoeur, Bakhtin and Nabokov's *The Gift*'. Ed. Garry L. Hagberg. *Fictional Worlds and Philosophical Reflection*. London: Palgrave Macmillan, 2022. 129–151.

Blanchot, Maurice. *The Infinite Conversation*. Trans. Susan Hanson. Minneapolis: University of Minnesota Press, 2003.

Boxall, Peter. '"The Existence I Ascribe": Memory, Invention and Autobiography in Beckett's Fiction'. *The Yearbook of English Studies* 30 (2000): 137–158.

Boxall, Peter. *The Prosthetic Imagination: A History of the Novel as Artificial Life*. Cambridge: Cambridge University Press, 2020.

Boxall, Peter. *The Value of the Novel*. Cambridge: Cambridge University Press, 2015.

Boyer, Philippe. 'Vue en peinture d'Odette'. Ed. Sophie Bertho. *Proust et ses peintres*. Amsterdam: Rodopi, 2000. 17–27.

Boyd, Brian. *Nabokov's Ada: The Place of Consciousness*. Christchurch: Cybereditions Corporation, 2001.

Boym, Svetlana. The *Future of Nostalgia*. New York: Basic Books, 2001.

Brooks, Peter. *Reading for the Plot: Design and Intention in Narrative*. Cambridge, MA: Harvard University Press, 1992.

Brooks, Peter. *Realist Vision*. New Haven: Yale University Press, 2005.

Brosch, Renate. 'Ekphrasis in the Digital Age: Responses to Image'. *Poetics Today* 39.2 (June 2018): 225–243.

Brosch, Renate. 'Ekphrasis in Recent Popular Novels: Reaffirming the Power of Art Images'. *Poetics Today* 39.2 (June 2018): 403–423.

Bruss, Elizabeth W. *Autobiographical Acts: The Changing Situation of a Literary Genre*. Baltimore: Johns Hopkins University Press, 1976.

Burgin, Victor. *The Remembered Film*. London: Reaktion Books, 2010.

Carter, William C. 'The Vast Structure of Recollection: From Life to Literature'. Ed. Richard Bales. *The Cambridge Companion to Marcel Proust*. Cambridge: Cambridge University Press, 2010. 25–41.

Casey, Edward. 'Imagining and Remembering'. *The Review of Metaphysics* 31.2 (1977): 187–209.

Casey, Edward. *Remembering: A Phenomenological Study*. Bloomington: Indiana University Press, 2000.

Caws, Mary Ann. *Reading Frames in Modern Fiction*. Princeton: Princeton University Press, 1985.

Clark, Alex. "Ali Smith: 'There are two ways to read this novel, but you're stuck with it – you'll end up reading one of them'". *The Guardian*, 6 September 2014, https://www.theguardian.com/books/2014/sep/06/ali-smith-interview-how-to-be-both. Accessed 5 December 2019.

Colony, Tracy. 'The Future of Technics'. *Parrhesia* 27 (2017): 64–87.

Compagnon, Antoine. *Literature, Theory and Common Sense*. Trans. Carol Cosman. Princeton: Princeton University Press, 2004.

'constitute, v'. *OED Online*, Oxford University Press, June 2020, www.oed.com/view/Entry/39844. Accessed 9 July 2020.

Cook, Jon. *After Sebald: Essays and Illuminations*. Suffolk: Full Circle Editions, 2014.

Culler, Jonathan. *Flaubert: The Uses of Uncertainty*. Aurora: The Davies Group Publishers, 2006.

Currie, Mark. *About Time: Narrative, Fiction and the Philosophy of Time*. Edinburgh: Edinburgh University Press, 2010.

Currie, Mark. 'Ali Smith and the Philosophy of Grammar'. Ed. Monica Germana and Emily Horton. *Ali Smith*. London: Bloomsbury, 2013. 48–60.

Currie, Mark. *Postmodern Narrative Theory*. London: Palgrave Macmillan, 2011.

Currie, Mark. 'The Trace of the Future'. Ed. Sebastian Groes. *Memory in the Twenty-First Century: New Critical Perspectives from the Arts, Humanities and Sciences*. London: Palgrave Macmillan, 2016. 199–205.

Currie, Mark. *The Unexpected: Narrative Temporality and the Philosophy of Surprise*. Edinburgh: Edinburgh University Press, 2013.

Curtis, Neil. '"As if": Situating the Pictorial Turn'. *Culture, Theory & Critique* 50.2–3 (2009): 95–101.

Dandieu, Arnaud. *Marcel Proust: Sa Révélation Psychologique*. London: Maison d'édition de l'Université d'Oxford, 1930.

D'Angelo, Frank J. 'The Rhetoric of Ekphrasis'. *JAC* 18.3 (1998): 439–447.

Davies, Ben. 'The Darkness-within-the-light of Contemporary Fiction: Agamben's Missing Reader and Ben Lerner's *10:04*'. *Textual Practice* 34.10 (2020): 1729–1749.

Davis, Lydia. *The Collected Stories of Lydia Davis*. London: Penguin, 2013.

Davis, Lydia. *The End of the Story*. London: Penguin, 2015.

Davis, Lydia. *Essays One*. New York: Farrar, Straus and Giroux, 2019.

Davis, Lydia. 'Loaf or Hot-Water Bottle: Closely Translating Proust'. *The Yale Review* 92.2 (2004): 51–70.

De Man, Paul. *Blindness and Insight: Essays in the Rhetoric of Contemporary Criticism*. Minneapolis: University of Minnesota Press, 1983.

De Man, Paul. *The Rhetoric of Romanticism*. New York: Columbia University Press, 1984.

De Vries, Gerard and D. Barton Johnson. *Nabokov and the Art of Painting*. Amsterdam: Amsterdam University Press, 2006.

Deleuze, Gilles. *Bergsonism*. Trans. Hugh Tomlinson and Barbara Habberjam. New York: Zone Books, 2006.

Deleuze, Gilles. *Proust and Signs: The Complete Text*. Trans. Richard Howard. Minneapolis: University of Minnesota Press, 2014.

Derrida, Jacques. *Archive Fever: A Freudian Impression*. Trans. Eric Prenowitz Chicago: Chicago University Press, 1998.

Derrida, Jacques. *Memoires for Paul de Man*. Ed. Avital Ronell and Eduardo Cadava. Trans. Cecile Lindsay, Peggy Kamuf et al. New York: Columbia University Press, 1989.

Derrida, Jacques. *Memoirs of the Blind: The Self-Portrait and Other Ruins*. Trans. Pascale-Anne Brault and Michael Naas. Chicago: University of Chicago Press, 1993.

Derrida, Jacques. 'The Parergon'. Trans. Craig Owens. *October* 9 (1979): 3–41.

Derrida, Jacques. 'White Mythology: Metaphor in the Text of Philosophy'. Trans. F. C. T. Moore. *New Literary History* 6.1 (1974): 5–74.

Descombes, Vincent. *Proust: Philosophy and the Novel*. Trans. Catherine Chance Macksey. Stanford: Stanford University Press, 1992.

'DNA cycle'. *Nature* 447.911 (2007). https://www.nature.com/articles/447911a#article-info. Accessed 22 June 2020.

Dowd, Garin. 'Apprenticeship, Philosophy, and "The Secret Pressures of the Work of Art" in Deleuze, Beckett, Proust and Ruiz; or Remaking the *Recherche*'. Ed. Mary Bryden and Margaret Topping. *Beckett's Proust/Deleuze's Proust*. London: Palgrave Macmillan, 2009. 89–103.

Dowling, W. C. *Ricoeur on Time and Narrative*. Indiana: University of Notre Dame Press, 2011.

Dyer, Nathalie Mauriac. 'Composition and Publication of *À la recherche du temps perdu*'. Ed. Adam Watt. *Marcel Proust in Context*. Cambridge: Cambridge University Press, 2013. 34–40.

Elkins, Amy E. 'Has Art Anything to Do with Life? A Conversation with Ali Smith on *Spring*'. *Los Angeles Review of Books*, 3 September 2019, https://lareviewofbooks.org/article/has-art-anything-to-do-with-life-a-conversation-with-ali-smith-on-spring/. Accessed 5 December 2019.

Elkins, Katherine. 'Middling Memories and Dreams of Oblivion: Configurations of a Non-Archival Memory in Baudelaire and Proust'. *Discourse* 24.3 (2002): 47–66.

Ellison, David R. *The Reading of Proust*. Baltimore: Johns Hopkins University Press, 1984.

Elsner, Jas. *Roman Eyes: Visuality and Subjectivity in Art and Text*. Princeton: Princeton University Press, 2007.

Emerson, Caryl and Gary Saul Morson. *Mikhail Bakhtin: Creation of a Prosaics*. Stanford: Stanford University Press, 1990.

Evans, Jonathan. 'Lydia Davis's Rewritings of Proust'. *Translation and Literature* 21.2 (2012): 175–195.

Evans, Jonathan. *The Many Voices of Lydia Davis: Translation, Rewriting, Intertextuality*. Edinburgh: Edinburgh University Press, 2016.

Evans, Jonathan. 'Translation and Response between Maurice Blanchot and Lydia Davis'. *TranscUlturAl* 4.1 (2011): 49–61.

Felski, Rita. *The Limits of Critique*. Chicago: University of Chicago Press, 2015.

Flaubert, Gustave. *Memoirs of a Madman and November*. Trans. Andrew Brown. Richmond: Alma Classics, 2013.

Flaubert, Gustave. *Novembre*. Neuchatel: Ides et Calendes, 1961.
Flaubert, Gustave. *Selected Letters*. Trans. and ed. Geoffrey Wall. London: Penguin, 1997.
Foster, John Burt, Jr. *Nabokov's Art of Memory and European Modernism*. Princeton: Princeton University Press, 1993.
Foucault, Michel. *The Order of Things: An Archaeology of the Human Sciences*. Trans. Anon. London: Routledge, 2002.
Fowler, D. P. 'Narrate and Describe: The Problem of Ekphrasis'. *The Journal of Roman Studies* 81 (1991): 25–35.
Genette, Gérard. *Figures of Literary Discourse*. Trans. Alan Sheridan. New York: Columbia University Press, 1982.
Genette, Gérard. *Narrative Discourse: An Essay in Method*. Trans. Jane E. Lewin. Foreword by Jonathan Culler. Ithaca: Cornell University Press, 1983.
Gibbons, Alison. 'Autonarration, I, and Odd Address in Ben Lerner's Autofictional Novel *10:04*'. Ed. Alison Gibbons and Andrea Macrae. *Pronouns in Literature: Positions and Perspectives in Language*. London: Palgrave Macmillan, 2018. 75–96.
Gibson, E. Leigh. 'Proust Recalled: A Psychological Revisiting of That Madeleine Memory Moment'. Ed. Sebastian Groes. *Memory in the Twenty-First Century: New Critical Perspectives from the Arts, Humanities and Sciences*. London: Palgrave Macmillan, 2016. 42–51.
Graham, Victor E. *The Imagery of Proust*. Oxford: Blackwell, 1966.
Grishakova, Marina. *The Models of Space, Time and Vision in V. Nabokov's Fiction*. Tartu: Tartu University Press, 2006.
Haddad, Karen. 'Images Come Alive (How to Make Images with Words)'. Ed. Nathalie Aubert. *Proust and the Visual*. Cardiff: University of Wales Press, 2013. 115–130.
Hägglund, Martin. *Dying for Time: Proust, Woolf, Nabokov*. Cambridge, MA: Harvard University Press, 2012.
Hamilton, Paul. *Historicism*. London: Routledge, 2003.
Hedley, Jane. 'Introduction: The Subject of Ekphrasis'. Ed. Jane Hedley et al. *In the Frame: Women's Ekphrastic Poetry from Marianne Moore to Susan Wheeler*. Newark: University of Delaware Press, 2009. 15–40.
Heffernan, James. 'Ekphrasis and Representation'. *New Literary History* 22.2 (1991): 297–316.
Heidegger, Martin. *The Question Concerning Technology and Other Essays*. Trans. William Lovitt. New York: Harper Perennial, 1977.
Hirsch, Marianne. *The Generation of Postmemory: Writing and Visual Culture after the Holocaust*. New York: Columbia University Press, 2012.
'history, n.' *OED Online*, Oxford University Press, June 2020, www.oed.com/view/Entry/87324. Accessed 9 July 2020.
Homer. *The Iliad*. Trans. Robert Fagles. London: Penguin, 1990.
Horace. 'The Art of Poetry'. Ed. Penelope Murray. Trans. T. Dorsch. *Classical Literary Criticism*. London: Penguin, 2004. 98–113.

Horstkotte, Silke. 'Visual Memory and Ekphrasis in W.G. Sebald's *The Rings of Saturn*'. *English Language Notes* 44.2 (2006): 117–128.
Hoy, David Couzens. *The Time of Our Lives: A Critical History of Temporality*. Cambridge, MA: MIT Press, 2009.
Hughes, Edward J. *Marcel Proust: A Study in the Quality of Awareness*. Cambridge: Cambridge University Press, 1983.
Husserl, Edmund. *On the Phenomenology of the Consciousness of Internal Time (1893–1917)*. Trans. John Barnett Brough. Ed. Rudolf Bernet. Dordrecht: Kluwer Academic Publishers, 1991.
'impeller, n.' *OED Online*, Oxford University Press, June 2020, www.oed.com/view/Entry/92207. Accessed 9 July 2020.
'inform, v.' *OED Online*, Oxford University Press, June 2020, www.oed.com/view/Entry/95559. Accessed 9 July 2020.
Ingarden, Roman. *The Cognition of the Literary Work of Art*. Trans. Ann Crowley and Kenneth R. Olson. Ed. James M. Edie, Paul Ricoeur and Emmanuel Levinas. Evanston: Northwestern University Press, 1973.
Iser, Wolfgang. 'The Reading Process: A Phenomenological Approach'. *New Literary History* 3.2 (1972): 279–299.
Jacobs, Carol. *Sebald's Vision*. New York: Columbia University Press, 2015.
Jameson, Fredric. *The Antinomies of Realism*. London: Verso, 2013.
Jay, Martin. *Downcast Eyes: The Denigration of Vision in Twentieth-Century French Thought*. Berkeley: University of California Press, 1994.
Karpeles, Eric. *Paintings in Proust: A Visual Companion to* In Search of Lost Time. London: Thames and Hudson, 2017.
Kilbourn, Russell J. A. and Eleanor Ty, eds. *The Memory Effect: The Remediation of Memory in Film and Literature*. Waterloo: Wilfrid Laurier University Press, 2012.
Kilmartin, Terence. 'Introduction'. *Marcel Proust on Art and Literature 1896–1919*. Trans. Sylvia Townsend Warner. New York: Carroll & Graf, 1997. 9–16.
Knausgård, Karl Ove. *A Death in the Family: My* Struggle, *Book 1*. Trans. Don Bartlett. London: Vintage, 2014.
Knight, Christopher J. 'An Interview with Lydia Davis'. *Contemporary Literature* 40.4 (1999): 525–551.
Knight, Christopher J. 'Lydia Davis's Own Philosophical Investigation: *The End of the Story*'. *Journal of Narrative Theory* 38.2 (2008): 198–228.
Koelb, Janice Hewlett. *The Poetics of Description: Imagined Places in European Literature*. London: Palgrave Macmillan, 2006.
Kouvaros, George. 'Images that Remember Us: Photography and Memory in *Austerlitz*'. Ed. Gerhard Fischer. *W.G. Sebald: Schreiben ex Patria/Expatriate Writing*. Amsterdam: Rodopi, 2009. 389–413.
Krasznahorkai, László. *Satantango*. Trans. George Szirtes. London: Atlantic Books, 2013.

Krell, David Farrell. *Of Memory, Reminiscence and Writing: On the Verge*. Indianapolis: Indiana University Press, 1990.

Krieger, Murray. *Ekphrasis: The Illusion of the Natural Sign*. Baltimore: Johns Hopkins University Press, 1992.

Lacan, Jacques. *Écrits: The First Complete Edition in English*. Trans. Bruce Fink. London: W. W. Norton, 2007.

Landy, Joshua. *Philosophy as Fiction: Self, Deception, and Knowledge in Proust*. Oxford: Oxford University Press, 2004.

Lanham, Richard. *A Handlist of Rhetorical Terms: A Guide for Students of English Literature*. Berkeley: University of California Press, 1969.

Latour, Bruno. 'The Berlin Key or How to Do Words with Things'. Ed. P. M. Graves-Brown. *Matter, Materiality and Modern Culture*. London: Routledge, 2000. 10–22.

Lennon, Thomas M. 'Proust and the Phenomenology of Memory'. *Philosophy and Literature* 31 (2007): 52–66.

Lerner, Ben. *10:04*. London: Granta, 2015.

Lerner, Ben. 'Each Cornflake'. *London Review of Books*, 22 May 2014, https://www.lrb.co.uk/v36/n10/ben-lerner/each-cornflake. Accessed 10 February 2018.

Lerner, Ben. *Leaving the Atocha Station*. London: Granta, 2012.

Lerner, Ben. 'The Polish Rider'. *The New Yorker*, 6 June 2016, http://www.newyorker.com/magazine/2016/06/06/the-polish-rider-by-ben-lerner. Accessed 5 September 2017.

Leslie, Esther. 'Introduction: Walter Benjamin and the Birth of Photography'. Trans. Esther Leslie. *On Photography* by Walter Benjamin. London: Reaktion Books, 2015. 7–53.

Lewis, Cara L. 'Beholding: Visuality and Postcritical Reading in Ali Smith's *How to Be Both*'. *Journal of Modern Literature* 42.3 (2019): 129–150.

Lewis, Cara L. *Dynamic Form: How Intermediality Made Modernism*. Ithaca: Cornell University Press, 2020.

Leyshon, Cressida. 'Ben Lerner on Art, Language and Uber'. *The New Yorker*, 31 May 2016, http://www.newyorker.com/books/page-turner/fiction-this-week-ben-lerner-2016-06-06. Accessed 1 June 2017.

Lingis, Alphonso. *The Imperative*. Bloomington: Indiana University Press, 1998.

Long, J. J. *W.G. Sebald: Image, Archive and Modernity*. Edinburgh: Edinburgh UP, 2007.

Louvel, Liliane. *The Pictorial Third: An Essay into Intermedial Criticism*. Trans. and ed. Angeliki Tseti. London: Routledge, 2018.

Louvel, Liliane. *Poetics of the Iconotext*. Trans. Laurence Petit. Ed. Karen Jacobs. London: Routledge, 2016.

Louvel, Liliane. 'Types of Ekphrasis: An Attempt at Classification'. *Poetics Today* 39.2 (June 2018): 245–263.

Lukács, Georg. *Writer & Critic and Other Essays*. Trans. and ed. Arthur D. Kahn. New York: Grosset and Dunlap, 1971.

Macé, Marielle. 'Ways of Reading, Modes of Being'. Trans. Marlon Jones. *New Literary History* 44 (2013): 213–229.

McLuhan, Marshall. *Understanding Media: The Extensions of Man*. London: Routledge, 2001.

McQuire, Scott. *Visions of Modernity: Representation, Memory, Time and Space in the Age of the Camera*. London: Sage Publications, 1998.

Medvedev, P. M. *The Formal Method in Literary Scholarship: A Critical Introduction to Sociological Poetics*. Trans. Albert J. Wehrle. Ed. Wlad Godzich. Cambridge, MA: Harvard University Press, 1985.

Mendelsund, Peter. *What We See When We Read*. New York: Vintage Books, 2014.

Mitchell, W. J. T. 'Image'. Ed. W. J. T. Mitchell and Mark Hansen. *Critical Terms for Media Studies*. Chicago: Chicago UP, 2010. 35–48.

Mitchell, W. J. T. *Image Science: Iconology, Visual Culture and Media Aesthetics*. Chicago: Chicago University Press, 2018.

Mitchell, W. J. T. *Picture Theory: Essays on Verbal and Visual Representation*. Chicago: Chicago University Press, 1994.

Mitchell, W. J. T. *What Do Pictures Want: The Lives and Loves of Images*. Chicago: Chicago University Press, 2005.

Morales, Helen. *Vision and Narrative in Achilles Tatius' Leucippe and Clitophon*. Cambridge: Cambridge University Press, 2004.

Mulvey, Laura. *Death 24x a Second*. London: Reaktion Books, 2015.

Nalbantian, Suzanne. *Aesthetic Autobiography: From Life to Art in Marcel Proust, James Joyce, Virginia Woolf and Anaïs Nin*. London: MacMillan Press, 1994.

Nabokov, Vladimir. *Ada or Ardor: A Family Chronicle*. London: McGraw Hill International, 1969.

Nabokov, Vladimir. *The Gift*. Trans. Michael Scammell and Dmitri Nabokov. London: Penguin, 2012.

Nabokov, Vladimir. *Lectures on Literature*. New York: Harcourt, 1982.

Nabokov, Vladimir. *Speak, Memory*. London: Penguin, 2000.

Nabokov, Vladimir. *Strong Opinions*. London: Penguin, 2011.

Nabokov, Vladimir. *Transparent Things*. New York: Random House, 1989.

Nancy, Jean-Luc. *The Ground of the Image*. Trans. Jeff Fort. New York: Fordham University Press, 2005.

Nancy, Jean-Luc. 'The Image: Mimesis and Methexis'. Trans. Adrienne Janus. Ed. Carrie Giunta and Adrienne Janus. *Nancy and Visual Culture*. Edinburgh: Edinburgh University Press, 2016. 73–92.

Nelson, Victoria. *The Secret Life of Puppets*. Cambridge, MA: Harvard University Press, 2003.

Olney, James. *Memory and Narrative: The Weave of Life-Writing*. Chicago: University of Chicago Press, 1998.

Olney, James. *Metaphors of Self: The Meaning of Autobiography*. Princeton: Princeton University Press, 1972.

'osmosis, n.' Ed. Lesley Brown. *The New Shorter OED, Volume II.* Oxford: Oxford University Press, 1993. 2029.

Pamuk, Orhan. *The Naïve and the Sentimental Novelist.* Trans. Nazim Dikbas. London: Faber, 2011.

Poulet, Georges. *Proustian Space.* Trans. Elliott Coleman. Baltimore: Johns Hopkins University Press, 1977.

Prendergast, Christopher. *The Triangle of Representation.* New York: Columbia University Press, 2000.

Proust, Marcel. *À la recherche du temps perdu, tome I.* Ed. Pierre Clarac and André Ferré. Paris: Éditions Gallimard, 1954.

Proust, Marcel. 'Chardin'. Trans. and ed. Sylvia Townsend Warner. *Marcel Proust on Art and Literature 1896–1919.* New York: Carroll & Graf, 1997. 19–276. 323–336.

Proust, Marcel. 'Contre Sainte-Beuve'. Trans. and ed. Sylvia Townsend Warner. *Marcel Proust on Art and Literature 1896–1919.* New York: Carroll & Graf, 1997. 19–276.

Proust, Marcel. *Le Temps retrouvé.* Ed. Pierre-Louis Rey and Brian G. Rogers. Paris: Éditions Gallimard, 1990.

Proust, Marcel. 'On Reading: Translator's Preface to *Sesame and Lilies*'. Trans. and ed. Damion Searls. *Marcel Proust and John Ruskin on Reading.* London: Hesperus, 2011. 3–43.

Proust, Marcel. *In Search of Lost Time, I: Swann's Way.* Trans. C. K. Scott Moncrieff and Terence Kilmartin. Revised by D. J. Enright. London: Vintage, 2005.

Proust, Marcel. *In Search of Lost Time, II: Within a Budding Grove.* Trans. C. K. Moncrieff and Terence Kilmartin. Revised by D. J. Enright. London: Vintage, 2005.

Proust, Marcel. *In Search of Lost Time, III: The Guermantes Way.* Trans. C. K. Scott Moncrieff and Terence Kilmartin. Revised D. J. Enright. London: Vintage, 2000.

Proust, Marcel. *In Search of Lost Time, IV: Sodom and Gomorrah.* Trans. C. K. Scott Moncrieff and Terence Kilmartin. Revised by D. J. Enright. London: Vintage, 2000.

Proust, Marcel. *In Search of Lost Time, V: The Captive/The Fugitive.* Trans. C. K. Scott Moncrieff and Terence Kilmartin. Revised by D. J. Enright. London: Vintage, 2000.

Proust, Marcel. *In Search of Lost Time, VI: Time Regained.* Trans. C. K. Scott Moncrieff, Andreas Mayor and Terence Kilmartin. Revised by D. J. Enright. London: Vintage, 2000.

Rancière, Jacques. *The Emancipated Spectator.* Trans. Gregory Elliott. London: Verso Books, 2014.

Rancière, Jacques. *The Future of the Image.* Trans. Gregory Elliott. London: Verso Books, 2009.

Reid, James H. *Proust, Beckett, and Narration.* Cambridge: Cambridge University Press, 2003.

Ricoeur, Paul. 'The Function of Fiction in Shaping Reality'. *Man and World* 12.2 (1979): 123–141.

Ricoeur, Paul. *Memory, History, Forgetting*. Trans. Kathleen Blamey and David Pellauer. Chicago: University of Chicago Press, 2006.
Ricoeur, Paul. *Oneself as Another*. Trans. Kathleen Blamey. Chicago: University of Chicago Press, 1992.
Ricoeur, Paul. *The Rule of Metaphor: The Creation of Meaning in Language*. Trans. Robert Czerny. London: Routledge, 2004.
Ricoeur, Paul. *Time and Narrative: Volume 1*. Trans. Kathleen McLaughlin and David Pellauer. Chicago: University of Chicago Press, 1990.
Ricoeur, Paul. *Time and Narrative: Volume 2*. Trans. Kathleen McLaughlin and David Pellauer. Chicago: University of Chicago Press, 1985.
Ricoeur, Paul. *Time and Narrative: Volume 3*. Trans. Kathleen Blamey and David Pellauer. Chicago: University of Chicago Press, 1988.
Rivers, J. E. 'Proust, Nabokov and *Ada*'. Ed. Phyllis A. Roth. *Critical Essays on Vladimir Nabokov*. Boston: G.K. Hall & Co., 1984. 134–156.
Rousseau, Jean-Jacques. *Confessions*. Trans. Angela Scholar. Ed. Patrick Coleman. Oxford: Oxford University Press, 2008.
Schwartz, L. S. *The Emergence of Memory: Conversations with W.G. Sebald*. London: Seven Stories Press, 2010.
Scott, Clive. 'Sebald's Photographic Annotations'. Ed. Jo Catling. *Saturn's Moons: W.G. Sebald: A Handbook*. London: Legenda, 2011. 217–247.
Scott, Clive. 'W.G. Sebald: Enumeration, Photography and the Hermeneutics of History'. Ed. Jon Cook. *After Sebald: Essays and Illuminations*. Woodbridge: Full Circle Editions, 2014. 125–143.
Scranton, Roy. *We're Doomed, Now What?* New York: Soho Press, 2018.
Sebald, W. G. *Austerlitz*. Trans. Anthea Bell. Introduction by James Wood. London: Penguin, 2011.
Sebald, W. G. *Campo Santo*. Trans. Anthea Bell. Ed. Sven Meyer. London: Penguin, 2006.
Sebald, W. G. *The Emigrants*. Trans. Michael Hulse. London: Vintage, 2002.
Sebald, W. G. *Vertigo*. Trans. Michael Hulse. London: Vintage, 2002.
Setina, Emily. 'Proust's Darkroom'. *MLN* 131.4 (2016, French issue): 1080–1112.
Silverman, Kaja. *The Miracle of Analogy: Or the History of Photography, Part 1*. Stanford: Stanford University Press, 2015.
Silverman, Kaja. *The Threshold of the Visible World*. London: Routledge, 1996.
Shklovsky, Viktor. *Viktor Shklovsky: A Reader*. Trans. and ed. Alexandra Berlina. London: Bloomsbury, 2017.
Smith, Ali. *Artful*. London: Penguin, 2013.
Smith, Ali. 'He Looked Like the Finest Man Who Ever Lived'. *The Guardian*, 24 August 2014, https://www.theguardian.com/books/2014/aug/24/ali-smith-the-finest-man-who-ever-lived-palazzo-schifanoia-how-to-be-both. Accessed 5 December 2019.
Smith, Ali. *Hotel World*. London: Penguin, 2002.

Smith, Ali. *How to Be Both*. London: Penguin, 2015.

Smith, Ali. 'Loosed in Translation'. Ed. Jon Cook. *After Sebald: Essays and Illuminations*. Norwich: Full Circle Editions, 2014. 71–85.

Smith, Barry C. 'Proust, the Madeleine and Memory'. Ed. Sebastian Groes. *Memory in the Twenty-First Century: New Critical Perspectives from the Arts, Humanities and Sciences*. London: Palgrave Macmillan, 2016. 38–42.

Sontag, Susan. *On Photography*. London: Penguin Books, 2008.

Sorabji, Richard. *Aristotle on Memory*. London: Bristol Classical Press, 2012.

Spitzer, Leo. 'The "Ode on a Grecian Urn," or Content vs. Metagrammar'. *Comparative Literature* 7 (1955): 203–225. Rpt. *Essays on English and American Literature*. Ed. Anna Hatcher. Princeton: Princeton University Press, 1962. 67–97.

Squire, Michael. 'Ekphrasis at the Forge and the Forging of Ekphrasis: The "Shield of Achilles" in Graeco–Roman Word and Image'. *Word & Image* 29.2 (2013): 157–191.

Stelmach, Kathryn. 'From Text to Tableau: Ekphrastic Enchantment in *Mrs Dalloway* and *To the Lighthouse*'. *Studies in the Novel* 38.3 (2006): 304–326.

Stendhal. *The Life of Henry Brulard*. Trans. John Sturrock. New York: The New York Review of Books, 2002.

'stereotype, n.' Ed. Lesley Brown. *The New Shorter OED, Volume II*. Oxford: Oxford University Press, 1993. 3052–3053.

Stiegler, Bernard. 'Memory'. Ed. W. J. T. Mitchell and Mark Hansen. *Critical Terms for Media Studies*. Chicago: Chicago University Press, 2010. 64–88.

Stiegler, Bernard. *Symbolic Misery, 2: The* Katastrophē *of the Sensible*. Trans. Barnaby Norman. Cambridge: Polity Press, 2014.

Stiegler, Bernard. *Technics and Time, 1: The Fault of Epimetheus*. Trans. Richard Beardsworth and George Collins. Stanford: Stanford University Press, 1998.

Stiegler, Bernard. *Technics and Time, 2: Disorientation*. Trans. Stephen Barker. Stanford: Stanford University Press, 2009.

Stiegler, Bernard. *Technics and Time, 3: Cinematic Time and the Question of Malaise*. Trans. Stephen Barker. Stanford: Stanford University Press, 2011.

Tatius, Achilles. *Leucippe and Clitophon*. Trans. S. Gaselee. Loeb Classical Library 45. Cambridge, MA: Harvard University Press, 1969.

Tarr, Béla, director. *Sátántangó*. Von Vietinghoff Filmproduktion, 1994.

Townsend, Gabrielle. 'Painting'. Ed. Adam Watt. *Marcel Proust in Context*. Cambridge: Cambridge University Press, 2013. 83–89.

Vaihinger, Hans. *The Philosophy of the 'As If': A System of the Theoretical, Practical and Religious Fictions of Mankind*. Trans. C. K. Ogdon. Edinburg: Edinburg University Press, 1924.

Van Campen, Cretien. *The Proust Effect: The Senses as Doorways to Lost Memories*. Trans. Julian Ross. Oxford: Oxford University Press, 2014.

Vitale, Serena. *Shklovsky: Witness to an Era*. Trans. Jamie Richards. Champaign: Dalkey Archive Press, 2013.

Walsh, Lauren. 'The *Madeleine* Revisualized: Proustian Memory and Sebaldian Visuality'. Ed. Ofra Amihay and Lauren Walsh. *The Future of Text and Image*. Newcastle upon Tyne: Cambridge Scholars Publishing, 2012. 93–131.

Warnock, Mary. *Memory*. London: Faber and Faber, 1987.

Watt, Adam. *The Cambridge Introduction to Marcel Proust*. Cambridge: Cambridge University Press, 2011.

Watt, Adam. 'Late Twentieth- and Twenty-First-Century Responses'. Ed. Adam Watt. *Marcel Proust in Context*. Cambridge: Cambridge University Press, 2013. 206–213.

Webb, Ruth. 'Ekphrasis Ancient and Modern: The Invention of a Genre'. *Word & Image* 15.1 (1999): 7–18.

Webb, Ruth. *Ekphrasis, Imagination and Persuasion in Ancient Rhetorical Theory and Practice*. London: Routledge, 2016.

Webb, Ruth. 'The Model Ekphraseis of Nikolaos the Sophist as Memory Images'. Ed. Michael Grünbart. *Theatron*. Berlin: De Gruyter, 2012. 463–476.

Weinrich, Harold. *Lethe: The Art and Critique of Forgetting*. Trans. Steven Rendall. Ithaca: Cornell University Press, 2004.

White, Hayden. *The Content of the Form: Narrative Discourse and Historical Representation*. Baltimore: Johns Hopkins University Press, 1990.

White, Hayden. *Metahistory: The Historical Imagination in 19th Century Europe*. Baltimore: Johns Hopkins University Press, 2014.

White, Hayden. *The Practical Past*. Evanston: Northwestern University Press, 2014.

White, Hayden. *Tropics of Discourse: Essays in Cultural Criticism*. Baltimore: Johns Hopkins University Press, 1992.

Williams, Luke. 'A Watch on Each Wrist: Twelve Seminars with W.G. Sebald'. Ed. Jo Catling. *Saturn's Moons: W.G. Sebald: A Handbook*. London: Legenda, 2011. 143–154.

Wilson, Mary Griffin. 'Sheets of Past: Reading the Image in W.G. Sebald's *Austerlitz*'. *Contemporary Literature* 54.1 (2013): 49–76.

Wolff, Lynn. 'Literary Historiography: W.G. Sebald's Fiction'. Ed. Gerhard Fischer, *W.G. Sebald: Schreiben ex Patria/Expatriate Writing*. Amsterdam: Rodopi, 2009. 317–333.

Wood, James. 'Introduction'. *Austerlitz* by W. G. Sebald. Trans. Anthea Bell. London: Penguin, 2011. vii–xxvii.

Wood, Michael. *Literature and the Taste of Knowledge*. Cambridge: Cambridge University Press, 2005.

Wood, Michael. *The Magician's Doubts: Nabokov and the Risks of Fiction*. London: Chatto & Windus, 1994.

Wood, Michael. 'Translations'. Ed. Adam Watt. *Marcel Proust in Context*. Cambridge: Cambridge University Press, 2013. 230–240.

Yacobi, Tamara. 'Pictorial Models and Narrative Ekphrasis'. *Poetics Today* 16.4 (1995): 599–649.

Yates, Frances. *The Art of Memory: Selected Works of Frances Yates, Volume III*. London: Routledge, 2007.

Zalasiewicz, Jan. *The Earth after Us: What Legacy Will Humans Leave in the Rocks?* Oxford: Oxford University Press, 2008.

Zwicky, Jan. *Wisdom & Metaphor*. Kentville: Gaspereau Press, 2003.

Index

absence 158, 175, 183, 197–201, 211–12
Agamben, Giorgio 168, 218
'Age of the World Picture' 21, 168
Angier, Carole 117, 118 n.1
archive
　commemoration and 133
　external memory 128, 132, 135–6, 137
　　(*see also* Derrida)
　photography and (*see under*
　　photography)
　postmemory as 134–5
Aristotle 77 n. 11, 98 n.8, 192
as if
　Aristotle on 77 n.11
　mimesis and 5, 76 n.10, 168
　present, as if 5, 20, 30–1, 52, 58, 65,
　　179
　self-narration and 76, 77–8, 82–3, 119,
　　160
Attridge, Derek 120
Auerbach, Erich 2, 41–2
Augustine 12, 34 n.7, 79
autobiography 11, 13, 83–4, 106 n.14, 149

Bakhtin, Mikhail 145 n.15
Bal, Mieke 4 n.2, 60, 163 n.1
Baldwin, Thomas 39–40, 103–4
Bales, Richard 4 n.2
Balzac, Honoré de 42, 153
Barthes, Roland 7, 41 n.14, 149
　Camera Lucida 124, 126, 141, 163 n.1
　Image, Music, Text 16, 22
Barton Johnson, D. 94
Baudelaire, Charles 81 n.19, 81–2, 135 n.10
Baxter, James 206 n.9
Beckett, Samuel 205, 208 n.11, 210 n.13,
　　211 n.14
　Malone Dies 206–7, 209–11
　Proust 190–1, 201
Benjamin, Walter 81 n.19, 122–3, 128,
　　129 n.7, 135, 146, 201
Bergson, Henri 9, 33, 57 n.29, 68–9, 93, 116
Bergstein, Mary 51 n.21

Bewes, Timothy 3–4
Bilmes, Leonid 78 n.12, 151 n.3
Blanchot, Maurice 197–8, 200, 202–3, 209,
　　212
blindness 26, 85, 155, 158, 161, 214
Boyd, Brian 92, 104, 111–12
Boxall, Peter 80 n.17, 158, 197, 217
Boym, Svetlana 75, 122 n.3
Brooks, Peter 40–1, 76, 197 n.6
Brosch, Renate 5 n.3, 104, 154
Bruss, Elizabeth 85 n.21
Burgin, Victor 151 n.2

Carter, William C. 11 n.8
Casey, Edward 97–100, 106–7, 110–11, 114
Caws, Mary Ann 17, 37, 48, 65
Cicero 27–8
Compagnon, Antoine 16
confession 12, 24, 79, 141
Culler Jonathan 42 n.15, 43
Currie, Mark 185 n.8
　About Time 72, 108, 115, 152
　Postmodern Narrative Theory 6, 16
　The Unexpected 109, 115
Curtis, Neil 7

Dandieu, Arnaud 70 n.5, 78
D'Angelo, Frank J. 31 n.3
Davies, Ben 218 n.4
Davis, Lydia
　The Collected Stories 188–9
　The End of the Story 191–3, 195–6,
　　198–200, 202–3, 204, 206–8
　Essays One 189, 194–5, 198 n.7, 201,
　　205 n.8
　'Loaf or Hot-Water Bottle' 187–8
De Man, Paul 82, 106 n.14
De Vries, Gerard 94
Deleuze, Gilles 66 n.36, 71 n.7, 127
Derrida, Jacques 21 n.17, 85, 106, 197,
　　214
　Archive Fever 131–3, 141
Descombes, Vincent 23 n.19

description
  delay of 2, 12, 18, 23, 29, 83, 97, 115, 137, 152, 215
  as opposed to narration 5, 9, 29–30, 31, 42 n.16, 43–4, 65, 93–4, 97, 112, 115, 138
  pictorial description 137, 171, 177, 181
Dowd, Garin 206 n.10
Dowling, W.C. 192
Dyer, Nathalie Mauriac 32 n.6

ekphrasis
  as aide-memoire 49
  antiquity, uses of 14, 17, 31–2, 31 n.4, 40 n.13, 49
  deixis and 170, 174
  ekphrastic *ostranenie* 54, 56, 85, 177
  as imagetext 101, 104, 145, 155
  memory and 6–7, 11–13
  metaphor and 3, 11, 19, 35–6, 47–8, 49 n. 20, 50, 52, 54, 62–3, 103, 192, 215
  mnemonic ekphrasis 5, 28, 30–2, 49 n.20, 52, 58, 69, 75, 82, 150, 162, 215–16
  reading and 9–10, 15, 17–19, 26, 30, 32, 41 n.14, 48, 53 n.23, 65, 69, 87, 95, 152, 194–95, 204, 214
Elkins, Amy E. 173
Elkins, Katherine 81 n.18
Elsner, Jas 103
Emerson, Caryl 80 n.16
enargeia (vividness)
  enargeiac voice 28, 174, 176, 180–2, 184, 216
  as inner sight 15, 27–8, 166, 178, 180, 212
Evans, Jonathan 190, 192, 198 n.7, 201–2, 205 n.8
eye/eyes 14–15, 20, 21 n.17, 26, 34 n.7, 43, 52–3, 61, 65, 176, 218
  reader's eye 51 n.22, 84, 94, 139, 178–80, 182, 185, 190, 195–6, 197–8

Felski, Rita 4 n.1
Flaubert, Gustave 41–2, 76, 195
  November/Novembre 43–5
  Selected Letters 42
forgetting
  agency of 25, 190, 202, 211
  memory's potentiality/reserve 127, 201
Foster, John Burt Jr. 13 n.10
Foucault, Michel 20–1

Fowler, D. P. 30, 32
fragment 139, 189–90, 194, 211
frame/framing 13, 17–18, 21 n.17, 21–2, 41 n.14
  ekphrasis as 28–9, 170, 175, 196, 211
  in Proust 34, 47, 58–9, 64–5
future 72–3, 94, 107–8, 114–15, 219–20
  past's shaping of 24, 110–11, 150–2
  in Proust 2, 42, 75, 149, 163–4, 191 n.4, 203

Genette, Gérard 16–17, 29–30, 31, 42, 83, 92–3, 93 n.6
genre 3, 22, 40 n.13, 82, 145, 145 n.15, 149, 152 n.4
Gibbons, Alison 155 n.6
Graham, Victor E. 37
Grishakova, Marina 105

habit
  habit memory 9, 93, 127
  Proust on 33, 52–3, 56, 201
Haddad, Karen 4, 61 n.33
Hägglund, Martin 78 n.13, 92, 113–14, 114 n.18
Hamilton, Paul 123
hearing 9, 14, 213–14, 216
  in Davis 197, 205, 209, 211
  in Proust 34, 38, 38 n.11
  in Smith 165–6, 178, 181
Hedley, Jane 103 n.10
Heffernan, James 94, 105
Heidegger, Martin 22 n.18
Hirsch, Marianne 134
Homer 13, 29–30
Horace 13, 26
Horstkotte, Silke 137 n.11
Hoy, David Couzens 71 n.7
Hughes, Edward J. 6 n.4
Husserl, Edmund 109–10, 151
hypotaxis 18, 138, 140, 144–5, 161

image (*see under* memory)
imagetext
  and ekphrasis (*see under* ekphrasis)
  Mitchell on 7–8, 87, 99, 104
imagination (*see under* memory)
Ingarden, Roman 18–19
intermedial/intermediality 4, 5, 7, 20, 46, 51, 119, 159, 162–4, 166, 173, 216–17

irony 24, 54, 76, 80–2, 83
Iser, Wolfgang 115 n. 19

Jacobs, Carol 117
Jameson, Fredric 49 n.20
Jay, Martin 21 n. 17

Karpeles, Eric 51, 51 n.22, 90 n.4, 103 n.9
Kilbourn, Russell 117–18
Knausgård, Karl Ove 157 n.9
Knight, Christopher J. 194, 203
Koelb, Janice Hewlett 14, 16 n.15
Kouvaros, George 129 n.7
Krasznahorkai, László 213
Krell, David Farrell 87 n.1
Krieger, Murray 14, 17, 26

Lacan, Jacques 115 n. 20
Landy, Joshua 9 n.7, 62 n.34, 64 n.35
Lanham, Richard 15 n.14
Latour, Bruno 217 n.3
Lennon, Thomas M. 35–6
Lerner, Ben 156–7, 157 n.9, 158–9, 215
    10:04 149, 150, 151–2, 155–7
    Leaving the Atocha Station 159–60
    'The Polish Rider' 153–4
Leslie, Esther 122
Lewis, Cara L. 4, 174 n.4, 217 n.2
Lingis, Alphonso 45 n.19
Long, J. J. 130, 132
Louvel, Liliane 5, 51
    The Pictorial Third 5, 50, 166, 170, 173
    Poetics of the Iconotext 22, 162, 172, 179
Lukács, Georg 42 n.16

Macé, Marielle 45 n.18
madeleine 10, 33–4, 36–7, 56, 81 n.19
McLuhan, Marshall 105 n.12, 138
McQuire, Scott 121, 122 n.3, 123, 126
memory
    anticipatory memory 151–2
    imagination and 75–6, 84, 85, 97–9, 100–1, 103, 117, 165, 185, 203, 206, 215
    involuntary memory 9 n.7, 32–6, 37, 55–6, 58, 68–9, 74, 77, 78 n.13, 135, 201, 203
    memory cone (Bergson) 67–9, 127, 201

memory image 5, 12, 22, 32, 51–2, 75, 82, 98 n.8, 123, 135, 165, 186, 216
memory theatre 88–90, 90 n.3, 91, 95, 109, 116
mnemonic ekphrasis (*see under* ekphrasis)
painting as metaphor of 50–1, 92, 98
reminiscence 106–7, 134
Mendelsund, Peter 18
metaphor
    perception as impacted by 40 n.12, 41 n.14, 53, 56
    Proust on 53, 57, 69–70
    visual metaphor 23, 35–6, 39, 49, 52–3, 55, 84, 70, 75, 107, 175–6
methexis 177, 180
mimesis 6, 22, 28, 41 n.14, 73, 147, 158–9, 166, 177, 197, 220
Mitchell, W. J. T. 99, 104
    Image Science 171, 173, 186
    Picture Theory 7, 8–9, 12, 25 n.20, 87, 93–4, 107
    What Do Pictures Want 8
Morson, Gary Saul 80 n.16
Mulvey, Laura 138–9

Nabokov, Vladimir 118, 215
    Ada 94–7, 100, 102, 105–6, 107–8, 110–12, 113
    Lectures on Literature 78, 91, 95 n.7
    Speak, Memory 13, 83–5, 91, 105 n. 13, 120, 194
Nalbantian, Suzanne 11 n.8
Nancy, Jean-Luc 167, 170, 175–6, 177, 190, 199–200, 204–5, 211
narration (*see also* self-narration)
    description as opposed to (*see under* description)
    ending of 44 n.17, 72, 84, 109, 192–3
    primacy of 16, 30 n.2, 44
narrative identity 78 n.12, 78–80, 144, 151, 190–1
Nelson, Victoria 90 n.3
nostalgia 75–6, 80, 83, 121–2, 125, 131, 145

ocularcentrism 21, 21 n.17, 22 n.18
Olney, James 79, 80 n.17, 156 n.8

ostranenie
	Shklovsky on 23, 53–4
	and vision (*see under* ekphrasis)

painting
	in Lerner 153–4, 159
	and memory (*see under* memory)
	in Nabokov 91, 94–6, 98, 103–5
	in Proust 39, 50–3, 61, 75, 90 n.4
	in Smith 164–5, 167, 171, 174–9, 181–2
Pamuk, Orphan 119–20, 194
parataxis 18, 29, 46, 52, 120, 138, 140–1
past
	becoming-present 29–30, 34, 49 n. 20, 57–8, 71, 76, 85, 112, 152
	historical 120, 126, 129, 141, 142–4, 147
	personal 121, 129, 133, 135, 145
phenomenology 8, 34–5, 39, 45 n.19, 51, 76, 109–10, 173, 185 (*see also* reading)
photography
	as archive in Sebald 121–2, 126, 135–6, 141–2, 143, 152
	and forgetting 126–7, 129, 136, 145–6
	in Lerner 153–4, 155–6
	in Nabokov 98, 114, 117
	as parataxis 120, 138, 140, 143
	in Proust 51, 51 n.21, 162–3, 163 n.1
	in Smith 166, 178–81
pictorial model 96, 99, 101, 103, 105, 165
picture
	as opposed to image 8, 186
	as verb 3, 45, 89, 120, 166, 170, 185, 209, 220
Poulet, Georges 11, 11 n.9, 60 n.31, 74 n.8
Prendergast, Christopher 21–2, 53 n.24, 76–7
present 8, 15, 26, 28–9, 40, 73, 109–10, 152, 218 (*see also* as if)
	in Proust 42 n.16, 49 n.20, 58, 67–9
	the writing present 21, 190–1, 194, 200
prosthesis 21 n.17, 130, 132, 141, 152, 152 n.4, 215
Proust, Marcel
	À la recherche du temps perdu 10, 47, 50, 76, 95
	The Captive 38–9, 59–60, 61, 90
	'Chardin' 1–2, 9
	Contre Sainte-Beuve 32–3, 45 n.18, 53, 75–6
	The Fugitive 59, 61–2, 64, 84 n.20, 90
	The Guermantes Way 54–5, 90, 162
	Le Temps retrouvé 70, 75, 77, 78 n.14
	Sodom and Gomorrah 55 n.26, 90, 116, 163–4
	Swann's Way 10–11, 36–7, 38, 48–50, 62–3, 76, 78, 83, 90
	Time Regained 55–6, 59, 63, 67, 69–71, 74–5, 77–8, 90
	Within a Budding Grove 17–18, 33, 38 n.11, 46–7, 51, 52–3, 60 n.32, 78, 90, 162, 191 n.4, 192, 193 n.5, 201–2, 206
'Proust effect' 36–7

Rancière, Jacques 44 n. 17, 45–6, 58 n.30, 140
reading
	ekphrasis and (*see under* ekphrasis)
	phenomenology of 8, 18–19, 45 n.18, 87, 103, 165
	rereading 24, 91, 95 n.7, 214
realism 40–1, 41 n.14, 42 n.16, 45 n.19, 157–8, 197 n.6
Reid, James H. 206 n.10
Ricoeur, Paul 41 n.14, 52, 53 n.23, 67, 71, 76 n.10, 145
	Memory, History, Forgetting 127, 128, 133, 135, 136–7, 142 n.13, 144, 146–7
Rivers, J. E. 95
Rousseau, Jean-Jacques 12–13, 79–80

Scott, Clive 124 n.4, 140, 141
Scranton, Roy 219
Sebald, W. G. 118, 122, 124, 136, 143, 161, 215
	Austerlitz 126–6, 128–9, 133–4, 137, 139–40
	The Emigrants 127
	on Nabokov 120
	Vertigo 125
seeing-as (*see* metaphor)
self-narration 79–80, 191–2
Setina, Emily 51 n.21
shield of Achilles 13, 29–30
Shklovsky, Viktor 23, 53–4, 55
Silverman, Kaja 81 n.19, 163 n.1

sight 34–5, 50, 59, 176 (*see also enargeia*)
    retrospective 3, 28, 214
    sight/blindness 155, 199–200, 204
    textual sight/site 5, 19, 23–4, 50, 85, 185, 197, 211–12
Smith, Ali 167–8, 173
    Artful 185–6
    Hotel World 185 n.8
    How to be Both 164–6, 169–71, 173–6, 177–82, 183–5
    on Sebald 161
Smith, Barry C. 36–7
Sontag, Susan 121–2, 124, 125
Spitzer, Leo 13 n.12, 14
Squire, Michael 13 n.11
Stelmach, Kathryn 32 n.5
Stendhal 125 n.5
Stiegler, Bernard 80, 151, 152 n.4
superimposition 60, 62 n.34, 65, 71, 75–6, 91

Tatius, Achilles 40 n.13
time
    in narrative 29, 45, 67, 72–4, 109–10
    Proust on 69–70, 71 n.7, 71–2
Townsend, Gabrielle 51 n.22
Ty, Eleanor 118

Vaihinger, Hans 76 n.10
Van Campen, Cretien 36
vivid/vividness (*see enargeia*)

visual media 4, 8, 44, 87, 121, 154, 162, 164, 216
voice 99, 158, 202–4, 209, 211, 214, 216
    ekphrastic voicing 165–6, 168, 169, 175–6, 177–8, 182 (*see also enargeia*)
    in Proust 22, 64 n.35, 170

Walsh, Lauren 34, 119 n.2
Warnock, Mary 203–4
Watt, Adam 4 n.2, 57 n.28
Webb, Ruth 14, 31, 49
    Ekphrasis, Imagination and Persuasion 14–15, 27–8, 31, 40 n.13, 51, 91–2, 179
Weinrich, Harold 34
White, Hayden 80, 140 n.12, 142–3, 144, 147
Williams, Luke 120
Wilson, Mary Griffin 127 n.6
Wolff, Lynn 144 n.14
Wood, James 129, 130
Wood, Michael 67 n.2, 146 n.16, 187 n.2

Yacobi, Tamara 96, 97
Yates, Frances 87, 88–9, 91

Zalasiewicz, Jan 220
Zwicky, Jan 40 n.12, 56 n.27

www.ingramcontent.com/pod-product-compliance
Lightning Source LLC
Chambersburg PA
CBHW062140300426
44115CB00012BA/1990